Robert Bolton, Ph.D., is president of Ridge
Consultants, a Cazenovia, New York–based
firm that specializes in improving human
performance in industry, health care, education, and government. His staff has taught
communication skills to thousands of managers, salespersons, first-line supervisors, secretaries, customer-relations personnel,
teachers, members of the clergy, health-care
workers, couples, and others.

PEOPLE SKILLS

How to Assert Yourself, Listen to Others, and Resolve Conflicts

ROBERT BOLTON, PH.D.
President
Ridge Consultants
Cazenovia, New York 13035

A SPECTRUM BOOK

Prentice-Hall, Inc.
Englewood Cliffs, New Jersey 07632

Library of Congress Cataloging in Publication Data

Bolton, Robert.
  People skills.

  (A Spectrum Book)
  Bibliography: p.
  Includes index.
  1. Interpersonal relationships.   2. Interpersonal
communications.   I. Title.
HM132.B65   301.11   79-12517
ISBN 0-13-655779-1
ISBN 0-13-655761-9 pbk.

A Spectrum Book

20 19 18 17 16

Editorial/production supervision
and interior design by Eric Newman
Cover design by Vincent Ceci
Manufacturing buyer: Cathie Lenard

Prentice-Hall International, Inc., *London*
Prentice-Hall of Australia Pty. Limited, *Sydney*
Prentice-Hall of Canada, Ltd., *Toronto*
Prentice-Hall of India Private Limited, *New Delhi*
Prentice-Hall of Japan, Inc., *Tokyo*
Prentice-Hall of Southeast Asia Pte. Ltd., *Singapore*
Whitehall Books Limited, Wellington, *New Zealand*

TO DOT

My best friend,
closest companion, fun playmate.

Enabler of my various selves,
nurturer of my dreams.

Marvelous wife—
sensitive, loving, and genuine
with me, our children, parents, and friends.

Effective in tasks that sustain our common life—
colleague, teacher, partner.

I love it that when I am with you
I most often discover, choose, disclose
the selves I really am.

I love my experience of you as
a life-ful, love-ful,
value-ful person.

Imperfect, changing, growing, becoming,
yet rooted, consistent—
a friend for all seasons.

You are "something else."

Contents

PART TWO

Listening Skills, 27

CHAPTER FOURTEEN

Collaborative Problem Solving: Seeking an Elegant Solution, 232

CHAPTER FIFTEEN

Three Essentials for Effective Communication, 253

AFTERWORD

Training for Improved Communication, 275

Notes, 280

Index, 297

Preface

" 'Tis the good reader that makes the book," said Ralph Waldo Emerson. That truth applies especially to this type of book. A reader who only wants to toy with a few ideas will gain little from this volume. It is written for people with a strong enough desire to improve their relationships that they will *experiment* with the approaches to communication outlined in the following pages. It will do little good merely to read this book. However, those who persistently and creatively use these skills in their daily lives will notice significant changes in their relationships.

Effective communication is not something that has come easily to me. I suppose that if I had been especially capable in interpersonal communication from my childhood on, I would never have studied it so tenaciously. It was because communication was a problem for me that I researched it, tried out what I learned, taught it, and wrote about it.

I feel better qualified to teach these skills precisely because they do not come easily for me. I have struggled through many of the same impasses that block the typical learner from developing more fruitful ways of relating. Perhaps because of some of these initial deficits I can help you to overcome many of the pitfalls to learning and using these skills.

The writing of this book has gone on amidst the absorbing and incessant demands of managing a consulting firm. There are undoubtedly many advantages to writing in an unhurried, undemanding schedule. The daily pressure of an active business and teaching life, however, may be more of an advantage than a disadvantage. The skills have been used and tested daily in the hurly-burly of life as the book was written over a six-year period.

I write these pages with confidence that they will be of great benefit to the reader who applies them. Several thousand copies of earlier editions have been read by participants of our Communication Skills workshops. Literally hundreds who have read early editions of this book have written to say that these approaches to interpersonal relationships have worked for them and have greatly enriched their lives. Many say the book not only changed their ideas about human interaction, but it also helped them change their behaviors and enhance their relationships. This expanded volume should be even more useful.

This book, which began as a journey into myself and a study of how my interactions with people could be improved, was nourished by the thinking, research, teaching, and writing of Thomas Gordon, Carl Rogers, Allen Ivey, Gerard Egan, and Robert Carkhuff. The references in the "Notes" section indicate many of the other authors who have contributed to my understanding of interpersonal communication. Sometimes, when I am reading, the way a person has phrased his truth is as important to me as the truth itself. The wording is like a powerful painting that I would like to put on the wall. I want to share the statement with other people, not just for its truth, but also because the way it is worded somehow has a special meaning for me. So, sprinkled throughout these pages, you will find many quotations that resonate with my experience, taste, and values.

The concepts in this book have been discussed at length with colleagues at Ridge Consultants, especially Dot Bolton and Ed Lisbe. Their thinking and phrasing have contributed much to the book.

Special thanks too are due to the students in our communication-skills workshops who have contributed to my understanding. They have come from all walks of life: managers, salespeople, secretaries, teachers, health-care professionals, customer-relations personnel, construction workers, supervisors, psychologists, lawyers, members of the clergy, and many others. As they struggled to develop their communication skills, I found easier ways to teach these methods. As participants wrestled to apply the skills to particular situations, I discovered inadequacies in the theory and methods and was able to develop more helpful constructs. Many of the examples in the book come from their experiences. Names and some details have been disguised to preserve anonymity.

Many institutions have aided the development of this program. A cooperative venture with the College of Saint Rose, in Albany, New York, enabled thousands of educators to take graduate courses in which the methods taught in this book could be learned and applied in their daily work. Fortune 500 companies, small businesses, governmental agencies, religious orders, hospitals, universities, counseling centers, and other organizations afforded us the opportunity to teach these skills to people from a wide variety of backgrounds. The feedback we have received has helped sharpen the presentation in this book. It has also confirmed the importance of these skills and their relevance to a myriad of work situations as well as to family and other personal relationships.

Laura Weeks was of great help in the research of portions of this book and in polishing the phrasing of some sections. Pat Freeborn also polished the language in some of the chapters. Dot Bolton read the entire volume and made numerous improvements both large and small, and Ed Lisbe did the same with several key chapters.

Having traced just a portion of my indebtedness, it may seem strange that I still think of this as "my" book. The simile used by the author of one of the earliest English manuals of botany conveys my feelings very accurately:

> Some of [my readers] will say, seeing that I graunte that I have gathered this book of so many writers, that I offer unto you a heap of other mennis laboures, and nothing of mine owne. . . . To whome I answere that if the honeye that the bees gather out of so many floure of herbes, shrubbes and trees, that are growing in other mennis meadows, feldes, and closes may justelye be called the bee's honeye. . . . so may I call that I have learned and gathered of so many autores . . . my booke.[1]

In spite of the strong stimulus of others on my methods of communication and my thoughts about it, I, of course, am responsible for the material in these pages.

Until we develop a satisfactory set of unisex pronouns, the issue of whether to refer to a person in general as "he" or as "he/she" is one that must be settled. I was unhappy with either option. So all general references to human beings are made in feminine terms in the even-numbered chapters and in masculine terms in the odd-numbered chapters.

Some of the people familiar with the content of this volume say that Chapter Fifteen, "Three Essentials for Effective Communication," should be read first. Others say that it should be read in the middle of the book. Others believe that it should be read last. If at some point it seems to you that the book is too focused on methods of communication and not the spirit that infuses interactions with life, take a detour through Chapter Fifteen before continuing.

My wish for you, the reader, is that the skills taught in this book will benefit you as much as they have benefitted me.

PEOPLE
SKILLS

PART ONE

Introduction

As a result of a person's socialization, he has already acquired some interpersonal skills. However, one's level of functioning in terms of these skills can be raised. Everyone has a vast capacity for being more understanding, respectful, warm, genuine, open, direct, and concrete in his human relationships. With a sound body of theoretical knowledge, appropriate models, and numerous opportunities for personal experiencing, the process of becoming more fully human can be greatly accelerated.[1]

—George Gazda, educator

CHAPTER ONE

Skills for Bridging the Interpersonal Gap

I wish I had some way to make a bridge from man
to man. . . . Man is all we've got.[1]

> —Cross Daman in
> Richard Wright's
> *Outsider*

COMMUNICATION: HUMANITY'S
SUPREME ACHIEVEMENT

When one person communicates to another through the medium of language something takes place between them that is found nowhere else in nature. This ability to turn meaningless grunts into spoken and written words constitutes humanity's most important distinction. Language has made possible the development of those characteristics that differentiate *Homo sapiens* from all other creatures. No wonder the German philosopher Karl Jaspers claims, "Man's supreme achievement in the world is communication from personality to personality."[2]

THE INEFFECTIVENESS
OF MOST COMMUNICATION

Although interpersonal communication is humanity's greatest accomplishment, the average person does not communicate well. One of the ironies of modern civilization is that, though mechanical means of communication have been developed beyond the wildest flight of the imagination, people often find it difficult to communicate face-to-face. In this age of technological marvels we can bounce messages off the moon and land space probes on Mars, but we find it difficult to relate to those we love.

I have become increasingly aware of the inadequacy of most communication. In our society it is rare for persons to share what really matters—the tender, shy, reluctant feelings, the sensitive, fragile, intense disclosures. It is equally rare for persons to listen intently enough to really understand what another is saying. Sometimes people fix their gaze on a friend who is talking and allow their minds to wander off to other matters. Sometimes, while the friend speaks, they pretend to listen but are merely marking time, formulating what *they* will say as soon as they discover a way to begin talking. Nathan Miller caustically remarked that "conversation in the United States is a competitive exercise in which the first person to draw a breath is declared the listener."

Ineffective communication causes an interpersonal gap that is experienced in all facets of life and in all sectors of society. Loneliness, family problems, vocational incompetence and dissatisfaction, psychological stress, physical illness, and even death result when communication breaks down. In addition to the personal frustration and the heartache resulting from it, the interpersonal gap is now one of the major social problems of our troubled society.

THE ACHE OF LONELINESS

Many people today yearn for warm, positive, meaningful relatedness to others, but seem unable to experience it. The psychiatrist Harry Stack Sullivan put it this way:

> The deepest problem of people is loneliness, isolation, and difficulty of self-esteem in our society. Whereas the problem in Freud's early decades was sexual repression, and the chief problem in the early thirties, when Karen Horney wrote, was disguised hostility, today it is loneliness.[3]

There are two kinds of aloneness. Solitude can be a creative, joyous, full aloneness. But loneliness is a painful, dead, empty aloneness. Loneliness is being acutely aware of one's isolation and alienation from others. As David Riesman pointed out, when one is not vitally in touch with oneself or others, loneliness can occur even in the midst of a crowd.[4]

"Loneliness"—the sound of the word conveys some of the heartache associated with it. Try saying the word aloud several times in a sorrowful voice: "Loneliness . . . loneliness . . . loneliness . . ." The very word has a melancholy ring to it. It represents much pain for many people.

Several reasons have been given for the increased ache of loneliness in modern times. Materialism (finding one's solace in things rather than in people), the mobility of people, uprootedness of families and the bureaucratic structure of organizations—these are just a few. I am convinced that another major cause of this interpersonal gap, and the one that may be easiest to rectify, is inadequate methods of interpersonal communication.

SO MUCH LOST LOVE

Unfortunately, the most intense loneliness today is often found in the family where communication is breaking down or is in a shambles. Marriage, the most complicated of human relationships, cannot flourish without effective communication. Couples hoping to establish an enriching marriage often lack the needed relational skills and end up living parallel lives in a marriage without intimacy. The often-quoted words of the poet T. S. Eliot describe what may be a typical family:

> *Two people who know they do not understand each other,*
> *Breeding children whom they do not understand*
> *And who will never understand them.*[5]

Proximity without intimacy is inevitably destructive. When communication is blocked, love's energy turns to resentment and hostility. Frequent bickering, withering sarcasm, repetitious criticism, or an icy retreat into silence and sexual unresponsiveness result. One woman, after describing her family's dysfunctional patterns of communication said, "I live in a psychological slum, not a home."

As most parents can attest, it is no easy thing to raise children today. Virginia Satir, a leader in the family therapy field, writes:

> Parents teach in the toughest school in the world—The School for Making People. You are the board of education, the principal, the classroom teacher, and the janitor. . . . You are expected to be experts on all subjects pertaining to life and living. . . . There are few schools to train you for your job, and there is no general agreement on the curriculum. You have to make it up yourself. Your school has no holidays, no vacations, no unions, no automatic promotions or pay raises. You are on duty or at least on call 24 hours a day, 365 days a year, for at least 18 years for each child you have. Besides that, you have to contend with an administration that has two leaders or bosses, whichever the case may be—and you know the traps two bosses can get into with each other. Within this context you carry on your people-making. I regard this as the hardest, most complicated, anxiety-ridden, sweat and blood producing job in the world.[6]

Healthy communication is vitally important in raising a family. For couples who have competence in communication skills, parenthood can be one of the most rewarding and joyous experiences of their lifetime. When parents have not mastered skills for accurate, congruent communication, the resulting anguish, alienation, and loneliness for parents and children alike can be devastating.

Readers of Ann Landers's advice column were shocked when they read that 70 percent of the people responding to her survey said they were sorry they had children. Though her sample was not a true cross-section of the population, and though Landers admitted that readers with negative feelings had a stronger compulsion to respond than those with positive feelings, there was considerable evidence to support her survey's general results. Dr. Harcharan Sehdev, Director of the Children's Division of the Menninger Foundation in Topeka, Kansas, said, "The Landers letters appear to reflect the general changing trends and opinions of family systems and the place of children in our homes and society."[7]

Communication is the lifeblood of every relationship. When open, clear, sensitive communication takes place, the relationship is nurtured. When communication is guarded, hostile, or ineffective, the relationship falters. When the communication flow is largely obstructed, the relationship quickly deteriorates and ultimately dies. Where communication skills are lacking, there is so much lost love—between spouses, lovers, friends, parents and children. For satisfying relationships, it is essential to discover methods that will help us to at least partially bridge the interpersonal gaps that separate us from others.

A KEY TO SUCCESS AT WORK

Eighty percent of the people who fail at work do so for one reason: they do not relate well to other people. One's productivity as a supervisor or manager, nurse or secretary, mental health worker or janitor, laborer, attorney, physician, clerk, or minister is greatly enhanced by the ability to communicate well. In fact, it is difficult to think of a single job in which communication is unimportant.

A mechanical engineer mused, "I thought my engineering training was all I would need. But I spend most of my time on people problems." A teacher commented, "I was educated to be a physics teacher. Since I've been in the classroom, I discovered I teach people. I spend most of my energy trying to restore order. Why didn't my graduate program help me with this?" Communication skills are clearly keys to on-the-job success.

A LIFE-OR-DEATH MATTER

Most human interaction is for better or for worse. Each moment with another person can be an opportunity for discovery and growth or for the erosion of identity and the destruction of one's personhood. Our personality development and mental and physical health are linked to the caliber of our communication. One does not become fully human without interaction with other human beings. Indeed, the philosopher Martin Heidegger refers to language as "the dwelling place of being."

People need people. As the title of one book had it, "You can't be human alone." Each person matures through enhancing dialogues with others. In *The Mystery of Being*, Gabriel Marcel observes, "When somebody's presence does really make itself felt, it can refresh my inner being; it reveals me to myself, it makes me feel more fully myself than I should be if I were not exposed to its impact."[8]

Conversely, lack of communication or frequent exposure to poor communication diminishes one's selfhood both emotionally and physically. Many believe that mental illness is primarily a problem of inadequate communication. The psychologically sick individual has not achieved good human relationships. According to Carl Rogers, "The whole task of psychotherapy is the task of dealing with a failure in communication."[9]

Deficient communication can affect a person's physical health. The *extent* to which constructive or destructive dialogue influences bodily functions, however, comes as a surprise to many people.

Emperor Frederick, the thirteenth-century ruler of the Holy Roman Empire, wanted to know what language had been spoken at the birth of mankind in the Garden of Eden. Was it Hebrew, Greek, or Latin? He ordered an experiment in which the original circumstances would be re-created as closely as possible. A group of infants were to be isolated from hearing human speech from the moment of birth until they spoke their language. The babies were to be raised by wet nurses who were strictly charged to maintain complete silence when with the babies. All the conditions of the experiment were successfully carried out. The result? Every one of the babies died. The lack of communication is often toxic and can be lethal.

The film *Second Chance* provides a clinical portrayal of this type of physical deterioration in modern times. The fifteen-minute movie shows how lack of human interaction slowed the growth of twenty-two-month-old Susan so drastically that her size and weight were that of a child half her age. Susan's deterioration was dramatically arrested when, during hospitalization, she was given loving interaction and care for over six hours a day for two months.[10]

YOU CAN CHANGE

There is one thing certain about your methods and style of communication: they are primarily learned responses. Your most influential instructors were probably your parents, who in turn learned their approach to communication from their parents. Teachers, scout leaders, friends, and many others added their input. Through radio, television, and other sources, our culture has influenced the way you communicate.

Not many people have had models of effective communication in their home environments. The lucky few who have had such models seem to be "naturals" at communicating well. What seems natural, however, is usually the result of their good fortune at having learned to communicate effectively from early childhood. *Many of us, however, were taught to communicate poorly by well-intentioned people who themselves were taught inadequate ways of relating.* As far as communication is concerned, many of us are victims of victims.

We first experienced the training process at an early age. Parents or parent-substitutes rewarded some kinds of nonverbal behavior, like smiling, and they communicated displeasure over other kinds of nonverbal behavior such as "temper tantrums." When we were still quite young, they helped us frame our first words. Then they trained us to speak in certain ways. No matter how badly you hated the annual Thanksgiving visit to your aunt's house, you may have been told, "Thank your Aunt Edith for the lov ly time you had." When you interrupted two adults who were talking, you may have been taught, "Don't interrupt. Say, 'Excuse me.' " There are many other common training phrases like "Quit complaining" . . . "Stop that whining" . . . "Don't ever speak to your mother that way" . . . "Charles, stop using that horrible language."

Relatives, babysitters, Sunday school workers, and a host of others soon joined the process. "Why, Bobby, I am surprised at you for shouting at Johnny. You are usually such a good boy." "Raise your hand before you speak. I'll call on you when it is your turn." "Susan, don't tell Terry he can't play with your truck. You are not using it now. How can you be so selfish?" "There is no such word as 'ain't.' " "Mind your own business." "Don't contradict."

In addition to the admonitions they gave, the important adults in our lives were modeling certain ways of behaving. Perhaps they rarely disclosed their feelings. Or they may have been sarcastic, used put-downs, or screamed out polluted anger. As children, we learned by the example of the significant others in our lives as well as from their instructions to us. Cultural norms in our society reinforce much of the training we received. Some of these norms are less rigid than they were several decades ago, but many are still firmly entrenched.[11]

Numerous dysfunctional ways of relating that are typically learned by children in our culture are listed by Gerard Egan, a priest-psychologist:

how to remain superficial,
how to build façades,
how to play interpersonal games,
how to hide from [ourselves] and others,
how to downplay risk in human relating,
how to manipulate others (or endure being manipulated) . . .
how to hurt and punish others, if necessary.[12]

Some people may object that the processes and outcomes described are inaccurate. The portrayal is undoubtedly oversimplified. How one responds to the predominant communication patterns in one's early environment varies from individual to individual. Twin brothers growing up in a home where one parent has a volatile temper may develop very different approaches to handling anger. One twin may repress it, the other may express it belligerently. Many (and maybe most) of us, however, were trained in some very ineffective and destructive ways of relating. A vicious spiral has resulted where the communications faults of parents are visited upon their children. The spiral can be broken. You can unlearn those methods of relating that do not work well for you. This book can help you spot some of the areas that most need attention and help you learn specific skills that lead to more personal fulfillment, warmer and richer relationships, and greater effectiveness at work.

People are frequently fatalistic about their ways of communicating. They tend to think that their way of talking and listening, like the color of their eyes, is a "given" in their lives. To try to change one's style of communication, so the argument goes, is impossible. Or it leads to phoniness. As one physician said, "Relating to people is a gift. Either you have it or you don't. I don't have it and there is nothing I can do about it."

My experience and that of my colleagues in teaching communication skills to thousands of people leads us to just the opposite conclusion. We have noted major changes in our own lives and in the lives of trainees. Patterns that were acquired in childhood have been replaced by more effective responses. At any period of life, the average person of sound mind and determination can learn improved ways of communicating. The research of a number of highly regarded behavioral scientists documents the fact that adults can learn to communicate more effectively.[13]

Of course, it is not easy to alter methods of relating. Years of habit have ingrained certain tendencies for so long that it feels unnatural to relate differently. Any "new" approach seems awkward, and people are tempted to abandon their quest. But once they gain increased awareness of how dysfunctional some of their typical responses are, many people become highly motivated to change. After they have effectively used a communication skill, they often say with excitement, "It works! It really does work!"

YOU WILL CHANGE!

Change is inevitable. Erik Erikson, Robert Havighurst, and others have pointed out that people go through developmental stages from infancy to old age.[14] It is impossible to live the evening of life in the same manner as the morning.

The world is changing, too. We speak of the everlasting hills, but in the course of time they rise and sink. We refer to the eternal stars, but they too are in flux: they have their beginnings and ends, they expand or shrink, become brighter or descend toward darkness.

Change has been an integral part of human culture from the beginning. Nicholas Murray Butler insisted that in the Garden of Eden, Adam paused at one point to say, "Eve, we are living in a period of transition."

In this century, the changes in cultures have been so breath-takingly rapid and all-embracing that Alvin Toffler declares we are living in a period of "future shock." What he means is that change is avalanching down upon our heads at such a dizzying pace that we have great difficulty coping with it.[15]

With change continually occurring within us, in other people we relate to, in the physical world, and in our culture, it is impossible to remain the same.

Even when we try to cling to old ways, they are different. As H. Richard Niebuhr put it, "When we do today what we did yesterday, we actually do something different since in the interval both we and our environment have changed."[16]

The *law of change* says, "Things do not stay the same. If they don't get better, they get worse." If relationships do not get stronger, they will get weaker; if they do not become closer, they will become more distant; if they do not become more productive, they will become less productive.

You not only *can* change the way you relate with others, you inevitably *will* change your way of relating. It is better to manage changes skillfully than to just let life happen to you. This book teaches skills that allow for and indeed foster the kinds of changes that are desirable.

MANAGING YOUR RESISTANCE TO LEARNING

After years of trying to improve my own ways of relating and after teaching communication skills to many others, I have an awareness of and respect for the resistance most of us have to new learnings—especially if they demand behavioral change on our part. When the change is as fundamental as basic ways of relating to loved ones and business associates, the stakes are indeed high and reworking patterns of behavior can be an act of considerable courage.

When people begin to learn new skills of communication, they often say these kinds of things to themselves:

> Will these skills really work or is this just another of those psychological fads that come and go every few years? Suppose the skills are truly effective—will I be able to learn them? I've never been especially good at learning new things, especially skills where I must break one set of habits and develop a new set. Gosh, when I think of the trouble I had trying to stop smoking. . . . But suppose I do learn the skills, and they do change my relationships: how can I be sure the change will be an improvement? What I experience interpersonally right now may not be great, but things could be far worse. These skills could get me out of the frying pan and into the fire! Then, too, there is always the possibility that these skills will make me a different person. Though I'd really like to be a better me, suppose I end up as a casualty—a psychological disaster. Part of me is very leery of this whole venture.

Many of us have more resistance than we realize because much of it is buried in the subconscious.

We need to protect ourselves. *Homo sapiens* is a vulnerable creature in a dangerous world. However, some methods of protection arrest our development while others work positively for us. *One of the key elements in learning communication skills is to discover how to protect oneself adequately while reducing un-*

necessary defensiveness. Guidelines in various sections of this book will help you protect yourself from needless risk while you learn to use these new skills.

FIVE SETS OF SKILLS

Five clusters of skills critical to satisfying interpersonal relationships are taught in this book:

Listening skills: These methods enable a person to really understand what another person is saying. They include new ways of responding so that the other person feels his problems and feelings have been understood. When these methods are used appropriately, the other person often solves his problems without becoming dependent on you.

Assertion skills: These verbal and nonverbal behaviors enable you to maintain respect, satisfy your needs, and defend your rights without dominating, manipulating, abusing, or controling others.

Conflict-resolution skills: These abilities enable you to deal with the emotional turbulence that typically accompanies conflict—abilities that are likely to foster closer relationships when the strife is over.

Collaborative problem-solving skills: These constitute a way of resolving conflicting needs that satisfies all parties—it is a way of solving problems so they stay solved.

Skill selection: These guidelines enable you to decide what communication skills to use in any situation in which you find yourself.

These are the basic communication tools required for effective human relationships. They are the fundamentals.

Part of the strength of this program of communication training lies in the wide range of skills it includes. Many programs concentrate on listening skills, but do not teach people how to assert constructively. In recent years, people have been flocking to programs that help develop assertiveness, but ignore the need for attentive listening. Courses that combine listening and assertion seldom give adequate attention to methods of resolving the conflicts and solving the problems that are inevitable in all human relationships. It is even more unusual to find a communication skills program that helps you figure out when to use the skills being taught and when they are inappropriate. It is futile to use a skill well but use it in the wrong situation. Our program includes what we believe are the most fundamental skills of interpersonal communication.[17]

What is excluded from this book, however, is as important as what is included. Many books on interpersonal communication include such a broad range of skills to be developed and theories to be explored that the reader's energy is dissipated. Skill development requires a sharp focus—a concentration of energy. In the teaching of basic communication skills, as in so many other areas, the guideline of a famous architect holds true—"Less is more." One of the reasons for our success in helping people communicate better has been our insistence on sticking to the fundamentals. People learn best when they are not overwhelmed with too many topics and too much detail.

SUMMARY

Although interpersonal communication is humanity's greatest accomplishment, the average person does not communicate well. Low-level communication leads to loneliness and distance from friends, lovers, spouses, and children—as well as ineffectiveness at work.

Research studies indicate that, despite a tendency toward defensiveness, people of all ages can learn specific communication skills that lead to improved relationships and increased vocational competence. These more desirable ways of relating will be presented in succeeding chapters of this book.

CHAPTER TWO

Barriers
to Communication

A barrier to communication is something that
keeps meanings from meeting. Meaning barriers
exist between all people, making communication
much more difficult than most people seem to
realize. It is false to assume that if one can talk he
can communicate. Because so much of our education misleads people into thinking that communication is easier than it is, they become discouraged and give up when they run into difficulty. Because they do not understand the nature
of the problem, they do not know what to do. The
wonder is not that communicating is as difficult as
it is, but that it occurs as much as it does.[1]

—Reuel Howe,
theologian and educator

COMMON COMMUNICATION SPOILERS

Sue Maxwell, a woman in her mid-thirties, sighed as she said, "Well, I blew it again. We took the family to visit my parents over Thanksgiving weekend. They have been under heavy emotional and financial pressure this year, and I resolved to be very gentle and caring with them. But they started criticizing the way I handle the kids and I got mad. I told them they didn't do such a great job with me and my brother. We argued for half an hour. All three of us felt very hurt.

"This type of thing happens each time I return home," Sue continued. "Even though they have no right to say some of the things they do, I love them and want our visits to be pleasant. But somehow, we almost always say things that hurt each other."

Sue's experience is, unfortunately, a common one. Whether it is with parents, children, bosses, employees, colleagues, friends, or "all of the above," people usually long for better interpersonal results than they commonly achieve.

Since there is in most of us a strong desire for effective communication, why is it so rare and difficult to establish? One of the prime reasons is that, without realizing it, people typically inject communication barriers into their conversations. It has been estimated that *these barriers are used over 90 percent of the time* when one or both parties to a conversation has a problem to be dealt with or a need to be fulfilled.[2]

Communication barriers are *high-risk responses*—that is, responses whose impact on communication is frequently (though not inevitably) negative. These roadblocks are more likely to be destructive when one or more persons who are interacting are under stress. The unfortunate effects of communication blocks are many and varied. They frequently diminish the other's self-esteem. They tend to trigger defensiveness, resistance, and resentment. They can lead to dependency, withdrawal, feelings of defeat or of inadequacy. They decrease the likelihood that the other will find her own solution to her problem. Each roadblock is a "feeling-blocker"; it reduces the likelihood that the other will constructively express her true feelings. Because communication roadblocks carry a high risk of fostering these negative results, their repeated use can cause permanent damage to a relationship.

What specific barriers are apt to hinder a conversation? Experts in interpersonal communication like Carl Rogers, Reuel Howe, Haim Ginott, and Jack Gibb[3] have pinpointed responses that tend to block conversation. More recently, Thomas Gordon[4] devised a comprehensive list that he calls the "dirty dozen" of communication spoilers. These undesirable responses include:

Criticizing: Making a negative evaluation of the other person, her actions, or attitudes. "You brought it on yourself—you've got nobody else to blame for the mess you are in."

Name-calling: "Putting down" or stereotyping the other person "What a dope!" "Just like a woman. . . ." "Egghead." "You hardhats are all alike." "You are just another insensitive male."

Diagnosing: Analyzing why a person is behaving as she is; playing amateur psychiatrist. "I can read you like a book—you are just doing that to irritate me." "Just because you went to college, you think you are better than I."

Praising Evaluatively: Making a positive judgment of the other person, her actions, or attitudes. "You are always such a good girl. I know you will help me with the lawn tonight." Teacher to teenage student: "You are a great poet." (Many people find it difficult to believe that some of the barriers like praise are high-risk responses. Later, I will explain why I believe repeated use of these responses can be detrimental to relationships.)

Ordering: Commanding the other person to do what you want to have done. "Do your homework right now." "Why?! Because I said so. . . ."

Threatening: Trying to control the other's actions by warning of negative consequences that you will instigate. "You'll do it *or else* . . ." "Stop that noise right now or I will keep the whole class after school."

Moralizing: Telling another person what she *should* do. "Preaching" at the other. "You shouldn't get a divorce; think of what will happen to the children." "You ought to tell him you are sorry."

Excessive/Inappropriate Questioning: Closed-ended questions are often barriers in a relationship; these are those that can usually be answered in a few words—often with a simple yes or no. "When did it happen?" "Are you sorry that you did it?"

Advising: Giving the other person a solution to her problems. "If I were you, I'd sure tell him off." "That's an easy one to solve. First . . ."

Diverting: Pushing the other's problems aside through distraction. "Don't dwell on it, Sarah. Let's talk about something more pleasant." Or; "Think you've got it bad?! Let me tell you what happened to me."

Logical argument: Attempting to convince the other with an appeal to facts or logic, usually without consideration of the emotional factors involved. "Look at the facts; if you hadn't bought that new car, we could have made the down payment on the house."

Reassuring: Trying to stop the other person from feeling the negative emotions she is experiencing. "Don't worry, it is always darkest before the dawn." "It will all work out OK in the end."

WHY ROADBLOCKS
ARE HIGH-RISK RESPONSES

At first glance, some of these barriers seem quite innocent. Praise, reassurance, logical responses, questions, and well-intentioned advice are often thought of as positive factors in interpersonal relations. Why, then, do behavioral scientists think of these twelve types of responses as potentially damaging to communication?

These twelve ways of responding are viewed as *high-risk* responses, rather than *inevitably* destructive elements of all communication. They are more likely to block conversation, thwart the other person's problem-solving efficiency, and increase the emotional distance between people than other ways of communicating. However, a⁺ times, people use these responses with little or no obvious negative effect.

If one or two persons are experiencing a strong need or wrestling with a difficult problem, the likelihood of negative impact from roadblocks increases greatly. A useful guideline to follow is, "Whenever you or the other person is experiencing stress, avoid all roadblocks." Unfortunately, it is precisely when stress is experienced that we are most likely to use these high-risk responses.

The twelve barriers to communication can be divided into three major categories: judgment, sending solutions, and avoidance of the other's concerns:

1. Criticizing
2. Name-calling
3. Diagnosing
4. Praising Evaluatively $\biggr\}$ JUDGING

5. Ordering
6. Threatening
7. Moralizing
8. Excessive/Inappropriate Questioning
9. Advising $\biggr\}$ SENDING SOLUTIONS

10. Diverting
11. Logical Argument
12. Reassuring $\biggr\}$ AVOIDING THE OTHER'S CONCERNS

Let's look in greater detail at each of these major categories of high-risk responses.

JUDGING: THE MAJOR ROADBLOCK

Four roadblocks fall into this category—criticizing, name-calling, diagnosing, and praising. They are all variations on a common theme—judging the other person.

Psychologist Carl Rogers delivered a lecture on communication in which he said he believes the *major barrier* to interperpersonal communication lies in our *very natural tendency to judge*—to approve or disapprove of the statements of the other person.[5]

Few people think of themselves as judgmental. Yet in that lecture, Rogers convinced many of his listeners that the tendency to judge was more widespread than they realized:

> As you leave the meeting tonight, one of the statements you are likely to hear is, "I didn't like that man's talk." Now what do you respond? Almost invariably your reply will be either approval or disapproval of the attitude expressed. Either you respond, "I didn't either. I thought it was terrible." Or else you tend to reply, "Oh, I thought it was really good." In other words, your primary reaction is to evaluate what has just been said to you, to evaluate it from *your* point of view, your own frame of reference.
>
> Or, take another example. Suppose I say with some feeling, "I think the Republicans are behaving in ways that show a lot of good sound sense these days." What is the response that arises in your mind as you listen? The overwhelming likelihood is that it will be evaluative. You will find yourself agreeing, or disagreeing, or making some judgment about me such as "He must be a conservative," or "He seems solid in his thinking."

In that same speech, Rogers made another important point about the human inclination to be judgmental:

> Although the tendency to make evaluations is common in almost all interchange of language, it is very much heightened in those situations where feelings and emotions are deeply involved. So, the stronger our feelings, the more likely it is that there will be no mutual element in the communication. There will be just two ideas, two feelings, two judgments missing each other in psychological space. I'm sure you recognize this from your own experience. When you have not been emotionally involved yourself, and have listened to a heated discussion, you often go away thinking, "Well, they actually weren't talking about the same thing." And they were not. Each was making a judgment, an evaluation from his own frame of reference. There was really nothing which could be called communication in any genuine sense. This tendency to react to any emotionally meaningful statement by forming an evaluation of it from our own point of view is, I repeat, the major barrier to interpersonal communication.[6]

Criticizing

One of the judgmental roadblocks is criticism. Many of us feel we ought to be critical—or other people will never improve. Parents think they need to judge their children or they will never become hard-working, mannerly adults. Teachers think they must criticize their students or they will never learn. Supervisors think they must criticize their employees or production will slip. In later chapters we will see how some of the objectives we are trying to accomplish with criticism (and the other roadblocks) can be achieved more effectively by other means.

Meanwhile, it is worth observing our interactions with others to see how frequently we are critical. For some people, criticism is a way of life. One husband described his wife as being on a constant fault-finding safari. An admiral once gave White House aide Harry Hopkins the title of "Generalissimo of the Needle Brigade"[7] because of the latter's critical nature.

Name-Calling and Labeling

Name-calling and labeling usually have negative overtones to both the sender and receiver. "Nigger," "Wasp," "intellectual," "brat," "bitch," "shrew," "autocrat," "jerk," "dope," "nag"—these all attach a stigma to the other. Some other labels, however, provide halos: "bright," "hard worker," "dedicated," "a chip off the old block," "a real go-getter."

Labeling prevents us from getting to know ourselves and other individuals: there is no longer a person before us—only a type. The psychologist Clark Moustakas says:

> Labels and classifications make it appear that we know the other, when actually, we have caught the shadow and not the substance. Since we are convinced we know ourselves and others . . . [we] no longer actually see what is happening before us and in us, and, not knowing that we do not know, we make no effort to be in contact with the real. We continue to use labels to stereotype ourselves and others, and these labels have replaced human meanings, unique feelings and growing life within and between persons.[8]

Diagnosing

Diagnosis, a form of labeling, has plagued mankind through the centuries, but has been even more prevalent since the time of Freud. Some people, instead of listening to the substance of what a person is saying, play emotional detective, probing for hidden motives, psychological complexes, and the like.

A secretary who went to work for a psychologist resigned within a month. When a friend asked why she left the job, she explained, "He analyzed what motives were behind everything I did. I couldn't win. If I came to work late, it was because I was hostile; if I came early, it was because I was anxious; if I arrived on time, I was compulsive."

Perhaps you have found, as I have, that communication tends to be thwarted when one person informs another that she is being defensive, or self-deceiving, or that she is acting out of guilt or fear or some other unconscious motive or "complex."

Praising Evaluatively

There is a common belief that all honest praise is helpful. Many parents, teachers, managers, and others endorse praise without reservation. Praise "is supposed to build confidence, increase security, stimulate initiative, motivate learning, generate good will and improve human relations," says Haim Ginott.[9] Thus, at first sight, praise seems to be an unlikely candidate to qualify as a roadblock. However, positive evaluations often have negative results.

Praise is often used as a gimmick to try to get people to change their behavior. When someone with ulterior purposes offers praise, there is often resentment, not only of the effort to control, but also of the manipulativeness experienced. David Augsburger says that it is not always true that to be praised is to be loved. "To be praised more often is to be manipulated. To be praised is often to be used. To be praised is often to be outsmarted, outmaneuvered, out-sweet-talked."[10]

Even when it is not used manipulatively, praise often has deterimental effects. Have you ever noticed how people defend themselves against praise as though they were protecting themselves against a threat? Their guardedness and defensiveness cause them to come up with stock denials such as:

"I don't think it's that good."
"It wasn't much, really."
"I can't take the credit for it; my assistant, Charlie, thought it up."
"It was mainly luck."
"I could have done a lot better."

When people hear about the perils of evaluative praise, they often think behavioral scientists believe *all* forms of encouragement are detrimental. This is far from the case. Expressing positive feelings toward people is an important element of interpersonal communication. Constructive ways of doing this will be explained in Chapter 9.

SENDING SOLUTIONS CAN BE A PROBLEM!

Another group of roadblocks involves sending solutions to other persons. The solutions may be sent caringly as advice, indirectly by questioning, authoritatively as an order, aggressively as a threat, or with a halo around it as moralizing. Some ways of sending solutions obviously carry higher risks than others. *All* of these ways of sending solutions, however, are potential barriers to communication, especially when one or both of the persons is experiencing a need or a problem. Sending a solution often compounds a problem or creates new problems without resolving the original dilemma.

Ordering, threatening, moralizing, advising (and often asking closed-ended questions), are ways of sending solutions. I am not suggesting that sending solutions is never appropriate, but sending solutions can erect barriers and can thwart another person's growth.

Ordering

An order is a solution sent coercively and backed by force. When coercion is used, people often become resistant and resentful. Sabotage may result. Or people who are constantly given orders may become very compliant and submissive. Orders imply that the other's judgment is unsound and thus tend to undermine self-esteem.

Threatening

A threat is a solution that is sent with an emphasis on the punishment that will be forthcoming if the solution is not implemented. Threats produce the same kind of negative results that are produced by orders.

Moralizing

Many people love to put a halo around their solutions for others. They attempt to back their ideas with the force of social, moral, or theological authority. Moralizing speaks with "shoulds" and "oughts" but it chooses other wordings, too. "It's the right thing to do." "You don't visit me enough." "Shoulds" are often implied, even when they are not stated directly.

"Moralizing is demoralizing." It fosters anxiety, arouses resentment, tends to thwart honest self-expression, and invites pretense.

Excessive or Inappropriate Questioning

Some kinds of questions have their place in communication. But questions can be real conversation-stoppers, as illustrated in this familiar question-and-nonresponse routine:

"Where did you go?"
"Out."
"What did you do?"
"Nothing."

Day after day, parents in American homes ask, "How was school today?" and day after day they hear the droned nonresponse, "OK."

Some people ask questions constantly. When this happens, they experience an almost total drying up of conversation. When loved ones share so little with them, these questioners desperately resort to more questions to keep at least a trickle of disclosure coming from the other person. But the added questions retard the communication even more.

A large percentage of the population is addicted to questioning. While there are constructive ways of asking *occasional* questions (as will be seen in the next chapter), extensive questioning usually derails a conversation. Jacques Lalanne, president of the Institut de Developpement Humain in Quebec, says, "In everyday conversation, questions are usually a poor substitute for more direct communication. Questions are incomplete, indirect, veiled, impersonal and consequently ineffective messages that often breed defense reactions and resistance. They are rarely simple requests for information, but an indirect means of attaining an end, a way of manipulating the person being questioned."[11]

Advising

Advice is another of the most commonly used of the roadblocks. At its worst, it represents an "interfere-iority complex." Though I have known and taught others many of the important reasons why advice is rarely constructive, and though I have decreased my advice-giving enormously, I still find myself dispensing advice inappropriately. The advice-giving trap is a rather constant temptation to me, and I find I am most apt to give in to it when someone I love talks over a problem with me.

Well, what's wrong with advice? Advice is often a basic insult to the intelligence of the other person. It implies a lack of confidence in the capacity of the person with the problem to understand and cope with his or her own difficulties. As Norman Kagan puts it, "In essence, we implicitly say to someone, 'You have been making a "big deal" out of a problem whose solution is immediately apparent to me—how stupid you are!' "[12]

Another problem with advice is that the advisor seldom understands the full implications of the problem. When people share their concerns with us, they often display only the "tip of the iceberg." The advisor is unaware of the complexities, feelings, and the many other factors that lie hidden beneath the surface. Dag Hammarskjold, the introspective Swedish diplomat, said:

> Not knowing the question,
> It was easy for him
> To give the answer.[13]

AVOIDING THE OTHER'S CONCERNS

A journalist once commented that the first law of conversation is that if there is any possible way to derail the train of dialogue, someone will do it. The remaining three roadblocks—diverting, logical argument, and reassurance—are notable for getting conversations off the track.

Diverting

One of the most frequent ways of switching a conversation from the other person's concerns to your own topic is called "diverting." The phrase "Speaking of . . ." often signals the beginning of a diversion. Much of what passes for conversation is really little more than a series of diversions. For example, I overhead this interchange between four elderly ladies visiting a friend in a hospital:

> Patient: This was such a painful operation! I didn't think I would be able to stand it. It was just . . .
>
> Person A: Speaking of operations, I had my gallbladder out in Memorial Hospital in 1976. What a time I had . . .
>
> Person B: That's the hospital my grandson was taken to when he broke his arm. Dr. Beyer set it.
>
> Person C: Did you know that Dr. Beyer lives on my street? They say he has an alcohol problem.
>
> Person D: Well, alcohol is not nearly so bad as drugs. The son of the principal of the high school is really messed up by drugs. He shouldn't deal with other people's kids if he can't manage his own.

Whoa! What happened to the patient's concerns?

Sometimes people divert a conversation because they lack the awareness and skills to listen effectively. Sometimes they are grabbing the focus of attention for themselves. At other times people resort to diversion when they are uncomfortable with the emotions stimulated by the conversation. Many people dislike talking about affection, anger, conflict, death, sickness, divorce, and other topics that create tension in them. When these topics are the focus of conversation, they divert the conversation to a topic more comfortable for them.

Logical Argument

Logic has many important functions. When another person is under stress, however, or when there is conflict between people, providing logical solutions can be infuriating. Though it may seem that those are the very times we most need logic, it nevertheless has a high risk of alienating the other person.

One of the main problems with logic in situations of personal or interpersonal stress is that it keeps others at an emotional distance. Logic focuses on facts and typically avoids feelings. But when another person has a problem or when there is a problem in the relationship, feelings are the main issue. When persons use logic to avoid emotional involvement, they are withdrawing from another at a most inopportune moment.

Reassuring

"What on earth can be wrong with reassurance?" is a question we get from many people.

Like the other eleven barriers, reassurance can drive a wedge between people. Haim Ginott writes:

> Once in a blue moon, almost every parent hears his son or daughter declare, "I am stupid." Knowing that *his* child cannot be stupid, the parent sets out to convince him that he is bright.

> Son: I am stupid.
> Father: You are not stupid.
> Son: Yes, I am.
> Father: You are not. Remember how smart you were at camp? The counselor thought you were one of the brightest.
> Son: How do you know what he thought?
> Father: He told me so.
> Son: Yeah, how come he called me stupid all the time?
> Father: He was just kidding.
> Son: I am stupid, and I know it. Look at my grades in school.
> Father: You just have to work harder.
> Son: I already work harder, and it doesn't help. I have no brains.
> Father: You are smart, I know.
> Son: I am stupid, *I* know.
> Father: (loudly) You are not stupid!
> Son: Yes, I am!
> Father: You are not stupid, Stupid!

Ginott goes on to explain:

> When a child declares that he is stupid or ugly or bad, nothing that we can say or do will change his self-image immediately. A person's ingrained opinion of himself resists direct attempts at alteration. As one child said to his father, I know you mean well, Dad, but I am not *that* stupid to take your word that I am bright.[14]

Reassurance is a way of seeming to comfort another person while actually doing the opposite. The word *comfort* comes from two Latin words, *con* and *fortis*. The combination literally means "strengthened by being with." Reassurance does not allow the comforter to really be with the other. It can be a form of emotional withdrawal. Reassurance is often used by people who like the idea of being helpful but who do not want to experience the emotional demand that goes with it.

ROADBLOCK NUMBER THIRTEEN

When people are introduced to the roadblocks, a fairly typical reaction is, "That's just what my husband has been doing all these years! Wait till I tell him about all the roadblocks he sends." Or, "Gosh, my boss uses just about all of these barriers. The next time he does it, I'm going to point out how he's roadblocking me." This is Roadblock Thirteen: telling other people they are sending roadblocks. Roadblock Thirteen belongs in the judgment category. If you want to improve your communication, pointing the finger of judgment at others is a poor place to begin.

Guilt, Remorse, Regret

After hearing a presentation on the roadblocks, many people experience pangs of guilt. They suddenly become aware that some patterns of their communication are barriers in important relationships and have probably caused needless distance between them and other people. After presentations on communications barriers in our workshops, people typically make comments like these:

Awareness of the three major groupings of roadblocks was like a stab and I cringe for all the situations that I "blew" that could have been productive had I known how to respond properly. . . .

It's like suddenly knowing the enemy and finding out that it's *me!* . . .

I had always thought of myself as a "good listener," never realizing that I was often guilty of actually shutting off communication by the way I was listening. . . .

The responses you identified as barriers were things I'd always felt *helped* conversation, and I've been using many of them pretty consistently! As I listened to you talk about the roadblocks, I felt remorse and regret. These thoughts flew into my mind: "I've failed as a parent and a teacher." "I wish I could have learned this fifteen years ago." "How did I get to be forty years old without discovering that these were roadblocks?" After the guilt, however, I became hopeful. After all, it is practically impossible to counter a negative approach unless you know that it is destructive. Learning about the roadblocks is the first step to positive action for me.

We all use roadblocks sometimes. Their occasional usage rarely does much harm to a relationship. When employed frequently, however, there is a high probability that roadblocks will do considerable harm.

These conversational bad habits can be corrected. The awareness that comes from reading a chapter like this can help greatly. You can figure out which roadblock you most want to eliminate and concentrate on eradicating that one. It is difficult and discouraging work at first because roadblocks are habitual ways of responding and it requires time and effort to change any habit. At the same time that you try to eliminate the roadblocks, you can use the communication skills described in the remainder of this book. Several thousand years ago, a sage taught that it is much easier to stamp out a bad habit by supplanting it with a good one than it is to try to stamp out negative habits by willpower alone.[15] That wisdom still holds today. As you learn to listen, assert, resolve conflict, and solve interpersonal problems more effectively, your use of the roadblocks will inevitably diminish.

SUMMARY

Certain ways of verbalizing carry a high risk of putting a damper on the conversation, being harmful to the relationship, triggering feelings of inadequacy, anger, or dependency in the other person, or all of these things. As a result of one or more of the twelve roadblocks, the other may become more submissive and compliant. Or she may become more resistant, rebellious, and argumentative. These barriers to conversation tend to diminish the other's self-esteem and to undermine motivation. They decrease the likelihood that the other will be self-determining—they increase the likelihood that she will put the focus of evaluation outside herself. Roadblocks are prevalent in our culture; they are used in over 90 percent of the conversations where one or both persons have a problem or a strong need. Yet these conversational bad habits can be corrected, primarily through the use of the skills taught in the remainder of this book.

PART TWO

Listening Skills

One friend, one person who is truly understanding, who takes the trouble to listen to us
as we consider our problems, can change our
whole outlook on the world.

—Dr. Elton Mayo[1]

CHAPTER THREE

Listening Is More Than Merely Hearing

I often ponder over the nature of true human sincerity, true transparency. . . . It is a rare and difficult thing; and how much it depends on the person who is listening to us! There are those who pull down the barriers and make the way smooth; there are those who force the doors and enter our territory like invaders; there are those who barricade us in, shut us in upon ourselves, dig ditches and throw up walls around us; there are those who set us out of tune and listen only to our false notes; there are those for whom we always remain strangers, speaking an unknown tongue. And when it is our turn to listen, which of these are we . . .?[1]

—Anonymous

THE IMPORTANCE OF LISTENING

If you are at all typical, *listening takes up more of your waking hours than any other activity*. A study of persons of varied occupational backgrounds showed that 70 percent of their waking moments were spent in communication. And of that time, writing took 9 percent, reading absorbed 16 percent, talking accounted for 30 percent, and listening occupied 45 percent.[2] Other surveys underscore the large amount of time that people in different walks of life spend in listening.[3] It is important to listen effectively because of the sheer amount of it that you do each day.

Furthermore, many of the most important facets of your life are greatly influenced by your skills (or lack of skill) in listening. The quality of your friendships, the cohesiveness of your family relationships, your effectiveness at work—these hinge, in large measure, on your ability to listen.

Unfortunately, few people are good listeners. Even at the purely informational level, researchers claim that 75 percent of oral communication is ignored, misunderstood, or quickly forgotten. Rarer still is the ability to listen for the deepest meanings in what people say. How devastating, but how common, to talk with someone about subjects of intense interest to oneself only to experience the stifling realization that the other person was not really listening and that his responses were simply automatic and mechanical. Perhaps it was after an experience like this that Jesus was quoted as saying, "Thou hearest in thy one ear but the other Thou has closed."[4]

Dr. Ralph G. Nichols, who developed innovative classes on listening at the University of Minnesota, writes:

> It can be stated with practically no qualification that people in general do not know how to listen. They have ears that hear very well, but seldom have they acquired the necessary . . . skills which would allow those ears to be used effectively for what is called *listening*. . . . For several years, we have been testing the ability of people to understand and remember what they hear. . . . These extensive tests led to this general conclusion: immediately after the average person has listened to someone talk, he remembers only about half of what he has heard—no matter how carefully he thought he was listening. What happens as time passes? Our own testing shows . . . that . . . we tend to forget from one-half to one-third [more] *within eight hours.* . . .[5]

All too often the speaker's words go "in one ear and out the other."

A major reason for the poor listening in our society is that most of us receive a very rigorous early training in nonlistening. The therapist Franklin Ernst says that "from the earliest years of life, a person's listening activity is the most heavily trained of all activities. . . . The person's listening . . . is more attended to than his bowel training, his bladder activity, or his genital activity."[6] Ernst points out that the typical child, in his most impressionable years, receives a steady diet of antilistening edicts. Parents say things like:

"We don't listen to those things in our family."
"Don't pay any attention to him."
"Pretend you don't notice."
"Don't take it so seriously."
"He didn't mean what he said."
"Don't give them the satisfaction of knowing that you heard them" (and that it bothers you).

The typical parent not only verbalizes these antilistening comments, he demonstrates them daily in his own life. He is inattentive to persons speaking to him, may interrupt frequently, and responds with numerous roadblocks. By word and deed we are taught to be nonlisteners in our childhood.

Our schooling also conspires against the development of effective listening skills. About six years of training is given to reading in most school systems; additional opportunities are often available for remedial reading and speed reading. In the vast majority of schools, however, there are no effective training programs for developing listening skills. This makes little sense in a society where the graduated student will have to spend at least three times as much time listening as he spends reading.

Rather than receiving training in effective listening, the student in a typical school receives further antilistening training. Like his parents, most of his teachers will not be good listeners. They, too, will demonstrate inattentiveness, interruptions, and the use of many roadblocks throughout the school day. Furthermore, the typical classroom is structured for a larger ratio of listening time to talking time than the human being is capable of achieving. Some experts say that we can only listen effectively from one-third to two-thirds of the time. Whatever the specific ratio, each of us can recognize that when we listen for a long time without doing any talking or responding, our listening efficiency begins to drop drastically and finally our minds drift off to considering other topics than those about which the speaker is talking. Because the student cannot possibly listen effectively to all the talking to which school subjects him, he learns to turn off his mind when other people are speaking. This problem is compounded by the repetitions and boring nature of much teacher talk.

Most of us have been trained to be poor listeners. Yet ironically, we spend more time listening than doing anything else, and the quality of our listening greatly affects both the personal and the vocational dimensions of our lives. The remainder of this chapter is devoted to defining *listening*, outlining the major clusters of listening skills, and teaching the more elementary of the listening skills.

LISTENING DEFINED

It is helpful to note the distinction between *hearing* and *listening*. *"Hearing,"* says Professor John Drakeford, "is a word used to describe the physiological sensory processes by which auditory sensations are received by the ears and transmitted to the brain. *Listening,* on the other hand, refers to a more complex psychological procedure involving interpreting and understanding the significance of the sensory experience."[7] In other words, I can hear what another person is saying without really listening to him. A teenager put it this way: "My friends listen to what I say, but my parents only hear me talk."

I recall a time when I was talking with someone who seemed to ignore everything I said. "You are not listening to me!" I accused. "Oh, yes I am!" he said. He then repeated word for word what I had told him. He *heard* exactly. But he wasn't *listening*. He didn't understand the meanings I was trying to convey. Perhaps you have had a similar experience and know how frustrating it can be to be heard accurately by someone who isn't listening with understanding.

The distinction between merely hearing and really listening is deeply embedded in our language. The word *listen* is derived from two Anglo-Saxon words. One word is *hlystan*, which means "hearing." The other is *hlosnian*, which means "to wait in suspense." Listening, then, is the *combination* of hearing what the other person says *and* a suspenseful waiting, an intense psychological involvement with the other.

LISTENING SKILL CLUSTERS

Learning to be an effective listener is a difficult task for many people. Our approach simplifies the learning process by focusing on single skills or small clusters of skills so people can concentrate on one skill or one cluster at a time.

Focusing on a single skill when necessary, and on small clusters of skills when possible, enables people to learn most efficiently. This approach helps the reader master one cluster of skills, see himself readily improve in that area, and then move to a more advanced set of skills. When each of the separate listening skill clusters has been learned, the reader can integrate the various skills into a sensitive and unified way of listening.

The clusters of listening skills taught in this book include:

SKILL CLUSTERS	SPECIFIC SKILLS
Attending Skills	• A Posture of Involvement • Appropriate Body Motion • Eye Contact • Nondistracting Environment
Following Skills	• Door Openers • Minimal Encourages • Infrequent Questions • Attentive Silence
Reflecting Skills	• Paraphrasing • Reflecting Feelings • Reflecting Meanings (Tying Feelings to Content) • Summative Reflections

Definitions of each of the specific skills will be given as they are treated in this and the next chapter.

ATTENDING SKILLS

Attending is giving your physical attention to another person. I sometimes refer to it as listening with the whole body. Attending is nonverbal communication that indicates that you are paying careful attention to the person who is talking. Attending skills include a posture of involvement, appropriate body motion, eye contact, and a nondistracting environment.

The Impact of Attending and Nonattending

Effective attending works wonders in human relations. It shows the other that you are interested in him and in what he has to say. It facilitates the expression of the most important matters on his mind and in his heart. Nonattending, on the other hand, tends to thwart the speaker's expression.

Allen Ivey and John Hinkle describe the results of attending in a college psychology course. They trained six students in attending behavior. Then a session, taught by a visiting professor, was videotaped. The students started out in typical student nonattending classroom behaviors. The professor lectured, unaware of the students' prearranged plan. His presentation was centered on his notes. He used no gestures, spoke in a monotone, and paid little attention to the students. At a prearranged signal, however, the students began deliberately to physically attend. Within a half a minute, the lecturer gestured for the first time, his verbal rate increased, and a lively classroom session was born. Simple attending had changed the whole picture. At another signal, the students stopped attending, and the speaker, after awkwardly seeking continued response, resumed the unengaging lecture with which he began the class.[8]

It is an impressive experience to talk to a person who is directly and totally there for you. Norman Rockwell, the artist famed for his *Saturday Evening Post* covers, recounted his experience while painting a portrait of President Eisenhower:

> The general and I didn't discuss politics or the campaign. Mostly we talked about painting and fishing. But what I remember most about the hour and a half I spent with him was the way he gave me all his attention. He was listening to me and talking to me, just as if he hadn't a care in the world, hadn't been through the trials of a political convention, wasn't on the brink of a presidential campaign.[9]

Attending is often one of the most effective behaviors we can offer when listening to someone.

A Posture of Involvement

Because body language often speaks louder then words, a "posture of involvement" is extremely important in listening. In their book *Human Territories: How We Behave in Space-Time*, Drs. Albert Scheflen and Norman Ashcroft note, "Each region of the body can be oriented in such a way that it invites, facilitates, or holds an interpersonal relation. Or it can be oriented in order to break off, discourage, or avoid involvement."[10] Communication tends to be fostered when the listener demonstrates a relaxed alertness with the body leaning slightly forward, facing the other squarely, maintaining an "open" position and situating himself at an appropriate distance from the speaker.

The good listener communicates attentiveness through the *relaxed alertness* of his body during the conversation. What is sought is a balance between the relaxedness that communicates "I feel at home with you and accept you" and the alertness or productive tension that demonstrates "I sense the importance of what you are telling me and am very intent on understanding you." The blending of both of these body messages creates an effective listening presence.

Inclining one's body toward the speaker communicates more energy and attention than does leaning back or sprawling in the chair. When a public speaker has his audience enthralled, we say, "He has them on the edge of their seats." The people are not only leaning forward, but are sitting forward in their chairs. By contrast, some listeners slouch back in their chairs looking like propped-up cadavers. How demotivating that posture is to the speaker!

Facing the other squarely, your right shoulder to the other's left shoulder, helps communicate your involvement. The common phrase "He gave me the cold shoulder" suggests the indifference or rejection that can be communicated by not positioning yourself to face the other person. Because homes and offices are seldom arranged for good attending, you may have to rearrange some furniture to be able to position yourself properly.

Another aspect of facing the other squarely is to be at eye level with the speaker. This is especially important if you are an authority figure—a parent, teacher, or boss—of the speaker. Sitting on the edge of a desk when the other is in a chair or standing when he is sitting can be a major barrier to interpersonal contact. Parents of young children often comment on how important this aspect of attending is in their homes.

Maintaining an open position with arms and legs uncrossed is another important part of the posture of involvement. Tightly crossed arms or legs often communicate closedness and defensiveness. Baseball fans know what to expect when an umpire makes a call that is disputed by a team manager. The manager runs toward the umpire shouting and waving his arms. The umpire typically crosses his arms in a gesture of defensiveness, communicating that he will not budge from his position and that any argument will be fruitless. The very young do this same thing: they commonly cross their arms when defying their parents, indicating a psychological closedness to their parents' comments.

Positioning yourself at an appropriate distance from the speaker is an important aspect of attending. Too much distance between persons impedes communication. C. L. Lassen studied the effect of physical proximity in initial psychiatric interviews. The psychiatrists sat either three, six, or nine feet away from their clients. The clients' anxiety levels were measured, both by observable behaviors and through the clients' self-reports. Lassen discovered that a client's anxiety increased as the distance between himself and the psychiatrist increased.[11]

On the other hand, when a listener gets too close to another person, anxiety also increases. Some psychologists have demonstrated that the typical American feels uneasy when someone with whom he is not intimate positions himself closer than three feet for an extended time. Long periods of close physical proximity during a conversation can cause discomfort even when the persons are spouses or close friends. Cultural differences affect the optimal distance for conversing, as do individual differences within a given culture. The distance between yourself and another person that most facilitates communication can be discovered by watching for signs of anxiety and discomfort in the speaker and positioning yourself accordingly. Normally, about three feet is a comfortable distance in our society.

Appropriate Body Motion

Appropriate body movement is essential to good listening. In his book *Who's Listening?*, psychiatrist Franklin Ernst, Jr., writes:

> To listen is to move. To listen is to be moved by the talker—physically and psychologically. . . . The non-moving, unblinking person can reliably be estimated to be a non-listener. . . . When other visible moving has ceased and the eyeblink rate has fallen to less than once in six seconds, listening, for practical purposes, has stopped.[12]

One study of nonverbal listener behavior noted that the listener who remains still is seen as controlled, cold, aloof, and reserved. By contrast, the listener who is more active—but not in a fitful or nervous way—is experienced as friendly, warm, casual, and as not acting in a role. People prefer speaking to listeners whose bodies are not rigid and unmoving.[13] When watching videotapes of effective listeners, I discovered that they tend to have a rhythm of less activity when the speaker is talking and somewhat more activity when they are responding. Occasionally, the listener becomes so in tune with the speaker that his gestures synchronize with the speaker's.

The avoidance of distracting motions and gestures is also essential for effective attending. The good listener moves his body in *response* to the speaker. Ineffective listeners move their bodies in response to stimuli that are unrelated to the talker. Their distraction is demonstrated by their body language: fiddling with pencils or keys, jingling money, fidgeting nervously, drumming fingers, cracking knuckles, frequently shifting weight or crossing and uncrossing the legs, swinging a crossed leg up and down, and other nervous mannerisms. Watching a TV program, waving or nodding one's head to people passing by, continuing with one's activities, like preparing a meal, or reading the paper can be very distracting when someone is talking to you.

Eye Contact

Effective eye contact expresses interest and a desire to listen. It involves focusing one's eyes softly on the speaker and occasionally shifting the gaze from his face to other parts of the body, to a gesturing hand, for example, and then back to the face and then to eye contact once again. Poor eye contact occurs when a listener repeatedly looks away from the speaker, stares at him constantly or blankly, or looks away as soon as the speaker looks at the listener.

Eye contact enables the speaker to appraise your receptiveness to him and his message. It helps him figure out how safe he is with you. Equally important, you can "hear" the speaker's deeper meanings through eye contact. Indeed, if effective listening means getting inside the other's skin and understanding the person's experience from his perspective, one of the best ways to enter that inner world is through the "window" of the eyes. Ralph Waldo Emerson said, "The eyes of men converse as much as their tongues, but with the advantage that the ocular dialect needs no dictionary, but is understood the world over."[14]

Many people have a difficult time establishing eye contact. Just as some people have a hard time knowing what to do with their hands in social interactions, other people do not know what to do with their eyes. People sometimes look away from another's face at the moment they sense he will show emotion on his face. Part of the reason for that behavior may be a desire not to be intrusive or embarrass the other.[15] (As we will see later, however, the effective listener hears feelings as well as content and understands what the other says with his body language as well as through words.) Another reason for not looking into the speaker's eyes is that it is one of the most intimate ways of relating to a person, and the fear of escalation of affection has made it somewhat taboo in many societies.[16]

Despite the fact that some people find it difficult to look into another's eyes, few of us enjoy carrying on a conversation with a person whose glance continually darts about the room. When I am listened to by that kind of a person, I am distracted from what I am saying. For example, when a person talking with me at a party keeps looking around the room at other people, I often interpret that to mean that he would rather be someplace else—and I personally wish he would find out where he would rather be and go there! Lack of eye contact may be a sign of indifference or hostility. It can be experienced as a put-down.

The ability to have good eye contact is essential for effective interpersonal communication in our society. Sometimes it cannot be used maximally because others are uncomfortable with it. Often, however, it is one of the most effective of the listening skills. People who are uncomfortable with eye contact can develop the ability to communicate through the eyes. Awareness of the importance of eye contact helps many people overcome the inhibition. Additionally, people with this problem may have to work at looking at a person's face more often until they become more comfortable with this way of relating.

Nondistracting Environment

Attending involves giving the other person one's undivided attention. This is virtually impossible in environments that have a high level of distraction. An undistracting environment, one without significant physical barriers between people and one that is inviting rather than ugly—these conditions facilitate conversation.

The attending listener attempts to *cut environmental distractions to the minimum.* At home, the TV or stereo may be turned off in the room to provide the interruption-free and distraction-free environment that is so important for human interaction. If need be, the telephone receiver can be taken off the hook or unplugged, and a "Do Not Disturb" sign can even be placed on the door. In many offices, the door can be closed, the music or intercom turned off, and the secretary can hold telephone calls until the conversation is completed. In the factory, finding an undistracting setting is difficult but not impossible. Good attending in a manufacturing plant may involve using the feet before using the ears—to get to an office or some other place where you will not be disturbed and where the environment is not distracting.

Removing sizable physical barriers fosters better communication. In offices the desk typically intrudes between the speaker and the listener. A. G. White's study of medical case-history interviewing discovered that 55 percent of the patients initially sat at ease when no desk separated the patient and the doctor; only 10 percent were at ease when a desk separated the patient from the doctor.[17] For some people, a desk is associated with a position of authority and can trigger feelings of weakness or hostility. When a listener sits behind a desk, the interaction is more likely to be role-to-role rather than person-to-person. If an office is too small to place two chairs away from the desk for conversation, it is desirable to have the visitor's chair beside the desk rather than across the desk.

Good attending fosters improved observation of the other's body language, which is an important part of listening. When a desk or other large physical barrier stands between you and the speaker, it is extremely difficult to note what the other's body is communicating.

Psychological Attention

What a person wants most of all from a listener is a sense of psychological presence. He wants the listener to really be there for him. Physical attending fosters psychological presence. When I am in a good environmental setting, have comfortable eye contact, appropriate body motion, and maintain the posture of involvement, my psychological attending usually improves. My physical attending skill also helps the other feel my psychological presence.

However, if I try to fake attention when listening to another, I deceive only myself. The listener who is truly present to another displays a vitality that registers on face and body his interest and concern for what the other is saying. The person who is not really "there," even though his body takes an attending position, is inevitably detected. The speaker notes the glazed eyes, and his "antenna" picks up other signals that reveal that the listener's heart and mind are not with him. Without psychological presence, no attending technique will work.

Consciously Working At Attending

Surprisingly, we find that most people have a fairly accurate informal knowledge of attending before we teach them any attending skills. In our seminars, the trainer often says, "Position yourselves to show me that you are really interested in what I am saying." Most people in the group assume a fairly good attending position. Then the leader says, "Show me by your body posture that you couldn't care less about me or about what I am telling you." Virtually everyone demonstrates a clear idea of what nonattending behavior is like. So why do we make such an effort to teach attending skills? There are basically two reasons.

First of all, because the teaching of these skills does sharpen understanding of attending. People raise to the level of their awareness some understandings that were previously vague and hazy. People invariably learn something new and/or develop a deepened insight into what they already know.

Secondly, and more important, we find that a focus on the methods and merits of attending motivates many people to do what they already know how to do but often neglect to do. A focus on attending serves as a consciousness-raising experience that often motivates people to utilize these skills. Once people start attending at appropriate times, they are rewarded by a new quality of interpersonal relationships. Allan Ivey puts it this way:

> Some may question the possible artificiality of attending behavior or other skills. . . . They validly object to seeing life as a series of exercises in which the individual constantly dredges into a "handbag of skills" so he can adapt to each life situation. Our experience has been that individuals may sometimes begin attending in an artificial, deliberate manner. However, once attending has been initiated, the person to whom one is listening tends to become more animated, and this in turn reinforces the attender who very quickly forgets about attending deliberately and soon attends naturally. A variety of our clients and trainees have engaged in conscious attending behavior only to find themselves so interested in the person with whom they are talking that they lose themselves in the other.[18]

People tend to think of communication as a verbal process. Students of communication are convinced that most communication is nonverbal. The most commonly quoted estimate, based on research, is that 85 percent of our communication is nonverbal! So attending, the nonverbal part of listening, is a basic building block of the listening process.

FOLLOWING SKILLS

Beatrice Glass's car collided with another auto. As soon after the accident as possible she telephoned her husband, Charlie, and reported that she had been in an accident. "How much damage did it do to the car?" was his immediate response. When he had that information, Charlie asked, "Whose fault was it?" Then he said, "Don't admit a thing. You phone the insurance company and I'll call our lawyer. Just a minute and I'll give you the number."

"Any more questions?" she asked.

"No," he replied, "that just about covers it."

"Oh, it does, does it?" she screamed. "Well, just in case you are interested, I'm in the hospital with four broken ribs!"

Charlie's responses may have been more callous and blatant than those of the average husband, but what he did is typical for many people. Because Charlie's wife had a problem (an automobile accident that resulted in her hospitalization), Charlie's role in the conversation should have been primarily that of a listener. But he did most of the talking.

One of the primary tasks of a listener is to stay out of the other's way so the listener can discover how the speaker views his situation. Unfortunately, the average "listener" interrupts and diverts the speaker by asking many questions or making many statements. Researchers tell us that it is not at all uncommon for "listeners" to lead and direct a conversation through the frequent use of questions. It is also common for the "listener" to talk so much that he monopolizes the conversation!

Four following skills foster effective listening: door openers, minimal encourages, open questions, and attentive silence.

Door Openers

People often send *nonverbal clues* when they are burdened or excited about something. Their feelings are telegraphed in facial expressions, tone of voice, body posture, and energy level. For example, Jerry, who is normally exuberant, had not laughed or entered into the family repartee for four days. When they were alone, his wife, Darlene, said, "You don't seem yourself these past few days. You seem burdened by something. Care to talk about it?" That was Darlene's way of sending a door opener.

A door opener is a noncoercive invitation to talk. There are times when door openers are not necessary. The speaker plunges right into his theme. Sometimes, however, you will sense that the other person wants to talk but needs encouragement as Jerry did. At other times, the speaker will be in the midst of a conversation and will show signs that he is unsure about continuing. A door opener like this may help him proceed: "I'm interested in hearing more about it."

People often send door closers (roadblocks) when door openers are much more appropriate. When a child comes home from school with dragging steps and an unhappy expression on his face, parents often respond in ways that tend to make the child withdraw into himself. *Judgmental* statements are apt to pour forth.

> "What a sourpuss you have on today."
> "What did you do this time?"
> "Don't inflict your lousy mood on me."
> "What did you do, lose your best friend?"

Sometimes, they try to *reassure:*

> "Cheer up."
> "Things will get better. They always do."
> "Next week you won't even remember what happened."

At such times, *advice giving* is another favorite tactic:

> "Why don't you do something you like to do?"
> "Don't mope around all day. That won't help anything."
> "I'm sure that whatever happened wasn't worth ruining your day over."

Instead of yielding to the temptation to use roadblocks, parents could send a door opener:

> "Looks like things didn't go well for you today. I've got time if you'd like to talk."
> "Something unpleasant happen to you? Want to talk about it?"

Door openers typically have four elements:

1. A *description of the other person's body language.* "Your face is beaming today." "You look like you are not feeling up to par."
2. An *invitation to talk or to continue talking.* "Care to talk about it?" "Please go on." "I'm interested in what you are saying."
3. *Silence*—giving the other person time to decide whether to talk and/or what he wants to say.
4. *Attending*—eye contact and a posture of involvement that demonstrates your interest in and concern for the other person.

All four parts are not necessarily present in every door opener. One day, a friend with whom I had shared a great deal of my thoughts and feelings saw that I was troubled. He motioned to a chair and said quietly, "Let's hear about it." On another occasion, he simply said, "Shoot." These brief door openers worked well because of the trust and frequent self-disclosure in the relationship. If other people had said those things to me, I might have clammed up. The personality of the listener, the nature of the relationship, and other factors will determine the most effective door opener in a given situation.

Silence and attending alone often constitute a strong inducement to talk. A housewife who complained that her husband seldom talked with her decided to try attending to him when *he* wanted to talk. She discovered, to her dismay, that he seemed most ready to converse when he got home from work—and that's when she was in the midst of dinner preparations! For years she had continued attending to her cooking while calling questions over her shoulder about how his day had gone—but received virtually no response. Her new approach was to serve dinner forty-five minutes later, to take fifteen minutes to relax before her husband came home, and to spend a half-hour talking with him alone. For that half-hour, both the children and her cooking tasks were excluded. She says her husband now engages in significant conversations with her.

Another housewife who found it inconvenient to postpone the dinner hour planned to cook much of the meal earlier in the day on three days a week so she could attend to her husband's conversation when he arrived home. She says, "What a difference that has made! Some days we talk the whole time. On other occasions, our conversations are quite brief—but even these are not the forced exchanges we had when I used to grill him with questions while I prepared dinner. Some days, of course, we do no more than exchange greetings. But the whole interpersonal atmosphere of our house is changing because of my quiet, attentive availability during those three half-hour periods a week before dinner."

A person sending door openers needs an awareness of and a respect for the other person's probable feelings of ambivalence—he may want to self-disclose, yet be hesitant to do so.

One way to deal with ambivalence is to recognize and reflect back to the speaker how difficult it is to talk about painful experiences. When the speaker seems to find it difficult to speak about the things he is saying, a listener can reflect:

"It's pretty hard to talk about."

Another way of dealing with a person who is feeling very ambivalent is to make sure your door opener is an invitation rather than a directive to talk. Door openers should always be noncoercive.

Unfortunately, some people not only open the door, they try to drag the other through:

Sam: You look sad, John. Feel like talking?

John: Not really.

Sam: I can tell you are troubled. You know you can talk to me.
John: I don't feel like it right now.
Sam: You really ought to get it off your chest, you know.
John: Yeah, I know. Later maybe.
Sam: But the time to talk is when you are feeling things . . .

The empathic person respects the privacy of other people and is careful not to be intrusive. He honors rather than violates the other individual's separateness. When appropriate, empathic listeners invite conversation. They do not try to compel it.

It is difficult to offer a door opener, not to be taken up on it, and still let it go. However, in relationships where there is little trust or where communication has not been flowing well for some time, door openers will probably find little response from the other person. It takes time, skill, and goodwill to rebuild trust. Use of listening skills can help nurture this trust once more. If and when the relationship is restored, the door openers will probably find a welcome response.

Minimal Encourages

We have already stated that one of the listener's responsibilities is to allow the speaker room to talk about a situation as he sees and feels it. Many people, in their effort to stay out of the speaker's way, lapse into nonparticipation. Simple responses that encourage the speaker to tell his story in his way yet keep the listener active in the process are called *minimal encourages*. Minimal encourages are brief indicators to other persons that you are with them. The word *minimal* refers to the amount the listener says, which is very little, and to the amount of direction given to the conversation, which is also very little. The word *encourages* is used because these words and phrases aid the speaker to continue speaking. Just a few words can let the other know you are listening without interrupting the flow of talk or breaking the mood. Minimal encourages will be sprinkled throughout a conversation. In the early stages of an interaction, they may be used more frequently to help the conversation gain momentum.

The simple "mm-hmm" is probably the most frequently used of the minimal encourages. That brief phrase can suggest, "Please continue. I'm listening and I understand." There are many brief responses that the listener can use:

Tell me more.	You betcha!
Oh?	Yes.
For instance . . .	Really?
I see.	Gosh.
Right.	And?
Then?	Go on.

So?	Sure.
I hear you.	Darn!

You undoubtedly have your own favorites. Repeating one or two of the speaker's key words or the last word or two of the speaker's statement also constitutes minimal encourages. When the speaker says, "I can't figure out what to do. I guess I'm just confused," the listener may respond "Confused."

A skilled listener can communicate much empathy through voice and facial expressions even when only one or two words are said. I watched a film of one of America's leading therapists listening to a woman tell how furious she was at things her mother had done to her. His empathic "You betcha" seemed to give her the feeling, "He understands how angry I am and he still accepts me." When one of our children told my wife of a big disappointment at school, Dot simply said, "Darn!" but her tone of voice, facial expression, and other nonverbals made it a very feeling-ful response.

Minimal encourages do not imply either agreement or disagreement with what the speaker said. Rather, they let the other know he has been heard and that the listener will try to follow his meaning if the speaker chooses to continue. Thus, when I respond to a speaker with "Right," it does not mean that I agree with the speaker. Rather, it means, "Yes, I hear what you are saying—go on."

This kind of response has often been parodied. We hear tales of the psychiatrist who says nothing but "mm-hmm" for fifty minutes and at the end of the session says, "That will be fifty dollars, please." Obviously, these expressions can be overdone or used mechanically. However, when sensitively orchestrated with a variety of other responses, they assist the speaker's self-exploration.

Infrequent Questions

Questions are an integral part of verbal interaction in our society. As with many other kinds of responses, questions have their strengths and their limitations. Comparatively few people in our culture know how to question effectively. We often rely on questions excessively and use them poorly. Questions usually focus on the intent, perspective, and concerns of the listener rather than on the speaker's orientation. When that happens, questions are a barrier to communication.

We distinguish between "closed" questions and "open" questions. *Closed questions* direct the speaker to give a specific, short response. They are often answered with one word like "yes" or "no." *Open questions*, on the other hand, provide *space* for the speaker to explore his thoughts without being hemmed in too much by the listener's categories. Closed questions are like true/false or multiple-choice test questions, while open questions are like essay questions. When an employee walks into her boss's office, the latter could ask either a closed or an open question:

Closed question: "Do you want to see me about the Rumsford job?"
Open question: "What's on your mind, Ann?"

The open question is usually preferable because it does not suggest the agenda to the person who initiated the interaction.

When used skillfully and infrequently, open questions may help the listener better understand the speaker without directing the conversation. In the report on their study of open and closed questions, Moreland, Phillips, and Lockhart write:

> Crucial to the giving of open-ended questions is the concept of who is to lead the interview. While the interviewer does ask questions while using this skill, his questions are centered around concerns of the client rather than around concerns of the interviewer for the client. Questions should be designed to help the client clarify his own problems, rather than provide information for the interviewer. . . . If the interviewer relies on closed questions to structure his interview, he usually is forced to concentrate so hard on thinking up the next question that he fails to listen to and attend to the client. [19]

In addition to asking open rather than closed questions, it is important to *ask only one question at a time*. When two or more questions are asked in quick succession, the latter questions are usually closed questions. The tendency to ask more than one question seems related to the questioner's inner uncertainty. It rarely facilitates the conversation.

My experience in teaching communication skills leads me to conclude that *most people ask far too many questions*. Putting several questions in a conversation is risky to the interaction; it tends to put the listener opposite rather than beside the speaker, dictating the direction the conversation takes rather than giving the speaker an opportunity to explore his situation in his own way. Almost everyone I have taught would have been a better listener if he asked fewer questions. Furthermore, I believe that most questions can be expressed as statements and that doing so generally is far more productive in a conversation than repeated questioning.

When people try to give up their overreliance on questions, they usually feel very uncomfortable. They may feel the conversation is floundering because of more periods of silence. Skills taught in this part of the book will help you refrain from asking too many questions and at the same time not feel too much of a void in the conversation.

Attentive Silence

The beginning listener needs to learn the value of silence in freeing the speaker to think, feel, and express himself. "The beginning of wisdom is silence," said a Hebrew sage. "The second stage is listening."

Most listeners talk too much. They may speak as much or even more than the person trying to talk. Learning the art of silent responsiveness is essential to good listening. After all, another person cannot describe a problem if you are doing all the talking.

Silence on the part of the listener gives the speaker time to think about what he is going to say and thus enables him to go deeper into himself. It gives a person space to experience the feelings churning within. Silence also allows the speaker to proceed at his own pace. It provides time to deal with his ambivalence about sharing. In the frequent silences, he can choose whether or not to continue talking and at what depth. Silence often serves as a gentle nudge to go further into a conversation. When an interaction is studded with significant silences and backed by good attending, the results can be very impressive.

Through the years, I have returned again and again to these words of Eugene Herrigel that describe why silence can be such a powerful force for a person whose emotions are intense:

> The real meaning of suffering discloses itself only to him who has learned the art of compassion. . . . Gradually, he will fall silent, and in the end will sit there wordless, for a long time sunk deep in himself. And the strange thing is that this silence is not felt by the other person as indifference, as a desolate emptiness which disturbs rather than calms. It is as if this silence had more meaning than countless words could ever have. It is as if he were being drawn into a field of force from which fresh strength flows into him. He feels suffused with a strange confidence. . . . And it may be that in these hours, the resolve will be born to set out on the path that turns a wretched existence into a life of happiness.[20]

Silence can be a balm for sufferers; it is also important in moments of great joy. How beautiful are the silences of intimacy. Thomas Carlyle and Ralph Waldo Emerson sat together for hours one night in utter silence until one rose to go and said, "We've had a grand evening!" I've had many experiences like that with my wife, Dot, when we sat quietly before a fire or gazed silently into each other's eyes, basking in each other's affection. As Halford Luccock says:

> This silence of love is not indifference; it is not merely poverty of something to say. It is a positive form of self-communication. Just as silence is needed to hear a watch ticking, so silence is the medium through which heartbeats are heard.[21]

More than half the people who take communication skills training with us are initially uncomfortable with silence. Even a few seconds' pause in a conversation causes many of them to squirm. These people feel so ill at ease with silences that they have a strong inner compulsion to shatter the quiet with questions, advice, or any other sound that will end their discomfort by ending the silence. For these people, the focus of attention is not on the speaker but rather on their own inner disquiet. They are like the character in Samuel Becket's *Waiting for Godot* who said, "Let us try to converse calmly since we are incapable of keeping silent."[22]

Fortunately, most people can increase their comfort with silence in a relatively short period of time. When people find out what to *do* in silence, they become far less uptight in the verbal lulls that are so important to vital communication. During the pauses in an interaction, a good listener does the following:

Attends to the other. His body posture demonstrates that he is really there for the other person.

Observes the other. He sees that the speaker's eyes, facial expressions, posture, and gestures are all communicating. When you are not distracted by the other's words, you may "hear" his body language more clearly.

Thinks about what the other is communicating. He ponders what the other has said. He wonders what the speaker is feeling. He considers the variety of responses he might make. Then he selects the one that he thinks will be most facilitative.

When he is busy doing these things, the listener does not have time to become anxious about the silence.

Some people are helped in their quest for comfort with silences by realizing that when the other person is conversing about a pressing need, the focus of attention is on him—not on the listener. If he does not want to talk further, that's his prerogative. Why should it bother a listener if the speaker doesn't want to continue the conversation? Many people believe that once a problem has been stated, it should be solved—in one sitting. Human behavior simply isn't that neat and efficient.

Before the birth of Jesus, the author of the Book Ecclesiastes said there is a "time to keep silent and a time to speak."[23] The effective listener can do both. Some people sit quietly during a whole conversation, pushing the other into a monologue. Excessive silence can be as undesirable as no silence. To sit mute like a "bump on a log" does not constitute effective listening. It is rarely possible to listen effectively for a long time without making some kind of verbal response. Soon the mind of such an unresponsive "listener" dulls, his eyes become glazed, and it becomes obvious to the speaker that the "listener" is not with him. Silence, when overdone, is not golden—it is then merely a lack of response to the person with needs.

The effective listener learns to speak when that is appropriate, can be silent when that is a fitting response, and feels comfortable with either activity. The good listener becomes adept at verbal responses while at the same time recognizing the immense importance of silence in creative conversation. He frequently emulates Robert Benchley, who once said, "Drawing on my fine command of language, I said nothing."

SUMMARY

Listening is a combination of hearing what another person says and involvement with the person who is talking. Its importance can be gauged by the fact that we spend more time listening than anything else we do in our waking hours and because our ability to listen directly influences our friendships, our family relationships, and our effectiveness at work. For ease of learning, this book treats listening in three skill clusters: attending skills, following skills, and reflecting skills. Attending is demonstrating by a posture of involvement, eye contact, appropriate body movement, and assurance of a nondistracting environment that the listener is psychologically present to the speaker. The skills of using door openers, minimal encourages, open questions, and attentive silence enable the listener to keep the focus on the speaker's communication. The cluster of reflective listening skills will be taught in the next chapter.

Four Skills
of Reflective Listening

Listening in dialogue is listening more to meanings than to words. . . . In true listening, we
reach behind the words, see through them, to find
the person who is being revealed. Listening is a
search to find the treasure of the true person as
revealed verbally and nonverbally. There is the
semantic problem, of course. The words bear a
different connotation for you than they do for me.
Consequently, I can never tell you *what you said*,
but only *what I heard*. I will have to rephrase what
you have said, and check it out with you to make
sure that what left your mind and heart arrived in
my mind and heart *intact* and without distortion.[1]

—John Powell, theologian

There are three major clusters of listening methods—attending skills, following skills, and reflecting skills. This chapter defines what is meant by the phrase *reflective responses* and examines four kinds of reflection: paraphrasing, reflecting feelings, reflecting meanings, and summative reflections.

REFLECTIVE RESPONSES
PROVIDE A MIRROR
TO THE SPEAKER

The art of good listening involves the ability to respond reflectively. *In a reflective response, the listener restates the feeling and/or content of what the speaker has communicated and does so in a way that demonstrates understanding and acceptance.*

A child psychologist, speaking to a group of mothers, contrasted a nonjudgmental reflective response with the kind of interaction that is more common in our society:

Leader:	Suppose it is one of those mornings when everything seems to go wrong. The telephone rings, the baby cries, and before you know it, the toast is burnt. Your husband looks over the toaster and says: "My God! When will you learn to make toast?" What is your reaction?
Mrs. A:	I would throw the toast in his face!
Mrs. B:	I would say, "Fix your own damned toast!"
Mrs. C:	I would be so hurt I could only cry.
Leader:	What would your husband's words make you feel toward him?
Parents:	Anger, hate, resentment.
Leader:	Would it be easy for you to fix another batch of toast?
Mrs. A:	Only if I could put some poison in it!
Leader:	And when he left for work, would it be easy to clean up the house?
Mrs. A:	No, the whole day would be ruined.
Leader:	Suppose the situation is the same: the toast is burnt but your husband, looking over the situation, says, "Gee, honey, it's a rough morning for you—the baby, the phone, and now the toast." [This is a reflective response. It says in a few nonjudgmental words what the listener thinks the other person is experiencing.]
Mrs. A:	I would drop dead if my husband said that to me.
Mrs. B:	I would feel wonderful!
Mrs. C:	I would feel so good I would hug him and kiss him.
Leader:	Why?—That baby is still crying and the toast is still burnt?
Parents:	That wouldn't matter.
Leader:	What would make the difference?
Mrs. B:	You feel kind of grateful that he didn't criticize you—that he was with you, not against you.[2]

From that brief interaction in a mothers' group, we can distill the essentials of reflective listening. First, the reflective response in the leader's example was nonjudgmental. Second, it was an accurate reflection of what the other person was experiencing. Third, it was concise. Fourth, as is sometimes appropriate, the husband reflected more than the words that were spoken.

PARAPHRASING

A *paraphrase* is a *concise response* to the speaker which states the *essence* of the other's *content* in the *listener's own words*. The italicized portions of this definition highlight the essential ingredients of an effective paraphrase.

First, a good paraphrase is concise. When people begin using this skill, they tend to be too wordy. Sometimes the paraphrase is even longer than the speaker's message. When a paraphrase is not succinct, the speaker's train of thought can be derailed. The effective listener learns to condense her responses.

Secondly, an effective paraphrase reflects only the essentials of the speaker's message. She cuts through the clutter of details that encumber many conversations and focuses on the heart of the matter. The good listener develops a sense of what is central in the speaker's message and mirrors that. Twenty-five centuries ago, the Greek philosopher Heraclitus put it this way: "Listen to the essence of things."

Another characteristic of a paraphrase is that it focuses on the content of the speaker's message. It deals with the facts or ideas rather than the emotions the sender is expressing. Even though a firm distinction between content and feelings is artificial, paraphrasing focuses on the content of the message.

Finally, an effective paraphrase is stated in the listener's own words. This skill involves understanding the speaker's frame of reference. It requires getting "into the other's skin" for a while and looking at the situation from her perspective. The listener's understanding is then summarized in her own words. There is an enormous difference between parroting (repeating exactly the speaker's words) and paraphrasing. Parroting usually stifles a conversation, while paraphrasing, when used appropriately, can contribute greatly to the communication between people.

Let's eavesdrop for a moment on a fragment of a conversation between Maureen and her friend Kim. Maureen was trying to decide whether to start a family or continue her career with a public-relations firm.

> Maureen: I don't know whether to have a baby or not. George isn't sure either. I love my work . . . it's stimulating and challenging and I'm well paid. But sometimes I yearn to have a child and be a full-time mother.
>
> Kim: You enjoy your work so much, but sometimes you feel a strong pull toward motherhood.

Maureen: (*Nods affirmatively.*)

Kim restated the crux of Maureen's content. She did it concisely and in her own words. Her response was a paraphrase. Indeed, some authorities call parapharases "concise, own-word responses."[3]

When the paraphrase is "on target," the speaker almost always says, "Yes," "Right," "Exactly." Or she may nod her head or in some other way indicate that the response was accurate. In the snatch of conversation above, Maureen let Kim know that she understood correctly. When a paraphrase is inaccurate, the speaker will usually correct the misunderstanding.

Most people who learn listening skills feel awkward when they first try to reflect the essence of the other's statement. Furthermore, many do not believe it will "work." They think people will be insulted or worse if they use reflecting skills.

"My husband will think I'm crazy if I say back to him what he just finished telling me."

"Are you kidding? Me use reflective responses with those guys on the assembly line? I'd be the laughingstock of the whole plant."

"My kid will say, 'You're really weird—I just said that.' "

Actually, most people already do more reflecting of content than they realize. If someone tells you her telephone number, you probably repeat it as you write it down to make sure you heard correctly. If someone gives you directions to a location a couple of miles and a few turns away, you will probably repeat the directions to be sure you have them straight. When dealing with specifics like that, most of us know from sad experience that communication is often unreliable unless it is checked out. We've dialed too many wrong numbers and taken too many wrong turns in the past. Communications experts believe that this method, which most people use only occasionally, could be applied more frequently and more skillfully in our interpersonal relationships. Most of us would benefit from more accuracy in our daily interactions. Paraphrasing greatly reduces the likelihood of misunderstandings. The kind of accuracy check that we make when we repeat a telephone number could well be used more frequently.

REFLECTING FEELINGS

The reflection of feelings involves mirroring back to the speaker, in succinct statements, the emotions which she is communicating. Fred, 34, told a friend:

Fred: I was so sure I'd be married by now. One relationship after another fails.
Rick: It's really discouraging.
Fred: Sure is. Will I ever find the right person?

Rick realized that Fred could be experiencing a number of feelings—loneliness, anger, frustration, fear, discouragement, or a combination of these. As Fred talked, Rick "read" the body language and decided that discouragement was the principal emotion. The subsequent conversation confirmed Risk's guess about what his friend was feeling.

Listeners frequently miss many of the emotional dimensions of a conversation. There is a tendency to rivet attention on content. If any reflecting is done, the focus is more on facts than on feelings. Or the listeners ask questions which elicit fact-type answers: "What did you do?" "When did that happen?"

I was deeply involved in a writing project when the telephone rang. It was a colleague calling from Chicago. I was delighted to hear from him, but slow to leave my own frame of reference. Soon he was saying, "I just got word that the January workshop I was going to lead was cancelled." "Cancelled, eh?" I responded. "Yeah," he said before we drifted off to some other topic. After we hung up, I realized what a lazy listener I had been. I missed the whole point of what he was saying because I didn't know how he *felt* about the workshop's cancellation. I gave him no encouragement to talk about his feelings, thereby directing the conversation into a discussion of content.

Later, I began to put together what I knew about the January workshop. He had been hired to lead a workshop on a cruise ship in the Caribbean. Most of the time each day would be free for sun and play. How disappointed he must have been to learn the workshop was cancelled. I also remembered my friend had been very upset that he overscheduled himself that winter. He hadn't left enough time for rest, solitude, and friends. This large chunk of open time would enable him to get caught up with his work and enjoy a free period for solitude and friends. Very probably my friend experienced both of those feelings at the same time—sad that he couldn't go on the cruise; glad he had time to get his life squared away.

I never found out. I never gave him the encouragement to tell me how he felt about that situation. Though I didn't say it in so many words, and certainly didn't intend it, my way of listening encouraged him to relate facts and not feelings. It was as though I had said to him, "Stick to the facts. All I want is the facts."

When listening does not encourage disclosures of feeling, we tend to miss the speaker's personal reaction to the events she is describing—her joy, sorrow, frustration, anger, grief, ambivalence, and so on. Since, as William James put it, "Individuality is found in feeling,"[4] we miss the uniqueness of the other person when we have a low level of awareness of the other person's emotions.

If a speaker is talking about a problem, the reflection of feelings helps her understand her own emotions and thereby move toward a solution of the problem. Data is all around us. Feelings are the energizing force that help us sort our data, organize it, and use it effectively as we shape and implement relevant action steps.

Improving the Capacity To "Hear" Feelings

Though it is uncommon to reflect feelings in a conversation, each of us has, in the course of our maturation, learned to "read" the emotions of others. No doubt we could improve that skill. Still, it is important to realize that we are more accomplished at it than most of us realize. There have probably been times in your life when you were talking to individuals or groups and quickly realized that the listeners were bored. Interesting, isn't it, that you could identify their feelings when they never said they were bored or tuned out? You often know when a person is angry with you even when she doesn't say anything about it. Remember those times when people didn't mention it, but wanted something from you—and you figured out what they were really after? Then, too, there are those people that like you a lot but may never say it in words—yet you know. Sometimes a person may have been saying one thing to you but you were aware that she was thinking and feeling something very different. Psychiatrists and psychologists, with their years of training and intuition, are often able to understand or guess the gut reactions of people. What is remarkable, however, is that people with little formal education and no training in modern communication skills are able to decode much of what other people are feeling. How did this come about? How did you develop this incredibly complex ability?

Professor Norman Kagan, who teaches communication skills at Michigan State University, says there may be some inborn sensitivity that derives from heredity, but beyond that:

> You've probably had a lifetime of looking at other people and many reasons to have taught yourself well to recognize their moods. . . . As a child you had to learn to recognize your parents' mood. You learned to recognize when you could ask for something and when you could not. You learned to sense your parents' mood and to predict what they might do next. You learned to recognize when food was on its way or was not on its way to you. Throughout your entire life, you have learned to pay attention to other people's affect [emotions]. The first time you got punched by the class bully, because you didn't recognize the cues of another human being about to lose his temper, you certainly had good reason to learn next time to recognize the symptoms of anger. At school and on dates, you had to attend to some of the subtle messages you received or you suffered. The human mind is a fantastically complex nerve center. It would take volumes to write all of what each

of you already knows about identifying the "vibes" or feelings of other people.[5]

While it is true that each of us has enough emotional sensitivity to immediately begin to reflect feelings with some sense of accuracy, that is not the whole story. Judging from the thousands of participants in our communication skills training programs, the typical listener is apt to focus more on content than on feelings and frequently has some difficulty figuring out what the speaker is feeling, even when the emotions are quite obvious to the trained observer.

Sigmund Freud explained how some of our emotional insensitivity developed. Freud noted that if everyone acted on impulse and expressed feelings spontaneously, society would be disrupted. To prevent this disturbance, every society, to a greater or lesser degree, conspires against the expression of emotion. Our own highly organized society has especially strong sanctions against too free an expression of feelings. Major institutions like the home, school, business, and church or synagogue all tend to squelch the expression of emotion. The result of this pervasive conditioning is that many people find it relatively difficult to tune into and reflect the feelings of others. Yet the reflection of feeling lies at the heart of effective listening.

As I see it, each of us has a partially developed capacity to understand the feelings of others. In this important and difficult skill, no one starts from scratch. At the same time, living in an emotion-squelching society has blocked some of our sensitivity and made it more likely that people will feel awkward reflecting feelings in a conversation.

As they try to reflect feelings, most participants in our courses want to know how they can become more aware of the speaker's feelings. We teach them to concentrate on four things:

1. Focus on the feeling words.
2. Note the general content of the message.
3. Observe the body language.
4. Ask yourself, "If I were having that experience, *what would I be feeling?*"

Listening for Feeling Words

If the goal is to reflect emotions, one obvious way to do this is to identify the verbally expressed feelings in a conversation. People occasionally put their feelings directly into words.

A young career woman confided to her best friend:

I can't believe how much I'm enjoying my job. And I'm into a lot of fun things outside of work. I'm so busy I hardly have time to think. But when I'm alone I get tense because I have to face how lonely I am when all the activity stops.

Now reread that statement and note the words that most directly communicate the emotions that she was describing. I noted the words *enjoying, fun,* and *lonely.* A reflection of feelings, then, might be worded like this:

"Even though you're having lots of fun, there's loneliness. too."

Such feelings are easier to pick out when they can be read and reread on a printed page than in the give and take of a conversation. Even when the words are expressed as clearly and directly as in the above example, people may not notice them. We tend to get so absorbed in the facts that we overlook the verbal clues about feelings.

When the speaker gives verbal statements about her feelings, and when these are congruent with her body language, the reflection of feelings is the same as paraphrasing except that it focuses on the feeling words the speaker used.

Since our culture tends to thwart emotional expression, the verbal clues may not be nearly as clear-cut as in the above example. A mother asked her daughter how she enjoyed her date last night. The daughter replied, "Oh, it was OK." The word indicative of feelings was "OK." But what did that word mean in the context of the conversation? It may have meant "I am irritated that you are probing into my personal affairs." Or it could have meant that on a continuum between awful and great, the evening fell into the middle and was another of those acceptable but not very exciting times. The daughter's body language may have disclosed what she really meant.

Inferring Feelings
from the Overall Content

Because the suppression of feelings is so widespread in our culture, the speaker may not use feeling words at all. However, the overall content of what she is saying may give you clues about what she is feeling.

Read the following statement and guess what Eric's feelings are:

Eric: That customer sure led me down the primrose path. He had me come to his company for three appointments. Spent hours of my time going over every detail of my recommendations for a changeover in production methods. Then he purchased my competitor's line and won't even see me on sales calls now.

Eric probably felt angry at his customer and/or at himself. However, he could have been experiencing some other emotions like discouragement. Checking out Eric's body language would help the listener appraise Eric's emotions with greater accuracy.

Observing Body Language

One of the most effective ways of understanding what another person is feeling is to observe her body language. Because the reflection of feeling is so important to effective listening and because the observation of facial expression, tone of voice, gesture, and posture give such important clues to a person's feeling state, Chapter 6 is devoted to this topic alone.

What Would I Be Feeling?

As the listener notes the speaker's feeling words (if any are used), "reads between the lines" for feelings that might be implied in the general content of what is said, and observes the body language, she asks herself, *"What would I be feeling if I were saying and doing those things?"* Since each person's emotional experience is unique, we can't be sure we know what the speaker is feeling. The best we can do is to understand our own inner reactions and *guess* at the other's emotions. On the basis of this "guestimate," the listener reflects her understanding of the other's feelings. Normally, the speaker will automatically let us know whether or not we heard correctly—by nodding her head, saying "Yes" or "Right," or correcting what we said.

REFLECTING MEANINGS

When feelings and facts are joined in one succinct response, we have a reflection of meaning. For example, Marge, who is middle-aged, says to her husband Rob:

Marge: My supervisor keeps asking questions about my personal life. I wish she'd mind her own business.

Rob: You feel annoyed that she won't respect your privacy.

Feelings are often triggered by specific events. Note how my feelings in the left column of the following list are related to specific events listed in the right column:

Feeling	Event (Fact)
Happy	Prentice-Hall awarded me the contract for this book.
Sad	A good friend is moving away.
Irritated	The agreements we reached last week are not being observed by some of the other people involved.
Frustrated	The photocopy machine has broken down for the third time in three days.

We have seen how important it is for the listener to tune in to the speaker's feeling. We also noted that it is very helpful to understand the factual content of her message. As Robert Carkhuff says, things that we can frame in our minds are easier to act on than those which we only feel in our gut.[6] When we respond to the speaker's meanings—the feelings that paralyze or motivate and the content to which the feelings are associated—our listening is often most effective.

Once a person knows how to reflect feeling and content separately, it is relatively easy to put the two together into a reflection of meaning. When first learning to reflect meanings, people often find it useful to use the formula *"You feel* [insert the feeling word] *because* [insert the event or other content that is associated with the feeling]."

Let's take a look at how the *"You feel . . . because . . ."* formula works in some actual situations:

Earl: What a change! I feared I wouldn't get a promotion, but it came through. Our new home is just super. And Marie and the kids seem more content than they have ever been.

John: You feel happy because things are going well in all parts of your life.

Or:

Wilma: My husband drives me crazy. First he says we're doing fine and don't have any financial worries. The next day he blows up when I buy something for the house.

Harriet: You feel anxious because he is so inconsistent.

The formula "You feel . . . because . . ." is not very intrusive in a conversation. It helps people remember to reflect both the feelings and the content and it is an aid in keeping the responses brief. It is far different from encumbering conversations with jargon phrases like "What I think I hear you saying is. . . ."

Many people have strong negative feelings about using this formula for reflective listening. Actually, the formula is like scaffolding on a house that is being constructed. It can be very helpful to use it for awhile, but when it is not needed any longer, it may be removed from one's repertoire of responses. After using the "You feel . . . because . . ." formula until the brief reflection of meaning becomes second nature, you may wish to use more "natural" ways of reflecting meanings. The word "are" can be substituted for the word "feel." Words like "by," "since," "about," and "that" can be used in place of the "because" of the formula. With variations like these, the responses may sound less stilted.

"You are confused by his mixed messages."

"You are elated that things are going so well in your new job."

"You're angry about the recent schedule revisions."

"You are discouraged by his unresponsiveness."

In the rapid interchange of actual conversations, it is impossible and undesirable to use reflections of meanings continually. Reflections of feelings, reflections of content, minimal encourages to talk, active silence, and other responses will be orchestrated with the reflection of meaning. In some conversations, it may be most helpful to stress the reflection of feeling. Occasionally, it may be most appropriate for the listener to concentrate more on the reflection of content. In many situations, however, the most facilitative listener will rely heavily on reflecting meanings.

Sometimes a reflection of meaning is appropriate even though no words are exchanged. Norma, an office manager, has just taken on a new task for her company. She works hard all day long, but at the end of the day the stack of work to be accomplished seems just as high as it was at the beginning of the day. Barbara, an executive secretary in the same office, says to her, "You feel discouraged that you worked so hard and yet there is still so much to do."

The reflection of meaning is usually best when it is honed to a single succinct sentence. The shorter the better. A rambling response impedes communication.

SUMMATIVE REFLECTIONS

A summative reflection is a brief restatement of the main themes and feelings the speaker expressed over a longer period of conversation than would be covered by any of the other reflective skills. It may tie together a number of recent comments or highlight feelings and/or issues by concisely recapping them. The conversational landscape can become littered with bits of information that are useless until the most important fragments have been put together in a meaningful way. Sometimes the speaker gets lost in a welter of confusing thoughts and feelings. What a difference between the puzzle when it is only a jumble of parts in a box and when it is a compact picture on the table. Similarly, an effective summary can enable a speaker to see the fragments of her utterances gathered together in a meaningful unity. A summative response helps the speaker gain an integrated picture of what she has been saying. It states the important emphases that have been repeated over and over again or that have been stated with the most intensity.

Carl Jung, the famous Swiss psychotherapist, told a colleague about his first visit with Sigmund Freud in the year 1907. Jung had much that he wanted to talk about with Freud, and he spoke with intense animation for three whole hours. Finally Freud interrupted him and, to Jung's astonishment, proceeded to group the contents of Jung's monologue into several precise categories that enabled them to spend their remaining hours together in a more profitable give-and-take.[7]

A summary can help a speaker understand herself more clearly. Gerard Egan gives this example:

> Counselor: Let's go over what we have so far. You're down, depressed—not just a normal slump, but this time it's hanging on. You worry about your health, but this seems to be more of a symptom than a cause of your depression. There are some unresolved issues in your life. One is the fact that your recent change in jobs has meant that you don't see much of your old friends any more. Geography has made a big difference. Another issue—one you find painful and embarrassing—is your investment in trying to stay young. You don't want to face the fact of getting older. A third issue is the way you overinvest yourself in work—so much so that when you finish a long-term project, suddenly your life is empty.
>
> Client: It's painful to hear it all that baldly, but that about sums it up. I really have to look into my values. I feel I need a new life style, one in which there is more immediate involvement with people.[8]

This kind of summary has elements of confrontation in it. The listener must carefully judge whether the speaker is emotionally prepared to handle a somewhat confrontative summary.

Summaries are useful in situations where there are conflicts of needs or where problem solving is required. Bill was talking with his father about going on to graduate school or taking a year off from formal education a while to get some practical experience. After talking together for forty-five minutes, the father says:

> You feel that graduate school is a "must" sometime in your life, but you're not sure if going directly from your undergraduate work into more-formal education is wise. You worry about my financial situation because your education has cost me thousands of dollars already. You want to marry Lea, and you wonder if she'll wait for you for two years or if she'll think you're just a perennial schoolboy. You are feeling pressure from the graduate school to make a decision soon in order to receive the graduate assistanceship you would need if you decide to go on to school now.

A summary is also useful when the speaker seems to have exhausted everything she has to say on a topic. The recap of what the speaker said can help bring that part of a conversation to a conclusion and/or provide direction for the next segment.

When listening to someone over a period of more than one session, a summary can be used at the beginning of a new session. Since the speaker may have had important thoughts or experiences between sessions, it is important to ask if she has had any and, if so, whether she would like to discuss them. If not, the listener can summarize the last conversation. It demonstrates the listener's interest, helps prevent the speaker from repeating old material, and can help her build on the previous session.

One of the purposes of summarizing is to give the speaker a feeling of movement in exploring content and feelings. This sense of progress may lead more quickly to the development of action programs. Summarization also provides an accuracy check on the listener's overall impressions of what has been said.

A reflective summary is effective when the listener (1) gathers together points that the *speaker* brought up, and (2) selects *relevant* data—that which will help the speaker more clearly understand key elements of her situation. "A summary," says Egan, "is not a mechanical pulling together of a number of facts; it is a systematic presentation of relevant data."[9]

The use of the following sentence stems can help you get started using the skill of summarization:

"One theme you keep coming back to seems to be . . ."

"Let's recap the ground we have covered so far . . ."

"I've been thinking about what you've said. I see something that may be a pattern and I'd like to check it out. You . . ."

"As I've been listening to you, your main concern seems to be . . ." (Then give examples.)

The effectiveness of a summative reflection can be best judged by the other's reception and use of it. A good summation should enable the other to speak in more depth, with clearer directionality and/or greater coherence. A good summary often helps the speaker understand her situation more clearly even though it is a recap of what she had already said. Even though there is no new material in a summary, it may seem new to the speaker because she is hearing it all put together for the first time. Also, an effective summary can tie the loose strands of a conversation together at its conclusion.

SUMMARY

The good listener responds reflectively to what the speaker is saying. She restates, in her own words, the feeling and/or content that is being expressed—and in doing so, communicates understanding and acceptance. There are four basic reflecting skills. Paraphrasing, the first of the reflective responses, focuses on the speaker's content. The reflection of feeling occurs when the listener concentrates on feeling words, infers feelings from the general content, "reads" body language, asks, "How would I feel if I were doing and saying that?" and then mirrors the feeling back to the speaker. The combined reflection of feelings and content is called the reflection of meaning. Summative reflections are very condensed recaps of the most significant elements of a fairly long segment of conversation.

CHAPTER FIVE

Why Reflective Responses Work

At most points in communication where others would interpret, probe, advise, encourage, we reflect. . . . Reflection can be, in the hands of an imitating novice, a dull wooden mockery. On paper, it often looks particularly so. Yet, it can also be a profound, intimate, empathically understanding response, requiring great skill and sensitivity and intense involvement.[1]

—J. M. Shlien, therapist

People who are learning to listen more effectively often wonder why such importance is placed on reflective responses. I explain that what Winston Churchill said of democracy applies to reflective listening: it is the worst possible method—except for all the other alternatives! Most of the other options don't work nearly as well when the speaker is under stress or has a problem or other strong needs.

When people are first introduced to the concept of reflective responses, they often think that this way of listening is too structured, too mechanical, and not "natural" enough. This chapter will explore some of those concerns and then will examine six problems of human communication that can be alleviated by reflective listening. The chapter concludes with what I believe is the best method of dispelling one's doubts about the effectiveness of reflective listening.

STYLE AND STRUCTURE IN LISTENING

People in our seminars often say, "When I listen reflectively, I have to stop and think of how to respond. I'm not myself when I do this. Using these listening skills is too contrived and too lacking in spontaneity." One or more of three basic issues is usually relevant to this kind of concern.

First, when people learn a new set of skills, they usually go through an awkward and self-conscious stage before they are at home with the skills. A person's ability often decreases when he begins using a new method. When I went out for basketball, the coach made me change my method of taking a particular shot. For the next few days, my percentage of baskets dropped significantly. Soon, however, I was shooting better than ever. Similarly, when people first try using these listening skills, they often tell us that they are trying so hard not to send roadblocks and are working so diligently to phrase reflective responses that they miss what the speaker is saying! This does happen to many people, but fortunately only for a brief period.

Someone has said there are four stages in the process of improving communication. At first, when a person learns about the impact of the roadblocks he has been sending all his life, he feels *guilty*. Then he tries the skills but this "new" way of relating seems wooden and artificial. He feels *phony*. Fortunately, most people go through these two stages fairly quickly.

After using the methods for a few weeks, people often become quite *skillful* with them. They reflect fairly well, but they are still working at it and are conscious of what they are doing. Finally, after using the skills regularly for a couple of years, this way of relating becomes so *integrated* into the person's life style that he often does it well and without conscious awareness. He then is like a violinist who has mastered the techniques of his art. The skills become virtually automatic. He plays the music as though the problems of fingering and bowing never existed. Similarly, in time and with practice, these skills of communication can become so integrated into your life that they are natural to you.

A second issue that is relevant here is the amount of *structure* involved in this kind of listening. Beginners at listening skills often think that reflective responses are too rule-governed and therefore that they seem artificial and impede the free flow of a conversation. Actually, even the freest-flowing interactions are very structured, rule-governed interchanges. Richard Bandler and John Grinder write:

> When humans communicate—when we talk, discuss, write—we . . . are almost never conscious of the way in which we order and structure the words we select. Language so fills our world that we move through it as a fish swims through water. Although we have little or no consciousness of the way in which we form our communication, our activity—the process of using language—is highly structured.

For example, if we take this sentence which you are now reading and reverse the order of the words, the results would be nonsense. Here it is in reverse order: "Nonsense be would results the, words the of order the reverse and reading now are you which sentence this take we if, example for." Bandler and Grinder continue:

> Our behavior . . . when communicating is rule-governed behavior. Even though we are not normally aware of the structure in the process of . . . communication, that structure, the structure of language, can be understood in regular patterns.[2]

There is no such thing as unstructured communication. Some of the rules that foster clear communication have been transmitted fairly effectively in our society while other important structures of communication, like reflective listening skills, are rarely transmitted. As a result, when we learn these new skills, they seem strange and artificial at first. But they are no more artificial than the rules of sentence structure, spelling, and so on.

Even when I adhere to the patterns of language and the structure of listening skills, I can infuse my individuality into a conversation by what I call *style*. Style expresses my unique self through nonverbal elements, special wordings, rate of speaking, and other factors that disclose the real me. Though I may choose to use the same skills someone else uses, that does not mean we will communicate alike. Our styles will be very different, so each of our ways of relating will be unique.

This kind of distinction can be found in many fields. When learning to play the banjo, certain fingerings are recommended. Individual banjo players using identical methods (fingerings, etc.) may sound very different from one another, even when playing the same song, because their styles are so dissimilar.

The third issue is that while some kinds of spontaneity are highly desirable, other kinds are very destructive. People need to examine their "natural" reactions and learn what effects they have. At the least, roadblocks—which tend to be used very spontaneously—drive wedges between people and tend, when used repeatedly, to diminish both parties. At the worst, they psychologically maim people for life.

When people use reflective skills often enough to become proficient at it, when they realize how much all interpersonal communication is governed by rules, and when they realize the destructiveness of spontaneous use of roadblocks, they are often willing to discipline themselves to engage in reflective listening when it is appropriate.

SIX PECULIARITIES OF HUMAN COMMUNICATION

There are six problems of human communication that make reflective listening especially appropriate. Four of these problems are common to speakers, two to listeners. The first speaker problem is that words have different meanings for different people. The second problem is that people often "code" their messages so that their real meaning is masked. Third, people frequently "beat around the bush"—they talk about one thing when another agenda is far more important to them. Finally, many people have trouble getting in touch with and constructively handling their feelings. Listeners have their problems, too. They are easily distracted from the speaker's message and they often hear through filters which distort much of what was actually said. Let's take a closer look at each of these problems.

Words: Imprecise Vehicles of Communication

Often the experiences we most want to express do not fit into words and sentences very well. We are not able to say precisely what we mean. As philosopher Alfred North Whitehead said: "The success of language in conveying information is highly overrated. . . ."[3] Danish scientist Piet Hein also commented on this difficulty: "Ideas go in and out of words as air goes in and out of a room with all windows and doors widely open."[4] And T. S. Eliot tells us in poetry:

Words strain,
Crack and sometimes break, under the burden,
Under the tension, slip, slide, perish,
Decay with imprecision, will not stay in place,
Will not stay still. . . . [5]

Reflective listening enhances communication because it helps the listener verify his understanding of what the speaker said. At various points in the conversation, the reflective listener repeats in his own words his impression of what was said. If there is some misunderstanding, the speaker can correct it immediately.

Guesswork Is Involved in Understanding the Meaning of the Speaker's "Code"

When the president wants to convey directions to the Seventh Fleet and does not want other countries to know about his plans, he sends a coded message that he hopes will be unintelligible to agents of other countries. In the course of normal conversation, we frequently do a similar thing. At times we are very ambivalent about our desire to express ourselves accurately. Part of us desperately wants to make ourselves known and part of us wants to stay in hiding. So we often find ourselves speaking obscurely about our thoughts and even less clearly about our feelings. Just as the military conceals its messages in code for national security purposes, so each of us sometimes chooses ways to code our messages for personal security purposes.

Often we code our messages without trying. We have been trained from early childhood to express ourselves *indirectly* on many topics and feelings.

All of us have spent a lifetime coding our own messages and decoding the messages of others. When my children were young, for example, they asked a lot of questions at bedtime. Usually, those questions really meant, "Please stay with me a little longer." A husband brings his wife coffee in bed at the beginning of each day. She decodes the behavior and hears the message: "He loves me and wants to tell me daily in small ways." A manager informs his subordinate that he showed the subordinate's report to the president of the company. The subordinate decodes the messages and hears the meaning: "He is pleased with my ability."

Unfortunately, the unscrambling of coded messages does not always proceed this smoothly. For one thing, *we often forget to consider whether we need to decode the other person's message.*

A couple of years ago, I received a letter from friends who, unknown to me, were having serious marital problems. I thought it an interesting letter and showed it to a mutual friend. He said, "Their marriage is in trouble and they are sending this letter as a call for help." I reread the heavily coded letter and discovered the hidden signs of distress and the plea for help. I made it a point to visit them soon after and discovered that our friend was right—their marraige was on the verge of breakup and they desperately wanted to talk with me.

One of the basic reasons for miscommunication is that *decoding is always guesswork*. We can hear another person's words and we can observe his actions, but we can only infer what the words and actions mean.

The diagram in Figure 5.1 suggests that a person's *behaviors* are easily observable—they are on the outside. A person's *thoughts*, however, are not directly observable; our only clue to these are the person's behaviors (words and actions). The *emotions* are pictured in the core of the individual's being because they are often concealed very carefully. As with thoughts, our only clue to a person's feelings comes to us indirectly through his behaviors.

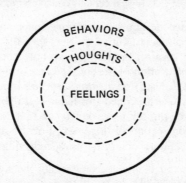

Figure 5.1. One person can see or hear another person's behaviors. The thoughts and/or feelings can only be guessed at.

When one person tries to say something to another, a very inexact process takes place. The way a statement is sent and received can be portrayed as in Figure 5.2.

HOW MEANT	HOW SENT	HOW RECEIVED
Speaker's Thoughts and Feelings (Private, known only to himself.)	Speaker's Actions and/or Words (These are often imprecise or veiled expressions of his thoughts and feelings or even attempts at concealment.)	Listener's Interpretation of the Meaning Behind the Speaker's Acts and Words (Private, known only to the listener.)

Figure 5.2. The inexactness of the communication process.

Let's take a look at how these imprecise sending and receiving processes work in daily life. A sales manager spoke sternly to his subordinate: "You've got to start getting serious about your job. You're just not on board like the rest of us!" As often happens, what was meant was not what was received. The coding (putting his feelings and/or thoughts into words and/or actions) and the decoding process for that comment went as pictured in Figure 5.3.

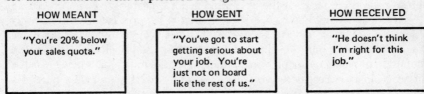

Figure 5.3. Typical coding–decoding process.

Our tendency to decode another's message inaccurately leads to needless misunderstanding on both sides. Since the speaker's thoughts and feelings are private and known only to him, the listener can only guess what they are. And since the listener's interpretation of the speaker's meaning is private and known only to the listener, *neither may be aware that a misunderstanding exists.*

Misunderstandings like this need not happen. In the above situation, the boss could have expressed himself more directly and accurately. We will work on that skill in the assertion section of this book. But the subordinate could have clarified the communication problem by using reflecting skills.

Sales manager: You've got to start getting serious about your job. You're just not on board like the rest of us.

Salesman: It sounds as if you didn't think I'm right for the job.

Sales manager: No, it's not that. I think you are the right man, but as of this date you are 20 percent below your sales quota and I'm worried about that.

Salesman: Basically, you've been satisfied with my work except for my falling 20 percent below my sales quota. That upsets you.

Sales manager: Yes, that's right. One of my top priority goals for this year is that every salesperson in this department achieve the sales quota set for him. What can I do to help?

Salesman: Well, I'm having trouble with one of my target accounts. How about coming with me on my next call? If I can get that one account, I'll be over my quota.

"Unreal!" That's what many people think to themselves when they read a dialogue like this. "People don't converse that way in real life." It's true, most people don't talk that way. And the misunderstandings that develop in their "normal" conversations are enormous. But in some companies, when one of the persons is under stress, the other listens this way and misunderstandings are kept to a minimum.

The Presenting Problem
May Not Be the Major Concern

People rarely begin a conversation by communicating the things that are of greatest concern. A woman involved in counseling said, "I was so afraid before the counseling began that I would get to that subject—and afraid that I wouldn't." This ambivalence about speaking of what is most significant to the person is very common. What is most important to share is often the area where we are most vulnerable.

Each person conceals much of himself from others. Everyone "travels incognito" to some degree. Yet it is often those very things that we sometimes most want to discuss that we hide most carefully. This results in a phenomenon popularly known as "beating around the bush." The speaker does not come directly to the point. In fact, he may not even hint at the real point of what he is saying. The speaker's drive to talk about one topic may impel him to converse with you, but his anxiety about that topic may keep him speaking about another subject altogether.

Psychologists sometimes speak of the "presenting problem" and the "basic problem." A parent may come to a teacher or guidance counselor with a complaint about the way his child is being treated in school. With skillful listening, the conversation may move to topics of greater concern to the parent. The child's treatment in school is probably a real concern, but something else, like a failing marriage or anxiety about inability to cope with the child at home, may be the most basic problem on the parent's mind—and the one he most needs to discuss.

Much like the swimmer who puts his foot into the water to test the temperature before deciding if he will take the plunge, many speakers "test the water"—to see whether they can trust the vulnerable areas of their lives to another. Research shows that empathic reflections which demonstrate understanding and acceptance are much more likely to foster exploration of these important areas than are the more typical responses in our culture. Unfortunately, most people are prone to zero in on and solve the least important problems—the presenting problems—while the more critical problems and issues remain hidden. *Coming up with good solutions to minor problems while the deeper concerns are not even addressed is one of the biggest sources of inefficiency in industry, government, schools, families, churches, counseling centers, and other institutions.*

The Speaker May Be Blind
to Her Emotions
or Blinded by Them

In our culture, people commonly have two types of problems with their feelings. On the one hand, they are often unaware of their own emotions. On the other hand, feelings sometimes surge through a person with such force that reason and other factors become impotent. The person finds himself dangerously out of control and is unable to direct his own destiny at that time. The first condition comes when we are blind to our emotions. The second condition is caused when we are blinded by our emotions. Reflective listening helps in both situations.

Ours is a culture that teaches people to repress their feelings. From an early age, children are taught to distort or repress their feelings. "Be nice to your sister" . . . "Stop crying" . . . "How many times have I told you not to get angry!" . . . "Let the other children play with your toys" . . . "I don't care how you feel—do it" . . . "You don't know what is good for you" . . . "Stop acting like a scaredy cat" . . . "Stop that silly laughter."

Men in our society tend to receive permission to feel some things but not others. Typically, it is acceptable for men to feel angry and act aggressively, but it is not all right for them to admit fear or to want sometimes to take a submissive role. Women, on the other hand, are often allowed to experience fear and cry, but are taught not to express or even be aware of anger when it is consuming them. Other cultural conditioning teaches women, as well as all people in certain religious subcultures, to place others' needs before their own.

To the extent that emotions are stifled, people lead dwarfed and stunted lives. Our emotions help shape our values. They are a fundamental part of our motivation and help to determine our direction and purpose in life. Emotions provide us with needed clues for solving our problems; they are central to our relatedness to others. As Haim Ginott points out, reflective responses help children (and adults) become aware of their inner world of emotion:

> How can we help a child to know his feelings? We can do so by serving as a mirror to his emotions. A child learns about his physical likeness by seeing his image in a mirror. He learns about his emotional likeness by hearing his feelings reflected by us.
>
> The function of a mirror is to reflect an image as it is, without adding flattery or faults. We do not want a mirror to tell us, "You look terrible. Your eyes are bloodshot and your face is puffy. Altogether you are a mess. You'd better do something about yourself." After a few exposures to such a magic mirror, we would avoid it like the plague. From a mirror we want an image, not a

sermon. We may not like the image we see; still, we would rather decide for ourselves our next cosmetic move.

The function of an emotional mirror is to reflect feelings as they are, without distortion:

> "It looks as though you are very angry."
> "It sounds like you hate him very much."
> "It seems that you are disgusted with the whole setup."

To a child who has such feelings, these statements are most helpful. They show him clearly what his feelings are. Clarity of image, whether in a looking glass or in an emotional mirror, provides opportunity for self-initiated grooming and change.[6]

The emotional mirror provided by reflective listening is of great worth to adults, too.

Sometimes, instead of being blind to our emotions, we are blinded by them. On these occasions, feelings block our rational capacity. We talk about "being in the grip of powerful emotions," implying that, for the moment, feelings have usurped our inner being and control us. When people are ruled by their emotions in such a way that neither reason nor willpower have any influence, they are apt to behave in ways detrimental to themselves and/or others. In such situations, reflective responses can help the person cope with his feelings and use his rational ability.

Many people believe that if a person inflamed with an emotion is encouraged to talk about it, the feeling will escalate. It is also widely thought that people in the grips of an emotion are more likely to act on the emotion if they verbalize it. For example, it is commonly believed that a person who is furious with another is more apt to harm him if the angry person speaks about his emotions. Actually, the reverse is more often true. When a person has a chance to talk about strong feelings to an empathic listener, the likelihood of acting irrationally on the basis of those feelings is diminished. The process of talking on a feeling level drains off much of the excess emotion so that the speaker has less need to act out the feelings irrationally.

Many Listeners
Are Easily Distracted

While speaking one's real meanings is not easy, at the other end of the conversation the listener is often beset by problems, too. Many listeners are easily distracted and slip off on a reverie while the speaker is talking. Also, everyone has at least a few emotional filters that block or distort some of the meanings being sent to us. Let's turn now to ways in which reflective responses can help the listener deal more effectively with these problems.

One of the reasons for poor listening (and also for good listening) is that people can think much faster than they can talk. The average rate of speech for most Americans is about 125 words per minute. This rate is slow for the ear and brain, which can process words about four times that fast. While we listen, we have a lot of spare time for thinking.

The typical listener uses this spare time poorly. After beginning to listen to a friend with interest, the listener's mind may grow bored with the slow pace of the conversation. He soon finds he can take a mental vacation and still get a bit of the message. So while his friend continues to talk, the "listener" plans the next day's work or relishes last week's tennis victory. He checks back with his friend from time to time, notes the drift of the conversation, and makes a few appropriate remarks, but spends most of the time with his own thoughts. Listeners sometimes stay out on a reverie too long and then miss a central point that was shared.

Remember the fable of the tortoise and the hare? Poor listeners often end up in the predicament of the hare who raced the slow-moving tortoise. The hare stopped by the side of the road to go to sleep; the tortoise finally passed him and won the race. When the hare awakened, it was too late to catch up. Poor listeners get off the track for a while and then find they cannot catch up to the thoughts being expressed by the tortoise-paced speaker.

There are many times, of course, when we manage to go off on mental tangents and still concentrate on the conversation enough to have a fairly good understanding of its content. This does not constitute good listening by my definition. The hearer is not deeply involved in the interaction. He is not personally present with the other in a rich and fulfilling way.

Filters Distort
What the Listener Hears

John Drakeford writes about "attention filters" that keep us from being overwhelmed by the increasing amount of sound in our modern world:

> The brain . . . is programmed by years of experience and conditioning to handle the auditory impressions with which it is fed. Like a busy executive's efficient secretary who sorts out the correspondence, keeping only the most important for his personal perusal, some sounds are summarily rejected, while others have the total attention focused on them. . . .

> Not unlike the ground crews of jet airlines who carefully position ear guards for protection against the earsplitting sounds of the whining engines, modern man has had to develop a self-protective mechanism to defend himself from the constant acoustical bombardment of twentieth-century living. Most hu-

mans are engaged in a lifelong process of gradually building up their own personal internal ear plugs and training themselves to ignore certain sounds. . . .

There is obviously wisdom in the natural tendency we have not to listen. The mechanism protects us in so many ways. But it also does us a disservice because it causes us to miss many of the things to which we should listen.[7]

In addition to the attention filters described by Drakeford, each of us has what might be called *emotional filters* that block or distort our understanding. Most people have heard of Pavlov's famous experiment in which he taught a dog to salivate at the sound of a bell. In the 1930s, Gregory Razran, of New York's Queens College, conditioned *people* to salivate in response to certain words like "style" and "urn."[8] Razran's experiments demonstrated that *it is possible to systematically give words emotional connotations that are totally unrelated to their rational meanings.*

The conditioning process by which most of us develop our emotional filters is often less systematic, but not necessarily less powerful than Razran's approach. In our childhood, parents, teachers, or other esteemed adults or peers may have coupled words like *communist, hospital, politician, black,* and *cop* with quiet sneers, scowls, frowns, or other gestures of contempt. Other seemingly neutral words and ideas may have been accompanied by smiles and other signs of pleasure. Once such conditioning takes place, often without design, the child (or adult) reacts to the words emotionally. The gut-level response to the now emotionally laden word interferes with the reception of messages containing that word.

In a training session for executive managers, the distortion from emotional filters was clearly demonstrated. Five executives were asked to leave the room. The people remaining were asked to study the picture shown in Figure 5.4, which was projected onto a screen.

After the group had examined the picture, the projector was turned off. One of the managers was asked to return from outside the room and listen to a description of the picture by a man who had studied it. Another manager was then called into the room and asked to listen to the description as it was repeated by the manager who just preceded him back into the room. This procedure was followed until all five men had returned individually and heard the description. The last man was asked to face the group with his back to the screen and tell what he had been told the picture contained. The projector was turned on so the group could visually compare the scene with the verbal description they heard.

The distortions that occurred in those descriptions were considerable. The black and the white man were now fighting. Some of the other passengers were involved in the fight. Others were frightened. The razor was in the hands of the

Figure 5.4. Projected picture from experiment on accuracy of communication. *Source:* Anti-Defamation League of B'nai B'rith, *Rumor Clinic.*

black. The white man wore the business suit and the black was dressed as a laborer.[9] Each executive heard the descriptions through his own emotional filters, resulting in gross misunderstanding. Emotional filters inevitably impede our listening ability.

Our expectations of others constitute another set of filters through which we listen. During sensitive union negotiations, a manager suddenly realized that he was not listening clearly. He asked a labor leader to repeat his comments and later admitted to a friend, "Sometimes I don't hear him clearly because of what I expect him to say." Numerous couples are in a similar boat. A husband may think he knows what his partner will say on a given topic and respond on the basis of his expectations rather than in terms of what his wife actually said. Parents and children misunderstand each other similarly.

A person's self-image may distort the reception of the other person's thoughts and feelings. Someone with low self-esteem may expect criticism from others and read that meaning into the most innocent of statements. One woman is defensive about her homemaking; when her husband praises his mother's hash, she thinks he is criticizing her cooking. The husband feels insecure about the amount of income he earns; when his wife mentions she is tired from house-

74

cleaning, he takes it as a slur on his ability to provide her with help. A woman who had very strong filters said, "My husband says I could read something into a cookbook."

In the *First and Last Freedom*, Krishnamurti says:

> To be able to really listen, one should abandon or put aside all pre-judices. . . . When you are in a receptive state of mind, things can be easily understood. . . . But, unfortunately, most of us listen through a screen of resistance. We are screened with prejudices, whether religious or spiritual, psychological or scientific; or, with daily worries, desires and fears. And with these fears for a screen, we listen. Therefore, we listen really to our own noise, our own sound, not to what is being said.[10]

Reflective responses are effective ways to correct the misunderstandings that occur because of our filters. If what we reflect back is inaccurate, the other person virtually always corrects it.

A Check on Accuracy:
A Channel for Warmth and Concern

Since it is so difficult for humans to say precisely what is on their minds and in their hearts, and since it is so hard for us to listen without distraction or distortion to what others are saying, we desperately need a check for accuracy in our conversations. To do this, the effective listener frequently reflects back the gist of what he has heard as a check that his understandings match the speaker's meanings.

As important as accuracy is in communication, most people want more than that. They crave the warmth and concern that can come to them from another human being. In moments of strong feeling, significant worries, or serious prob-lems, a person often feels alone and needs human contact and support. The empathic listener is there for the other in a unique way that communicates warmth and concern. The reflective listener helps the other person to experience community in the midst of a lonely struggle.

SKEPTICISM IS BEST DISSOLVED
BY ACTION

Explaining some of the rationale for reflective listening helps many people realize why this method of listening can foster better interpersonal understand-ing. Theory contributes to "informed consent" and thereby allows a person to experiment with new ways of relating, not just because some "authority" advo-cates those methods, but because his own mind agrees that these methods may make sense after all.

The ultimate test, however, is not in the mind but in the arena of daily life. Regardless of theory, the issue of whether effective reflections used appropriately tend to enhance or diminish communication must be determined in the rough and tumble of one's daily interactions. Ultimately the worth of reflective responses cannot be decided in the *mind* but must be decided on the basis of *experience*. As Thomas Carlyle, the English essayist, wrote, *"Doubt of any sort cannot be removed except by action."*[11] Constructive skepticism field-tests the hypotheses it is examining.

The next two chapters contain guidelines that will help you develop improved reflecting skills. They will help you develop sufficient ability to give this approach to listening a fair trial.

SUMMARY

When people are introduced to reflective listening skills, they are often skeptical about its appropriateness in their lives. They feel awkward and phony when they first use the skills. This, however, is only one stage of skill development, and will quickly pass if they continue developing the skills. Some people complain that this method is too "structured." That complaint seems less pertinent when we see that all communication is inevitably structured and when we realize that structure does not prevent the expression of individual style. Again, people say this method thwarts their spontaneity. While it may be good to value many kinds of spontaneity, the damage done by the impulsive use of roadblocks makes reflective responses seem more appealing.

Then, too, reflective listening makes more sense to some people when they consider six peculiarities of human communication:

1. Words have different meanings for different people.
2. People often "code" their messages.
3. People frequently talk about "presenting problems" when another topic is of greater concern to them.
4. The speaker may be blind to her emotions or blinded by them.
5. Listeners are often easily distracted.
6. Listeners hear through "filters" that distort much of what is being said.

Reflective listening provides a check for accuracy *and* a channel through which warmth and concern can be communicated.

While theory helps inform one's decision about whether to experiment with reflective responses, the ultimate test of the worth of these methods cannot be determined by the rationale developed in this chapter but only by your experience of using the skills appropriately and well in daily life.

CHAPTER SIX

Reading Body Language

We all, in one way or another, send our little
messages out to the world. . . . And rarely do we
send our messages consciously. We act out our
state of being with nonverbal body language. We
lift one eyebrow for disbelief. We rub our noses
for puzzlement. We clasp our arms to isolate ourselves or to protect ourselves. We shrug our
shoulders for indifference, wink one eye for intimacy, tap our fingers for impatience, slap our
foreheads for forgetfulness. The gestures are
numerous, and while some are deliberate . . . there are some, such as rubbing our
noses for puzzlement or clasping our arms to protect ourselves, that are mostly unconscious.[1]

—Julius Fast

THE IMPORTANCE
OF BODY LANGUAGE

A person cannot not communicate. Though she may decide to stop talking, it is impossible for her to stop behaving, The behavior of a person—her facial expressions, posture, gestures, and other actions—provide an uninterrupted stream of information and a constant source of clues to the feelings she is experiencing. The reading of body language, therefore, is one of the most significant skills of good listening.

Only a small portion of the understanding one gains in face-to-face interaction comes from words. One prominent authority claims that a mere 35 percent of the meaning of communication derives from words; the remainder comes from body language.[2] Albert Mehrabian stated in a widely quoted article that in situations he examined, only 7 percent of the impact was verbal—the remaining 93 percent was nonverbal.[3] You may question the specific percentages arrived at by these researchers, but few people dispute the general direction of their findings—that body language is a very important medium of communication. Psychotherapist Alexander Lowen puts it this way, "No words are so clear as the language of body expression once one has learned to read it."

Nonverbal communication was the only language used throughout most of humanity's existence. For many, many centuries there was absolutely no oral or written language. Therefore, body language was the sole means of communication.

When language finally developed, people commonly allowed themselves to be distracted from body communication. Some, however, continued to focus on nonverbal cues. An ancient Chinese proverb warns, "Watch out for the man whose stomach doesn't move when he laughs."[4] In the eighth century B.C., the prophet Isaiah commented, "The show of their countenance doth witness against them."[5]

While body language has been a source of interpersonal understanding from the very beginning of the human race, only in the past few decades have behavioral scientists started making systematic observations of nonverbal meanings. They have developed intricate notational systems, filmed people interacting for slow-motion frame-by-frame analysis, and conducted thousands of other experiments. The scientific study of body language is still in its infancy, and though conclusions are somewhat speculative, major contributions have already been made to our understanding of human interaction. When we add this research of modern scientists to the observations of sensitive people throughout history, we have a significant means of understanding others through reading body language.

NONVERBALS:
THE LANGUAGE OF FEELINGS

Though there is overlap in the type of information transmitted verbally and that which is transmitted nonverbally, there is a natural division of labor, so that each source is better at conveying certain types of messages.

Words are best for communicating factual information. If you are trying to tell someone the title of a book or the day's weather, the price of an article of clothing or the essence of Plato's philosophy, you rely primarily on words.

Words are also used to describe emotions and are typically used in combination with body language to do this. In the emotional realm, however, the advantage is with body language because, as Paul Ekman and Wallace Friesen note:

> The rapid facial signals are the primary system for expression of emotion. It is the face you search to know whether someone is angry, disgusted, afraid, sad, etc. Words cannot always describe the feelings people have; often words are not adequate to express what you see in the look on someone's face at an emotional moment.[6]

Nonverbals not only portray a person's feelings, they often indicate how the person is *coping* with her feelings. For example, the expression on a person's face may indicate that she is angry. The rest of her body shows what she is doing with those angry feelings. A person may approach another with menacing posture and clenched fists, ready for combat. Or she may try to repress the anger through muscular tension. Again, she may vent her feelings by stamping her feet, flailing her arms, slamming the door, and so on. You can gain insight into what a person is doing with her feelings by watching her body language.

People's feelings about their relationships are primarily communicated through their nonverbals. When people position themselves at a considerable distance from each other, tense their bodies, avoid facing each other and making eye contact, the relationship is probably not faring very well. As Gerard Egan says, the averted face may mean an averted heart.[7]

Our approach to communication stresses the primacy of feelings. Unquestionably the content of the conversation can be very important. When the emotions are strongly engaged, however, they should normally receive primary attention. Since nonverbals are the major means of communicating emotions, they are central to understanding many of the most important things that others communicate to us.

THE "LEAKAGE"
OF MASKED FEELINGS

There are times when each of us uses words in ways designed to hide our feelings. Sometimes these tendencies toward deception are buried in our subconscious and we are not even aware of our efforts to conceal. Similarly, each of us has learned to control our body language. Whether consciously or subconsciously, we try to control the expression of emotion that is communicated through our nonverbals. We may shrug our shoulders in feigned indifference when in fact the issue is very important to us. We may camouflage anger with a false smile. We may tense certain muscles to prevent crying when we are sad. We may put on a "poker face" to cover up the emotions that we are experiencing. In other words, under certain circumstances and in varying degrees, each of us tries to mask our feelings with deceptive body language.

We may be successful at choosing words to create a façade. But when we try to control our nonverbals, our bodies usually blab the truth about our feelings. Lie detectors are effective precisely because people who can concoct a very misleading story have a much more difficult time controlling their bodily responses.

Even when a person makes a determined effort not to show emotions in body language, her true feelings usually leak past the attempt at control, though sometimes only for a fleeting moment. In one experiment, researchers instructed a man not to show any emotion when viewing a film designed to arouse feelings. When interviewed later, he was confident that he had successfully concealed his feelings. The pictures taken as the subject viewed the film, demonstrated how his feeling of disgust temporarily "leaked" through all his efforts at control.[8]

The observation of body language is important to an effective listener because it communicates what is most important to the speaker. When a person is reluctant to put her feelings into words, or is unable to find the right phrases to describe her emotions, or has repressed her feelings to the extent that she is not consciously aware of her feelings—in each of these situations, the person's nonverbals usually indicate the person's true feelings. As Sigmund Freud said, "Self-betrayal oozes from all our pores."[9]

GUIDELINES FOR READING
BODY LANGUAGE

Five guidelines have helped me become more effective in responding to "our silent language—the language of behavior." First, I make a conscious effort to *focus my attention* on the cues that I think will be most helpful. Second, I try to see each of the nonverbals in proper *context*. Third, I *note incongruities* when they exist. Fourth, I *heighten my awareness of my own feelings* about the interaction. And finally, I often *reflect my understandings* back to the other for her confirmation or correction.

Focus Attention
on the Most Helpful Clues

Contrary to popular opinion, we are presented with too many rather than too few clues about feelings from the person to whom we are listening. As listeners, we receive information about the speaker's emotions from six sources.

In the *auditory channel* there are three sources: (1) the specific words that are spoken; (2) the sound of the voice; and (3) the rapidity of speech, the frequency and length of pauses, how often the speech is disrupted by words like "aah" and "mmm."

In the *visual channel* there are three additional sources of information about the person's feelings: (1) facial expression, (2) posture, and (3) gestures.

This bombardment of stimuli can be overwhelming to the listener. A person often misses some of the most significant messages coming from another person because she was distracted by other, more commanding sources of information. There is a common tendency to over-rely on what psychologist Wilson Van Dusen refers to as the most untrustworthy source—the words that are spoken. Greater sensitivity to and concentration on the nonverbal elements of communication will usually facilitate better understanding.

Facial expression. There is broad agreement among behavioral scientists that the face is the most important source of information about the emotions. To discover what the speaker is feeling, observe her changing facial expressions in a way that does not threaten her.

Over one hundred years ago, the naturalist Charles Darwin, who propounded the theory of evolution, wrote a pioneering book on body language entitled *The Expression of the Emotions in Man and Animals*. One of Darwin's key hypotheses, that people can decipher someone's emotions from facial expressions, has been confirmed by recent research.

The face not only discloses specific emotions, it telegraphs what really matters to a person. At times, a person's face will take on a natural and lively intensity. This may occur in the midst of a conversation that seems relatively unimportant. When this happens, the listener can zero in on the area of conversation that seemed to cause the reaction and thus converse about topics of high emotional priority to the other person. You can undoubtedly recall moments in otherwise mundane conversations when your companion's face lit up and she described a particular interest with great animation.

The eyes and facial tissue surrounding them can be most eloquent. Eyes twinkle with mirth, become red and watery with sadness, and glower with hostility. The eyes convey important information about how your relationship with another person is faring. They display affection and trust with one person, distance with another, and disengagement from a third person. In many cultures, warm eye contact is the purest form of reciprocity, the highest level of psychic union. Perhaps that is why the French novelist Victor Hugo advised, "When a woman is speaking to you, listen to what she says with her eyes."

As a person grows older, her most consistent emotional state tends to become permanently etched on her face. Some older faces are joyous and open, suggesting a lifetime of happiness. Others express chronic disapproval, as though nothing in the world ever was quite right for them. (Maybe it wasn't.)

Vocal clues. There is a passage in *The Journal of John Woolman* that describes the eighteenth-century Quaker's communication with Chief Papunehang, who commented to an interpreter about the prayer whose English words he had not understood: "I love to feel where words come from."[10]

The effective listener hears far more than the speaker's words; she listens to the pitch, rate, timbre, and the other subtle nuances of voice that communicate meaning. The voice provides one of the best ways of understanding an individual. That is why, when a patient enters the consulting room of psychotherapist Rollo May, the counselor often asks himself, "What does the voice say when I stop listening to the words and listen only to the tone?"[11]

At an elementary level, virtually everyone distinguishes meanings by noting differences in vocal qualities. For example, the statement "What a weekend I had" can have at least two different meanings depending on the tone of voice of the speaker. The ambiguous phrase might mean that it was a most enjoyable weekend. With different vocal qualities, however, the listener would assume that it was quite unpleasant. If an individual's voice is quavering when she says, "I quit my job," it might indicate she is sad, angry, or fearful about leaving. If, on the other hand, her voice is bright and bouncy, it would suggest that she is basically happy about the termination.

Feelings like anger, enthusiasm, and joy tend to be accompanied by increased rapidity of speech, higher volume, and higher pitch. A slower-than-normal rate of speech and lower volume and pitch tend to characterize feelings such as boredom or depression. Dr. Len Sperry suggests that the following voice characteristics (technically called *paralanguage*) are likely to have the meanings described in the right-hand column:[12]

Paralanguage	Probable Feeling/Meaning
Monotone voice	Boredom
Slow speed, low pitch	Depression

High voice, emphatic pitch	Enthusiasm
Ascending tone	Astonishment
Abrupt speech	Defensiveness
Terse speed, loud tone	Anger
High pitch, drawn-out speech	Disbelief

Some people become exceptionally proficient at understanding others by listening skillfully to their manner of speaking. Erle Stanley Gardner, the famous mystery writer and creator of Perry Mason, told of the skill his lawyer-partner developed in detecting critical information from vocal clues—information that went unnoticed by virtually everyone else. In an article in *Vogue* magazine, Gardner said:

> During the years that he was my partner, when we were in court together, he made it a point not to look at the witness on the stand; he kept his eyes on a piece of paper, sometimes taking down what the witness was saying in shorthand, sometimes simply doodling, but always listening to the voice of the witness.
>
> At some stage in the examination, my partner would nudge me with his elbow.
>
> Invariably that meant that the witness was either lying at that point in the testimony, or was trying to cover up something.
>
> My untrained ears were never able to detect these subtle changes of voice and tempo, but my partner could spot them with startling accuracy.[13]

Although you and I may never reach the proficiency of Gardner's partner, we can notice the pitch and timbre of a person's voice, the rhythm of speech, and the rapidity of expression. These vocal qualities help us to tune into the mood of the speaker. This feel for the speaker's emotions can then be reflected back to her.

Posture, gestures, and "actions." A person's posture and body movement can speak volumes about her feelings, self-image, and energy level. The movements of the head, arms, hands, legs, and feet can be very revealing. A person wanting to terminate a conversation, for instance, may stretch her legs, bob her foot, straighten the papers on the desk, close her briefcase, and/or sit in an upright position in preparation for leaving. One person discovered that when his boss wanted to terminate a conversation, he would make a "desperate looking grab for his cigarettes in his left-hand coat pocket."[14]

We can also learn about people's feelings by understanding the meaning of what, for want of a better word, I shall term *actions.* Child psychologists are aware that much "annoying" behavior at home can be a cry for help in veiled form. Parents of young children often discover that when a baby is born into a family and receives much attention, the older sibling(s) may revert to babyish ways. This behavior is usually an urgent plea for more attention. The child who consistently disrupts the classroom has probably decided that the only way she will be noticed is to misbehave. The executive who grows less productive may be demonstrating disappointment or anger at lack of mobility in the company or dissatisfaction with her relationship to her boss. The empathic listener observes these kinds of actions and devises ways of checking out the accuracy of her decoding.

People who teach, conduct meetings, do group sales interviews or presentations, or in other ways find themselves in a group leadership role need to be sensitive to the *corporate posture* of the group with which they are working. I teach many day-long seminars. Frequently there is a "body language consensus" in the class. At times, the group is erect and alert. At other times, there is a slump when the entire group demonstrates low energy. To maximize the learning climate, I need to note the "posture-talk" of the group and, when there is a slump, either terminate the session or utilize methods for energizing the group.

Clothing, grooming, and environment. The way a person dresses and grooms herself and the environment she selects or creates for herself is part of her message about herself to the world. The clean-shaven man in a pinstripe suit and conservative tie suggests a different life-style from that of a bearded, long-haired young man in faded jeans, T-shirt, and sandals. The appearance of a young woman who goes to the hairdresser every week and wears a classical cut of clothes communicates a very different impression than does the woman the same age who goes braless, wears jeans most of the time, and applies no makeup.

The location and style of a person's residence and the way she furnishes it—these also communicate something about a person. Though offices and other work spaces are often less susceptible than residences to personal influence, each person usually manages to put her personal stamp on that space in one way or another. The desk may be clean or cluttered. The space may be task-centered or people-oriented. The area may be spartan or aesthetic.

Read Nonverbals in Context

Much of the popular literature on body language is misleading when it suggests that certain gestures can be counted on to have specific and reliable meanings. In contrast, leading authorities claim that no gesture, in and of itself, has a specific meaning. No single motion ever stands alone. It is always part of a pattern and its meaning is best understood in context. A specific gesture is like a word in a paragraph. The word can have many meanings, but only in the context of the paragraph or chapter can we accurately understand its *intended* meaning. To a much greater extent, the meaning of a gesture becomes more understandable when it is viewed as a part of the larger pattern in which it occurs. Eisenberg and Smith write:

> Most words have only a few meanings, depending on who is using them in which circumstances. But the wrinkling of a nose is a sign which can have a thousand different meanings, each of which is dependent upon the set of signs which accompany it, the personality of the wrinkler, and the context of the wrinkling. For this reason, it is hard to assign general meaning to any isolated nonverbal sign, even though a specific meaning in a particular context is obvious. We would hazard no guess about what nose wrinkling means in general, but few people in the course of a conversation would take umbrage at a sentence such as, "Joan is wrinkling her nose because she can't stand the smell of fried mushrooms."[15]

Not only does a particular gesture need to be seen in the context of other body movements, it should be related to the person's words, too. If we listen only to words or only to body language, we are apt to receive a distorted impression. The goal of the effective listener is to receive cues from the whole person.

Note Discrepancies

You have probably noted occasions when a person's words communicated one message but her nonverbals suggested a very different meaning. The lyrics of an old song describe this kind of discrepancy: "Your lips tell me 'no, no,' but there's 'yes, yes,' in your eyes."

I once witnessed a conversation in which a wife said to her husband, "You seem upset with me." His face flushed red, he clenched his fist, pounded the table, and shouted, "I am *not* angry." His wife found her husband's body language more convincing than his words!

On the other hand, there are times when the body language is a smokescreen designed to hide the poignancy of the words a person hardly dares to speak. Some of the saddest utterances I have ever heard have been accompanied by the speaker's cover-up laugh. I have heard dozens of people tell the deepest griefs of their lives while cloaking their anguished feelings with a chuckle. When people hear the laugh and the tragic content, they are usually caught off guard or choose to avoid facing the pain. They typically laugh with the person. This behavior is so common in our society that we even have a phrase to describe it. The person who deals with sorrows this way is "laughing it off."

Actually, when there is a discrepancy between words and body language, *both* messages are important. When a woman's lips say, "no, no," but there is "yes, yes," in her eyes—it probably means that she is experiencing conflict between her desire to express affection and some "ought" or reservation that tells her to hold back. When a man shouts loudly that he is not angry, it may be that he does not want to admit these feelings to himself and/or others. When a person laughs as she tells of a personal tragedy, it may mean that she wants to share this part of her life but doesn't want to burden the other person—and/or she may be ambivalent about discovering and sharing her depth of feelings on the topic. Of course, there may be other meanings besides the ones I suggested. The point is that when there is a discrepancy between a person's words and nonverbals (or between two aspects of body language), it is helpful to search for the meanings in each of the channels of communicatioon.

Be Aware of Your Own Feelings and Bodily Reactions

Sigmund Freud noted that "the unconscious of one human being can react upon that of another without passing through the consciousness."[16] Much of that type of communication is transmitted through body language. These non-verbal communications can bypass the listener's conscious mind and still trigger responses in her body. By becoming more aware of what my body is experiencing, I can often be more sensitive to what other people are feeling.

One family therapist says that the atmosphere in a troubled family is easy to feel. When she is with such a family, she quickly senses her own discomfort. The atmosphere may be cold and icy, polite and boring, or very wary—as if waiting for an angry explosion. In those situations, the therapist's body develops its own discomfort. When her stomach feels queasy, her shoulders ache, or her head begins to throb, she tunes into those feelings and becomes more alert to what is happening in that family.

I was once with a teenager whose father launched into a twenty-minute verbal attack on the boy. I knew that most of the things the father was saying were not true. There was no opportunity for dialogue between father and son—there was just one long tirade. My whole body became tense; my stomach was upset. When I focused on the discomfort of my body, I was better able to understand what the young man was experiencing.

The therapist Frieda Fromm-Reichman devised a method that helped her sense what her clients were feeling. She knew that posture and body movement were clues to her clients' emotions. So she would sensitively try to match her clients' posture and gestures with her own body. Fromm-Reichman focused on what she was feeling when she assumed the client's position and her understanding of that client increased greatly. I am one of the many listeners who have used that method with much success. Obviously the listener must be sensitive about the manner in which she mirrors the other's position. When done clumsily or callously, it can be seen by the speaker as a put-down.

REFLECT THE FEELINGS
BACK TO THE SENDER

As a reflective listener, once you have discerned the feelings of the speaker by reading her body language, you will normally try to reflect them back to the speaker in your own words. In the process of verbalizing what you think the other may be feeling, several things may be achieved. First, you check on the accuracy of your assumptions about the other's feelings. Secondly, you may help the speaker become more aware of the feelings she is experiencing. Thirdly, your reflection encourages the other to speak about the feeling part of her situation. Fourthly, when the speaker hears her feelings reflected back by an accepting listener, she usually feels understood. The loneliness she may be experiencing can be diminished by the empathic response. Finally, if the person chooses to speak deeply and freely about her feelings, there may be a catharsis that brings about a release from tension and an emotional and/or spiritual renewal.

When Marion's husband, George, came home from work, he slumped into his chair and said in halting words and despondent voice, "Well, I finished that project I've been working on for the past two weeks." Marion recalled that before she began to pay increased attention to body language, she would have missed the whole point by responding, "Well, I'm glad that's behind you. Now maybe we can have supper on time for a while." This time was different. Marion noted her husband's nonverbals, sat facing him, and responded, "Even though it's completed, something is wrong and you're not satisfied." In that atmosphere of understanding and empathy, George began to talk about his frustration at work. They communicated at a depth they had seldom reached in their eight years of marriage.

A CLEAR BUT CONFUSING
LANGUAGE

Through the centuries, popular figures of speech have developed that coincide with the language of the body. Fearful people are said to be "frozen with terror." Angry people sometimes "tremble with rage." Belligerent people are apt to "bare their teeth." Reserved people seem "standoffish." Confident people are "bursting with enthusiasm" or "swollen with pride." Determined people "grit their teeth." When trying to control their feelings, people "keep a stiff upper lip." In spite of their efforts to hide their shame, some people "flush with embarrassment." The prominence of these clichés in our language suggests that we all have some expertise in reading body language.

Yet most of us can improve. We can focus more attention on the other's body language. We can read its meaning more sensitively. We can feed our perceptions back to the other with greater skill and empathy.

For most people, body language is a paradox. Sometimes nonverbals are so clear that nearly everyone can read them accurately. At other times, body language can be very difficult to decipher. People often misinterpret the meaning of the "silent language," and when they do not bother to check out their interpretation, alienation or conflict may be generated needlessly.

Commenting on the paradoxical state of the art of reading body language, Edward Sapir said it seems to operate "in accordance with an elaborate and secret code that is written nowhere, known by none, and understood by all."[17] Though the paradox will doubtless remain, the reader's increased attention to decoding nonverbals can effect a significant improvement in her communication.

SUMMARY

Since so much of interpersonal communication is nonverbal, the reading of body language is one of the most important skills of effective listening. The nonverbal elements of communication are especially important in understanding the other person's feelings. People often try to conceal their feelings by controlling their nonverbals. This is usually less successful than attempts at verbal camouflage; the emotions usually "leak" through our efforts to regulate nonverbal expression. Several guidelines foster improved "reading" of body language:

- Focus attention on the most helpful clues—facial expression, vocal expression, and posture, gestures and "actions."
- Read nonverbals in context.
- Note discrepancies.
- Be aware of your own feelings and bodily reactions.

Body language is sometimes very clear and unambiguous. At other times, however, it can be difficult to decipher. When the listener appropriately reflects her understanding of the sender's body language, communication can be improved significantly.

CHAPTER SEVEN

Improving Your Reflecting Skills

I want to hear you accurately, so I'll need to check out what I hear at crucial points to be as sure as I can that my meanings match your meanings. I get an inkling of what your meanings are from your words, your tone of voice, your face, gestures, and body movements. But it is only an inkling. I must check it out at times by replaying what I heard for your approval, until you agree that you have been heard.

I want to hear deeply, clearly, accurately enough that I am able—to some real extent—to feel what you feel, hurt a bit where you hurt, and want for you the freedom to be all you are becoming.[1]

—David Augsburger

There are some guidelines which, if followed, will make your reflections more accurate and helpful to the speaker. These will be the central focus of this chapter, which will also briefly explore what else the listener can do besides listen and will examine when reflective listening is and is not appropriate.

GUIDELINES
FOR IMPROVED LISTENING

Once people have learned to attend to the speaker, follow his lead in the conversation, and reflect the essence of his content and/or feeling, they are ready to improve their reflecting skills. The following guidelines can help you become an even better listener.

Don't Fake Understanding

There will be many times when you as a listener do not understand what the other person is saying. You may have daydreamed. You might be thinking of something that was said earlier in the conversation. The speaker may not be able to state clearly what he means. Though people commonly pretend that they are listening attentively and understand perfectly what is being said in those situations, I believe it is important not to be phony. Authenticity demands that the listener admit he is lost and then work to get back on the track again. "I seem to have lost you. Would you go over that once more?" "I was with you up to the point that your husband became sick. I'd like to hear again what happened next."

Don't Tell the Speaker
You Know How He Feels

When people begin to listen reflectively, many say something like, "I know just how you feel." There are several reasons why that is an inappropriate response. First, it is untrue. Our reading of another's feelings is at best an approximation. No one can ever fully know what it is like to walk in another person's shoes. Then too, that statement tends to block the speaker's attempt to present the details that would facilitate more specific understanding. Finally, the speaker will tend to doubt that you understand as much as you say you do. It is seldom helpful to *tell* another that you understand—what is needed is a *demonstration* that you do in fact have some degree of understanding of his feelings. The goal is to perceive the speaker's experience fairly accurately and reflect back in an accepting way that communicates nonverbally, "I'm with you." Then, without your ever saying, "I know how you feel," the other will sense, "He really understands me."

Vary Your Responses

There is no one "right" response to a given statement. We have already noted that a person can respond with silence, with a "minimal encourage," with a paraphrase, a reflection of meaning, or a summative reflection. We have seen how the wording of the formula for reflecting meanings can be altered slightly to make the response sound more natural. With practice, the formula can be obscured still more or dropped altogether.

Let's look at a statement and some of the possible reflective responses that would be appropriate. A woman in her late twenties complained to a friend, "My mother always butts into our affairs. I wish she would mind her own business." Possible responses include:

- "It bugs you to have your mother interfere so much."
- "You are annoyed that she intrudes in your life."
- "Such an intrusion!"
- "When your mother intrudes on your personal life, you feel your independence and privacy are threatened."
- "You wish she'd treat you like the grownup you are."
- "You hate it that she keeps putting in her 'two cents worth.' "

Focus on the Feelings

Charles Arribine visited his daughter's college on Parent's Weekend. When they had dinner alone, this conversation took place:

Kristy: I *don't* want to stay here. It's too hard for me. I'm afraid I'll flunk out. It would be awful to have to face my friends if I flunked out.

Charles: The work is too difficult.

Kristy: (*Tears in her eyes now*) I'm afraid I'll flunk out.

Charles totally ignored his daughter's *feelings*. He began to tell her that the freshman year was always the toughest, that she was smart, and that she would be able to regroup herself and make it through the semester. The interaction ended with Kristy's sobbing and going to the ladies' room to compose herself.

As he told me what happened, Charles said, "It wasn't until Kristy was sobbing that I remembered what you taught us about 'the primacy of feeling in conversation.' Kristy's feeling words fell on deaf ears. There have been many interactions like that, but I'm finally learning to tune into the feeling part of conversation."

Choose the Most Accurate Feeling Word

Emotions are the key to vital communication. In reflecting emotions, it is not only important to ascertain the right *kind* of emotion, but also the right *degree* of emotion. The feeling word should match the other's experience. A man stood at the rim of the Grand Canyon for the first time, awed by the beauty of the constantly changing hues of red and purple. After a long silence, he turned to his wife and with eyes full of wonder and a sense of amazement in his voice said, "This is magnificent. It is sublime."

His wife responded, "You think it's pretty."

It is a long emotional road from "magnificent" and "sublime" to merely "pretty."

The more accurate and specific the listener is in reflecting the other person's feelings, the more helpful the listening tends to be. Unfortunately, most people have very limited feeling-word vocabularies. By preceding feeling-word adjectives with appropriate adverbs, you can communicate with some accuracy the degree or intensity of feeling:

"You feel *a little* sad because your dog died."
"You feel *quite* sad over your dog's death."
"You feel *very* sad that your dog died."
"You feel *deeply* sad since your dog died."

While adverbs like *quite* and *very* can be used to specify the degree of feeling, they are imperfect substitutes for an adequate feeling-word vocabulary. "You are heartbroken" or "You are depressed," for example, tend to be better expressions of feeling than "You are extremely sad."

One way of developing a more accurate feeling-word vocabulary is to read and reread a list of feeling words like the one that follows.

affectionate	defeated	frantic
angry	despairing	guilty
annoyed	distraught	grief-stricken
betrayed	disturbed	happy
blissful	dominated	helpful
blue	eager	high
burdened	empathetic	horrible
charmed	energetic	hurt
cheated	enervated	hysterical
cheerful	exasperated	ignored
condemned	fearful	imposed upon
contented	flustered	infuriated
crushed	foolish	intimidated

isolated	pressured	tense
jealous	put upon	terrible
jumpy	rejected	thwarted
kind	relaxed	tired
left out	relieved	trapped
loving	sad	troubled
melancholy	satisfied	unfaired-against
miserable	scared	vulnerable
nervous	shocked	wonderful
OK	spiteful	worried
outraged	stunned	weepy
peaceful	stupid	
persecuted	sympathetic	

After doing that, you may wish to group "families" of feeling words according to levels of intensity. Figure 7.1 is a chart that will help you assign intensity levels to feeling words.

When the other person relates *facts* about a difficult decision, the productive listener often reflects the *feelings* of ambivalence. Charlene Adams was just offered a promotion to a very challenging job. If she accepted the new job, however, business trips would take her away from her family for several days every month. As she described her dilemma to her pastor, he reflected, "You feel very torn about this decision." This response enabled Charlene to explore her conflicted feelings at greater depth.

Develop Vocal Empathy

Empathy is listening with your heart as well as with your head. If the reflection of another's statement is made in cold, matter-of-fact tones, the person will seldom feel understood.

On the other hand, responsive sounds by themselves can demonstrate a high level of understanding. The composer Grieg set to music Ibsen's poem "To a Waterfowl." When Ibsen first heard the score, he gripped Grieg's hand and whispered, "Understood! Understood!" A similar experience takes place when a sensitive listener captures the mood of the speaker and reflects this back through tone qualities as well as through words.

There are two major aspects of voice quality to note. First is how much warmth is expressed by your voice. If it is harsh, sharp, and shrill, it is unlikely you will communicate caring acceptance and concern to the speaker. We sometimes ask people to think about how much they care for the person to whom they will be listening and then to think of him as burdened by some big problem. Then the listeners are to make wordless sounds to communicate their empathic

LEVELS OF INTENSITY	LOVE	JOY	STRENGTH	SADNESS	ANGER	FEAR	CONFUSION	WEAKNESS
Strong	Adore Love Cherish Devoted	Ecstatic Elated Overjoyed Jubilant	Dynamic Forceful Powerful Mighty	Desolate Anguished Despondent Depressed	Violent Enraged Furious Angry Seething	Terrified Horrified Panicky Desperate	Bewildered Disjointed Confused Muddled	Crushed Helpless Done for Washed up
Mild	Affection Desirable Friend Like	Turned on Happy Cheerful Up	Effective Strong Confident Able	Glum Blue Sad Out of sorts	Mad Frustrated Aggravated	Frightened Scared Apprehensive Alarmed	Mixed-up Foggy Baffled Lost	Powerless Vulnerable Inept Unqualified
Weak	Trusted Accepted Cared for O.K.	Glad Good Satisfied Contented	Capable Competent Adequate	Below par Displeased Dissatisfied Low	Irritated Annoyed Put out Perturbed	Worried On edge Nervous Timid	Undecided Unsure Vague Unclear	Weak Ineffective Feeble

Figure 7.1. Level of intensity. Feeling words grouped according to proximately the same degree of intensity to most people. The blank levels of intensity. Words have slightly different meanings for different spaces can be filled in with feeling words from Figure 7.1 (or other people. You may wish to move some of the words on the chart to a feeling words that come to mind). higher or lower level of intensity. Most words, however, convey ap-

feelings. When they do that, they normally reflect using low-pitched, full vocal tones in a slightly slowed pace of speech.

The listener's tone of voice and manner should also reflect the tone of voice of the speaker. If a person speaks excitedly about some success in his life and the listener responds in a dull monotone voice, the tone of the reflection detracts even when the words are on target. After a woman's outburst of anger about her husband's unfaithfulness, the listener said, "His affairs make you *furious.*" The speaker's manner of speaking and depth of emotionality are at least partly echoed in the listener's response. (At the same time, overdoing the effect on the response is very inappropriate.)

One of the problems of trying to learn communication skills from a book's printed page is that the vocal quality is missing. Tape-recording some conversations and role playing to see how empathic your voice is when you are listening to another can be instructive.

Strive for Concreteness and Relevance

Much of the time when we opt to listen, the other person has a problem. The goal of listening in such a situation is to facilitate the speaker's efforts to arrive at his own best solution to the problem. If the problem is discussed in vague generalities, it is difficult, if not impossible, to solve it. Vague solutions to vague problems do not lead to effective action.

There are three ways the listener can foster increased concreteness in a conversation. First, he can be very concrete in his responses. Sometimes listeners give a vague response to very specific statements. Obviously, we should try to at least match the speaker's level of concreteness in our responses. When the speaker is vague, however, the listener can reflect in a way that makes the conversation more concrete. In the following interaction, note the specificity of the listener's response:

> Joan: I can't go to that party. How can I face my friends? Trouble in a marriage is one thing. But separation—and now maybe divorce is too much.
>
> Helen: Going to the dinner party would hurt because of what your friends might think of you now that you are separated.

Another way to foster concreteness in a conversation is to ask a *few* fact-finding or feeling-finding questions. "Could you give me an example?" (fact-finding). "How did you feel when she said that?" (feeling-finding).

A third way to facilitate more concreteness in a conversation is to prevent the speaker from rambling. When the speaker becomes longwinded, he undermines the concreteness, the purposefulness, and the intensity of the interaction. If the listener punctuates the speaker's ramblings with nods, minimal encourages, and the like, he reinforces the fruitless rambling. Even when one is basically in a listening role, the conversation can be purposeful *dialogue*.

In order to respond frequently, it is sometimes necessary to *interrupt the speaker*. Many people find it ironic that good listening could involve interrupting the person doing the talking. It is possible, however, to interrupt the speaker's flow of words with a *brief* reflection, without making the speaker lose his train of thought.

When I as a listener interrupt rambling conversationalists with reflective responses, two things typically happen. After a few interruptions, the speaker and I develop a rhythm of speaking and reflection that promotes better conversation. Then, too, the speaker usually stops talking in circles and usually moves much more directly to the point.

Provide Nondogmatic but Firm Responses

The effective listener realizes that it is impossible to know another exactly. The best that is achievable is a reasonably correct but approximate understanding. For this reason, it is desirable to be continuously open-minded in seeking to understand the unique person to whom we are listening.

The nondogmatic way we word our reflection and the inflection of our voice should make it easy for the speaker to say, "No, that's not what I meant. Let me put it this way. . . ." The listener then tries to reflect the second statement more accurately.

While some novices at reflective listening make their reflections too dogmatically, more people make them excessively tentative. They often phrase their reflections as questions. Even when the reflections *read* like statements, the listener may raise his voice at the end of the sentence and thus turn it into a question. Excessive tentativeness in a listener is dysfunctional. Instead of mirroring a firm image of what he received from the other, the listener may merely demonstrate his own insecurity and unwillingness to risk a succinct and concrete reflection.

There will be times, of course, when you are quite confused about what the speaker meant. At those times, it is appropriate to say something like, "I'm not sure what you meant. Was it _____ or _____ that you meant?"

The effective listener can be tentative when appropriate, is not dogmatic, yet normally gives firm responses as befits a good "sounding board."

Reflect the Speaker's Resources

If the speaker is to resolve his problems, it is essential that he discover the resources available to handle these problems. The speaker may be so bogged down in problems that he is not aware of his resources even when he obliquely refers to them. The effective listener notes even the veiled reference to personal resources and reflects these back to the speaker:

Oliver: I'm no good at numbers. I freeze whenever I work with them. I'm afraid I'm going to screw up this forecast by some miscalculation. If I could ever get on top of the figures I could do a good job because I can see the big picture and have been able to forecast trends quite accurately.

Fritz: (*focusing on weaknesses*) Working with numbers is really difficult for you.

Fritz: (*focusing on resources*) You are frustrated with the figuring for this report, but you are pleased with your ability to anticipate future market trends.

A realistic focus on resources is extremely important. The basic characteristic of all troubled people is their sense of discouragement. The effective listener not only lightens the load of discouragement by listening acceptingly as the other talks, he listens for and reflects the speaker's resources that provide hope and will enable the speaker to solve his problems.

Reflect the Feelings That Are Implicit in Questions

Many times, beginners at reflective listening are at a loss to know what to do when the speaker asks them a direct question. Their resolve to continue reflecting falters in the face of a question because in our society it is rare to allow queries to go unanswered. For example, Morris Recupero told me he was able to resist his temptation to give advice and was able to continue reflecting Sean MacCarthy's meanings until Sean hit him with a question that was a definite request for advice.

Sean: I've thought about this a lot and I just don't know how to handle the situation. What would you do if you were in my shoes?

Morris: Well, I was in your shoes in 1972. I did this. . . . It really worked for me.

Later, he described the situation to me and said, "I know I used the advice roadblock then, but what can you do when someone makes a direct request for advice?"

This is a problem that stumps many people who are just beginning to use reflective listening skills. One option is to try to decode what the other person's question really means. What feeling lies behind it? Then reflect back the meaning. Morris and Sean's conversation could have proceeded like this:

Sean: I've thought about this a lot and I just don't know how to handle this situation. What would you do if you were in my shoes?

Morris: This one's really got you stumped!

Sean: It sure has. Maybe it's because it is the toughest thing I have ever faced in my life.

Let's see how a couple of other listeners handle questions reflectively.

Thad: It's been a year now since the death of my wife. I'm still grief-stricken. Will I ever get over it?

Dr. Brandon: You're afraid you never will.

Or:

Carol: When I'm really nervous I laugh. Sometimes I can't stop. Why do I do that?

Mr. Terry: This reaction puzzles and concerns you.

When the listener accurately reflects the feeling or meaning that lies behind the question, the speaker often forgets that he even asked a question and usually plunges into a deeper discussion of the matter and begins to grope toward a solution of his own devising.

Sometimes, however, when the question is decoded and the meaning reflected to the speaker, the speaker becomes irritated and asks the question again. When this happens, the listener may explain that his role as a listener is to serve as a sounding board, not to give advice. The other may say, "But you have more experience, wisdom, . . . [etc.]. I really need your advice." The listener committed to the reflective approach can reflect the other's feelings and then explain why he does not choose to give advice. If the speaker chooses to continue, he may initiate the conversation, or the listener may summarize as a means of getting the conversation started again. Occasionally you may mutually agree to terminate the conversation.

Accept That Many Interactions Will Be Inconclusive

Many listeners are impatient. They want to solve lifelong problems in one session. If a person sees a psychiatrist about a problem, the psychiatrist may expect to work with the client for several months or even years before an adequate solution is discovered and implemented. If that same person brings the identical problem to his next-door neighbor, the neighbor will probably expect everything to be resolved before the late news on TV!

Many times a person will discuss his problems with a spouse or friend and leave without any solution in sight. The speaker will often have greater insight into the problem and the alternatives facing him. He may need time to mull over these ideas and options before moving on to a firm decision.

Though it can be frustrating for the listener to get involved with another and not see the problem resolved immediately, that kind of tension is part of the cost of being a creative listener.

Reflect During Brief Interactions

One of the most common complaints about reflective listening is that it takes a lot of time. No question about it—attentive listening can consume a great deal of time. There are three ways in which I, a busy, task-oriented person, look at the problem.

First, I realize this is a value issue. If I really care for or am concerned about certain people, I know one of the demonstrations of my friendship is the amount and quality of time I devote to them. A value I hold is to spend more time listening to and disclosing to loved ones.

Second, I realize that this is an efficiency issue. When people are not heard and responded to, time can be saved in the short run, but in the long run, the resulting misunderstanding and alienation will often require far more time or take an enormous toll on efficiency. Experience has demonstrated that when employers do not take time to listen to employees, when salespersons do not understand their customers' needs, and when teachers do not hear the concerns of their students, they are far less efficient in accomplishing their tasks. Listening often seems to be inefficient, but when there are strong needs, deep feelings, or important concerns, the refusal to listen is very detrimental and can result in wasted time, effort, and money.

Finally, and very importantly, I realize that much reflective listening can be done in relatively short periods of time. I can listen with understanding without taking time out for an hour-long counseling session. A teacher noticed a student struggle unsuccessfully with a math problem and then slam his book shut. The teacher went to the student's desk and reflected the nonverbals: "The assignment is very difficult and you are frustrated." An employee who had been out sick is working under pressure. "It's tough trying to catch up when you're still not feeling well, isn't it?" said a colleague. In a family that shares household chores, the husband seemed very tired as he cleaned up the kitchen and did the dishes. His wife, who didn't pitch in because she had a lot of ironing to do, commented, "It's really tough to do the dishes after a hard day at work." Sometimes a smile, a nod, a wink, or a pat on the back is all that is needed to communicate understanding. People who experiment with these brief reflections often decide to use them at least once daily either at home or at work or both.

BEYOND REFLECTIVE LISTENING

Persons learning the discipline of reflective listening often ask, "Is it ever appropriate to do anything beyond reflective listening when the other person has a problem or a strong need?" It is common to be too eager to abandon listening and seek quicker but often less effective ways of helping a person in need. There are times, however, when it is appropriate to use other methods in conjunction with listening.

Subtractive, Interchangeable, and Additive Responses

The kinds of responses listeners make range on a continuum from "subtractive" through "interchangeable" or "additive." When the listener's response does not demonstrate accurate comprehension of the other person, we call the response *subtractive*. When the listener reflects the real feelings and specific content of the speaker with approximately the same intensity that they were expressed, the response is termed *interchangeable*. When the listener makes several interchangeable responses and then goes beyond what the speaker communicated, the response is *additive*. Before making additive responses, the listener gets into the speaker's frame of reference. Additive responses should relate to what the speaker has been saying about himself. They often help the speaker to see the world from a more objective point of view and/or to move more effectively into decision making and action.

Additive responses are risky. Some of them can damage the relationship or even prove harmful to the other person. Some therapists believe that only professional counselors should use additive responses.

I have found from my own experience and from observing others (including some of the most reputable therapists in our time) that additive responses, once used, can become addictive. The "listener" may "take over" the other's problem. Instead of being a facilitator to help the other solve his own problems, the listener often ceases to be a listener and becomes instead an authority doling out advice or pressuring the other to do problem solving when he is not emotionally ready for it.

While I recognize that additive responses are needed in many helping situations, I also recognize that they are often used inappropriately and inexpertly. A rule of thumb is: "When in doubt, leave additive responses out."

Building a Base
for Additive Responses

Many interchangeable responses by an effective listener build the base of trust and understanding before additive responses are used. When a person is in the midst of strong emotions, he is not psychologically ready to listen to anyone. Accurate and empathic reflections should always precede additive responses. Once additive responses have been made, the listener should rebuild the trust base by returning to a reflective-listening mode.

How do you know when you have listened long enough to begin to use some additive responses? You should listen until you are able to:

- view the other's situation from inside the speaker's frame of reference: understand the speaker's content, feelings, values, and so on;
- be sure that something other than continued listening is most appropriate; and
- figure out what possible next steps in the process might be most fruitful in facilitating the speaker's solution of his problem.

The speaker needs your continued reflective responses until he:

- moves beyond the presenting problem to the more basic problem;
- explores and begins to understand his basic problem;
- experiences the listener's acceptance and accurate empathy—senses that the listener is with him;
- accepts himself and his feelings; and
- experiences a readiness to launch into the difficult phases of the process that can be facilitated by additive responses.

Two Issues About
Additive Responses

Two issues are at stake in the question about whether and how much to use additive responses. One is a value issue—to what degree, if any, is it appropriate for me to try to mold and shape another person's life when he is wrestling with a problem? The other issue is a pragmatic one—what works best? It is a helpful corrective to my own impulse to be too additive to hear Carl Rogers address both of these topics:

> I become less and less inclined to hurry in to fix things, to set goals, to mould people, to manipulate and push them in the way that I would like them to go. I am much more content simply to be myself and to let another person be himself. I know very well that this must seem like a strange, almost an Oriental point of view. . . . What is life for if we are not going to teach [people] the things *we* think they should learn?

Yet the paradoxical aspect of my experience is that the more . . . I am willing to understand and accept the realities . . . in the other person, the more change seems to be stirred up. . . . At least this is a very vivid part of my experience and one of the deepest things I think I have learned in my personal and professional life.[2]

Other behavioral scientists have noted that the less a person is under pressure from others to change, the more likely it is that change will occur.

Despite the cautions and the problems, there will be times when additive responses are appropriate. In a specific conversation, it may be appropriate to use one or more of these responses that lie "beyond" reflective listening.

Responding with a Touch

There are times when a nonverbal response is far more appropriate than any words that might be spoken. The September 1968 issue of *McCall's* magazine described how David Kennedy witnessed, on the television screen, the death of his father, Robert Kennedy. The journalist Theodore White found the boy near shock from what he had seen. White "took David in his arms, held him close in bodily contact, and they wept together."[3]

Touching can also be an intrusion. It can impede the process of self-understanding. The speaker, like many in our culture, may be uptight about any form of physical contact. Still, there are many times when a pat on the back, a warm touch, or a caring hug are very appropriate.

Providing Factual Information

It is sometimes appropriate for a listener to share factual information with the person who is talking about his problems. After a base of trust and understanding has been built, information may be constructively shared *if*:

- the person is emotionally ready to receive your information;
- your information is relevant to the person's "basic" problem;
- you are confident that the other does not already have the facts nor does he have easy access to them; and
- you are confident of the validity of the information.

John, a management consultant, followed many of these guidelines in a conversation with a female intern:

John: You seem concerned that you weren't given that assignment to co-lead the training program for the Ridge National Bank.

Betsy: It's not just that one assignment. I sometimes wonder if a woman can make it in a man's world.

John: You want to work in a training department, yet you're not sure you'll be accepted.

Betsy: Yeah. Does any woman ever gain full acceptance leading a group of male managers? I doubt it.

John: You know, one of the best consultants on our staff is a woman. She works mainly with middle management, often with all male groups. And the evaluations are consistently higher than those of anyone else who works with that type of group.

Betsy: I'd love to be able to talk with her.

John: I'll tell her about our conversation and see if she'll make some time to be with you.

You will note that John reflected Betsy's concern, which he evidently read from her nonverbals. That served as a door opener. Then, after reflecting her concerns, he shared some pertinent information. Next, he offered to take action when he expressed his willingness to try to arrange an interview.

Taking Action

There are times when reflective listening discloses a situation that needs to be remedied. People may get so involved in the process of listening that they forget to take appropriate action! The "language of behavior" is sometimes the best response we can make to another person. When a child is struggling to fix his bike and the task is too complex for him, the parent needs to stop reflecting and start helping. When someone is stricken with grief at the loss of a loved one, reflective listening is very important—but so is an invitation to dinner. The First Epistle of John says, "Let us put our love into deeds and make it real."[4]

Facilitating Problem Solving

Active listening may be all that is required to help some people arrive at a resolution of their problems. Sometimes, however, the person with a strong need may lack problem-solving skills. Without taking over his problem solving for him, the effective listener may guide the speaker through a problem-solving process such as the one described in Chapter 14 of this book.

As always with additive responses, the listener needs to build a base of trust and understanding. He should also be confident that the speaker is dealing with the "basic" problem before assisting him in the use of an effective problem-solving method.

Referral

Sometimes the speaker will require information or a level of helping that you are unable to provide. In such situations you may decide to suggest he seek more qualified help.

Before recommending a referral, one needs to listen past the presenting problem. One needs to listen long enough to build a base of trust and understanding. When suggesting a referral, it is important to actively listen to the speaker's objections, resistance, and concerns. It is rarely easy to go to a strange person or visit an unknown agency about one's problems. Many people think something is wrong with them if they require this kind of help. Support by continued listening through the transition period is often an important part of the referral.

Self-Disclosure

The effective listener will occasionally tell the speaker some things about his own life. His self-disclosure, however, is not an end in itself when the other person has the stronger need. Rather, it is related to the goal of this particular helping relationship. The listener needs to determine whether his disclosure is apt to help the speaker understand himself more clearly. Effective self-disclosure by a listener is experienced much like a good reflective response. Gerard Egan gives these examples of effective and ineffective self-disclosure in a counseling situation:

Client: I seem to be most anxious when I wake up in the morning. I just don't want to face the day. It's too scary.

Counselor A: I experienced this kind of morning anxiety at one period of my life. It was when I was in graduate school and was not sure that I was good enough. I didn't know what I wanted out of life. But it all passed away.

Client: Do you think yours was related to the aimlessness of school life?

Or:

Client: I seem to be most anxious when I wake up in the morning. I just don't want to face the day. It's too scary.

Counselor B: It becomes a painful struggle just to get out on bed. I think I went through some of that in graduate school. It made the world seem pretty grim.

Client: It's just that it's such a painful struggle. But I think that the world would be even more grim if I were to give up that struggle.[5]

The self-disclosure of the first counselor shifted the attention from the client to his own situation. In response, the client went on a "head trip." Counselor B, on the other hand, related his disclosure to the client's situation and blended it with an empathic response. In response, the client's self-exploration went deeper.

Confrontation

As a helping skill, confrontation calls attention to discrepancies in the speaker's behavior:

- Between what he thinks and what he says.
- Between how he feels and what he says.
- Between what he says and what he does.
- Between his words and his body language.
- Between his self-image and the way he is seen by others.
- Between the life he lives and the life he would like to live.

Confrontation by a listener often utilizes the format "On the one hand, you say/feel/do _____, and on the other hand you say/feel/do _____." For example:

Greg: *(in slumped posture, sighs, speaks slowly)* I'm so excited about getting engaged. Carol is a wonderful girl.

Rodney: On the one hand you say you're excited; on the other hand, your body is slouched and you sound as if you're feeling pretty low.

Three conditions should be met before confrontation is attempted. First, a base of trust and understanding needs to be built. That base should be very firm before confrontation is attempted. Second, the listener must perceive incongruities which are essential to explore. And finally, the listener should be confident that the speaker is ready and able to do the difficult task of exploring these discrepancies. Timing and a nonjudgmental manner are important factors in aiding the speaker to utilize the confrontation effectively.

After a confrontation, the listener returns to reflective responses to rebuild the base of trust and understanding which may have been partly undermined. One should never initiate two or more confrontations in succession. Since confrontations are only useful in sensitive areas where people are very defended, the listener should use them rarely, cautiously, and skillfully—if at all.

You-Me Talk

"You-me" talk means conversing about the here-and-now feelings going on between the speaker and the listener. Most problems that people discuss with us are at least partially human relations problems. And the problems that are apt to trouble the speaker in his other relationships are likely to crop up in his talks with you. When this happens, it is advantageous to deal with what is happening currently between the speaker and the listener.

A husband was talking with his wife about his reluctance to take on a new assignment that would call for the entire family's moving to Latin America for two years:

John: I don't know if I'd be able to handle all the adjustments I'll need to make for this job. I'm worried about the kids too. Will they be angry at me for this move?

Pat: You could also be worried about how I'll feel toward you . . . will I adjust.

John: Well, yes, sure, that's a big concern.

Pat: Okay. Let's talk about that.

It requires a great deal of maturity to engage in "you-me" talk. The other person may be projecting hassles he has had with other people onto you. Or he may have some very legitimate concerns. Either way, the listener needs to be nondefensive and needs to guard against getting triggered if the discussion is to have positive results.

WHEN TO LISTEN REFLECTIVELY

There are many times when the skills of reflective listening can be used. Here are some of them.

Before You Act

Some business concerns have saved thousands of dollars by training all their employees to paraphrase before taking action. Interpersonal communication is often misleading. A simple paraphrase is one of the most efficient tools a person can use for an accuracy check when he has been asked to do a task.

Some companies program a time at the end of meetings so people can paraphrase the action steps they are expected to take or are responsible for as a result of the meeting. Some claim that this use of paraphrasing has greatly improved the results of the meetings.

Before You Argue or Criticize

Many arguments could be avoided if people really understood what the other person was saying. How often have you heard someone say during a heated argument, "That's what I was trying to say all along." People often argue because they don't realize they are both on the same side of the issue. Even when a person's opinion is different from mine, I may understand or learn from the disagreement when, by reflective listening, I discover how he arrived at that position. More detail on this will be found in Chapter 12 on conflict.

When the Other Person
Experiences Strong Feelings
or Wants to Talk Over a Problem

When another person is very excited, enthusiastic, or joyful—that is a time to reflect what he is saying. Likewise, when a person is depressed, confused, angry, or edgy—that is a time to be a reflective listener. When another person comes to me with a problem he wants to talk over, that is the time to listen reflectively while he arrives at his own best solution to his problem.

When the Other Person
Is Speaking in a "Code"

When you guess that the other is coding his message, it indicates that there are issues and/or feelings that are hard to express. The best way to help the person verbalize these feelings is to actively listen. Reflective listening can help at these times to decode the message and uncover the real point of what the speaker is struggling to say.

When Another Persons Wants
to Sort Out His Feelings
and Thoughts

Sometimes people want a solution to their problem. At other times, they are not solution-oriented and only want to explore a situation with a friend. It can be quite helpful at times just to share a dilemma with a friend without reaching any specific action plan. Unfortunately, some listeners grow frustrated when a speaker leaves without completing his problem solving.

During a "Direct Mutual
Conversation"

In many situations where listening is appropriate, the focus of attention is on the speaker. The resources of both parties are geared toward him. In direct mutual conversation, however, both parties share equally the focus of the dialogue. Both persons initiate conversation as well as reflect what the other says. In this case, a person shares his point of view after he reflects what the other has said. Direct mutual conversation is rarely appropriate for a light conversation. When talking about matters of great importance to one or both parties, or when conflict is involved, this type of conversation can be very meaningful.

When You Are Talking
to Yourself

Medical specialists tell me that we all talk to ourselves. When you talk to yourself about a significant problem, it is important to listen carefully enough to yourself to arrive at a sound decision.

Commonly, when a person talks to himself, he scarcely listens at all. Or he sends himself some gigantic roadblocks. Moralizing, for example, he says to himself, "You *should* do . . ." or he may give himself a put-down: "You'll never be able to do it." Or any other one of the dirty dozen.

More hopefully, you can reflect the content and especially the feelings of your conversations to yourself. You can summarize and psychologically attend to yourself during lulls and silences. It is simply amazing how helpful it can be to listen reflectively to yourself.

You can even listen to your body signals this way. A person getting a headache can reflect as though talking to his own body:

Me:	You've had it with me working so frantically today. You are beginning to throb now.
Neck and Head:	*(Sends more signals of physical discomfort.)*
Me:	This is just the beginning, you say? It will be much worse soon.
Neck & Head:	*(The muscles are still tense from the day's emotional pressure.)*
Me:	You want me to lay off and give you a rest before you develop into a full-blown headache. I bet you'd like a massage, too.

Now at least you have heard your body complain about the way you are abusing it. Simply taking a moment to listen sometimes helps. At other times, of course, change of behavior is required.

When Encountering New Ideas
in a Book or Lecture or at Work

I find that as I encounter new ideas, it helps to use active listening skills to decode the author's meaning. *I call this intellectual empathy.* I learned it as a graduate student writing a paper on John Calvin, a thinker known for his deterministic philosophy. I surprised myself at the excellence of my logic in demolishing Calvin's arguments, and my professor agreed that my logic was outstanding; but he added, "You haven't wrestled with the problem Calvin was facing." The professor was absolutely right. It is easy to criticize ideas even of an intellectual giant as long as one never addresses the complex problems he is trying to understand. I still don't agree with Calvin, but I now realize that he was facing a much deeper and more complex set of issues than I was. I respect him for his questions and have since learned from him.

I have to continually work at intellectual empathy. It is so easy to dismiss the ideas that do not find instant hospitality in my mind. As I teach communication skills and other courses to managers, salespersons, educators, and others, I find it is a rare person who does not have to struggle to be open to unfamiliar ideas and methods.

WHEN NOT
TO LISTEN REFLECTIVELY

Some people ruin a good thing by using it at the wrong time. This is particularly true about reflective listening. When there is no specific reason for reflective listening, don't work at doing it. There are times when the other's needs will signal you to discipline yourself to reflect. Reflective listening is work, however. It is unhealthy for a relationship if one or both parties are always working at the relationship when they are together. Relationships flourish when there are many hearty, carefree moments. When a relationship is always work for one person, it soon becomes a "drag" for both parties.

When You Are Not Able
to Be Accepting

When you listen reflectively, the other tends to let his guard down. He becomes more vulnerable to you. If you become moralistic or judgmental or in some way demonstrate nonacceptance, he will probably be hurt much more than if you had responded judgmentally right from the start. If you feel you must "zap" someone with your pronouncements, do it at the outset and without seeming to be in a helping mode.

When You Do Not Trust the Other
to Find His Own Solution

One of the basic theories underlying reflective listening is that when the other person has a problem, he is usually the best person to solve that problem. The primary purpose of active listening is to facilitate his solution of his own problem. There are several reasons why each person should retain the responsibility for solving his own problems:

- The other person with the problem has most of the data. No matter how effectively he discloses and I listen, the other will have more data on his situation than I can ever have.
- The other person takes all the risks. If the solution isn't as good as it looked on the surface, the other must suffer the consequences.

- The other must implement the solution.
- The other's confidence and sense of self-responsibility are strengthened when he makes and implements his own solutions. He takes a significant step toward shaping his own destiny.
- The other and I both benefit when he becomes less dependent on me as the listener/helper.

Some people don't "buy" this theory. Parents, teachers, bosses, and others often think their greater experience and/or intelligence should provide the solution. Sometimes people agree in the top of their minds with the theory that the person with a problem is in the best position to solve it. In practice, however, they look on their solution as better than anything the other could possibly imagine. So they "push" their solution. When I am tempted to impose my solutions on the person with the problem, I try to recall the words of Clark Moustakas, a psychologist at Detroit's Merrill-Palmer Institute:

> Ultimately, I cannot be responsible for another person. I can only participate in his life, no matter what that participation may come to mean to him. But, in the end, he discovers his own meanings, his own resources, his own nature, his own being.[6]

When You Are Not "Separate" from the Other

The good listener is able to get inside the other person's experience and yet remain separate. A boy told his father about an older "bully" who beat him up on the playground. The father was infuriated and insisted on calling the boy's parents. He allowed himself to get overinvolved. He took over his son's problem. A mother listened as her unmarried daughter said she was pregnant. The mother sobbed and said to this daughter, "How could you do this to us?" These "listeners" were not able to keep a healthy distance in the listening relationship. They were emotionally "triggered" by the other person's disclosure, which made it impossible for them to listen effectively.

When You Use Listening As a Way of Hiding Yourself

Some people consistently fall into the listener's role. They rarely disclose. They rarely impact on other people. They are not real, and their listening is usually dysfunctional for them and for the speaker. Other people use reflection to shield themselves from another's "negative" emotions. If the speaker is angry, and the listener doesn't want to experience the other's fury—he might simply reflect manipulatively. This seems to demonstrate how "mature" he is in handling the situation. If the listener doesn't feel the force of the other's anger, if he reflects without getting at least partially into the other's frame of reference, he will probably be creating distance in the relationship. That kind of "cowardly" listening has no place in a genuine relationship.

When You Feel Very Pressured, Hassled, or Depleted

It is important to be able to recognize those times when you may not be the best person to listen to a particular person. Maybe your inner self is out of kilter so that you can't be a good listener to anyone at the present time. It has taken me some time, but I've gradually come to accept that reality. Each person needs several listeners in his life. There will be times when each of us will not be inwardly ready to listen. If the other feels he has no one else to talk to, that is really unfortunate. But that is his problem to solve, not mine. I will probably do more harm than good if I try to listen when I am not inwardly ready to be there for that person.

There is no reason why you have to actively listen to any person. As much as I love my wife and want to be present for her as a listener, there are times when I am unwilling or unable to pay the price of empathic listening. If she starts a "heavy" conversation at one of those times, I tell her that I am not prepared to listen well right now.

THE GOOD NEWS AND THE BAD NEWS

The good news is that sometimes listening is a beautiful experience. The bad news is that it can be a heavy burden. As one listener admitted, "each act of listening that is not purely mechanical is a personal ordeal."[7] If you have made a disciplined attempt to utilize the skills described in previous chapters, you know something about the burden of listening empathically to another.

Listening is never easy. It involves overcoming the habitual tendency to roadblock. It requires a certain maturity, a certain self-transcendence, an openness to understand values and points of view very different from our own. When we really listen, our own ideas and values are sometimes altered. To listen well means to be vulnerable. If you listen empathically, your heart will certainly be wrung. Though the effective listener maintains some emotional distance from the speaker's pain, he is not insulated from experiencing some of the hurt that is crushing the other. Then, too, one's gift of listening may not be appreciated, or it may be exploited.

Listening is intensely demanding and therefore should not be entered into lightly. The experienced listener enters the helping relationship cautiously knowing that it involves time, effort, and sacrifice on his part. George Gazda points out that it is more respectful of the person with the problem or need if the listener weighs carefully the decision to help. Listening should not be entered into halfheartedly or carelessly. Nor should the listener enter a situation where it is likely that he will be ineffective. Such efforts are doomed to fail, and are likely to harm the speaker as well as disappoint the listener.[8]

SUMMARY

Guidelines for improved reflective listening include:

- Don't fake understanding.
- Don't tell the speaker you know how he feels.
- Vary your responses.
- Focus on the feelings.
- Choose the most accurate feeling word.
- Develop vocal empathy.
- Strive for concreteness and relevance.
- Provide nondogmatic but firm responses.
- Reflect the speaker's resources.
- Reflect the feelings that are implicit in questions.
- Reflect during brief interactions.

People often inquire if there is ever a time when it is OK to do more than exercise listening skills when the other has a problem. Additive responses tend to be risky, but may sometimes be used after a base of trust has been built. Additive responses include responding with a touch, providing factual information, taking action, leading the other through a problem-solving procedure, referral, appropriate self-disclosure, confrontation, and "you-me" talk. After an additive response has been made, further reflective responses are usually advisable.

There are many occasions that call for reflective listening:

- Before you act.
- Before you argue.
- When the other person experiences strong feelings or wants to talk over a problem.
- When the other person is speaking in a "code."
- When another person wants to sort out his feelings and thoughts.
- During a "direct mutual conversation."
- When you are talking to yourself
- When encountering new ideas in a book, lecture, or at work.

It is important to know when not to listen reflectively:

- When you are not able to be accepting.
- When you do not trust the other to find his own solution.
- When you are not "separate" from the other.
- When you use listening as a way of hiding yourself.
- When you feel very hassled or depleted.

While listening is often a delight, it is also a very demanding activity that should not be entered into lightly. If done well, it can be a burden for the listener; if done poorly, it may be a burden for the speaker.

PART THREE

Assertion Skills

If I am not for myself, who will be for me?
If I am for myself only, what am I?
If not now—When?[1]

—Hillel, ancient Jewish sage

CHAPTER EIGHT

Three Approaches to Relationships

Open, honest communication. Learning how to relax and reduce anxiety. Getting more of your needs met. Learning social skills that form closer interpersonal relationships. Being able to verbally and nonverbally communicate your positive and negative feelings, thoughts, and emotions without experiencing undue amounts of anxiety or guilt and without violating the dignity of others. Taking responsibility for what happens to you in life. Making more decisions and free choices. Being a friend to yourself and maintaining your own dignity and self-respect. Recognizing that you have certain rights and a value system that need not be sacrificed. Being able to protect yourself from being victimized and taken advantage of by others. Discriminating as to when assertive behaviors may lead to negative as well as positive consequences.

Essentially, this is what we believe assertion training is all about. It is not aggression training whereby you transgress upon the rights and dignity of another person. It is not a means of manipulating or deceiving others in order to just get ahead. On the contrary, assertion training, as we see it, rests upon a foundation of respect—respect for yourself, respect for others, and respect for your own value system.[1]

—Sherwin Cotler and Julio Guerra,
clinical psychologists

LISTENING AND ASSERTION: THE YIN AND YANG OF COMMUNICATION

In ancient Chinese thought, the terms *yin* and *yang* referred to polar categories, which, though very different, were interdependent and complementary facets of existence (see Figure 8.1). *Yin* and *yang* are necessary to each other. The goal of the *yin-yang* philosophers was the attainment of perfect balance between the two principles.

Figure 8.1. The *yin-yang* symbol.

I like to think of listening and assertion as the *yin* and *yang* of communication. Vital relationships involve both asserting and listening. The *yang* of assertion is the disclosure to another of what the speaker feels, needs, desires. The *yin* of listening is understanding and acceptance offered to another in times of stress or joy. Now *yin*, now *yang* is the way of vital communication. To the degree that a person is underdeveloped in either element, her maturation is incomplete. To the extent that either listening or assertion is missing from either person in their relationship—to that degree the relationship falls short of its potential.

We have already noted the deficiencies in listening that abound in our society. Unfortunately, assertion is also quite rare. Experts in communications skills estimate that less than 5 percent of the population can be expected to communicate assertively.[2] This means that nothing much of personal or interpersonal importance is being communicated in most conversations. Fairly typical is a novelist's portrayal of the interaction between a mother and her daughter at an especially poignant moment for both of them. The mother commented sadly, "The real things never get said."[3]

METHODS FOR DEVELOPING ASSERTIVENESS

Just as there are specific skills that increase listening ability, so there are practical methods for developing assertiveness. Since the 1960s, more research and experimentation have focused on how to increase one's assertiveness than at any

118

other period of history. The topic has become extremely popular, as books and magazine articles on assertion have flooded the marketplace. Many agencies have held workshops on assertiveness and some colleges report that courses dealing with this area receive the heaviest enrollment.

One of the primary appeals of assertion training (A.T.) is its effectiveness. For example, a study by the University of Missouri regarding the worth of some of its assertion training programs indicated that 85 percent of the participants experienced some changes in their lives as a result of A.T. A similar percentage of participants said they were able to maintain or increase their assertiveness skills in the six to eighteen months since they completed their training.[4] Obviously, there are significant qualitative differences between assertion training programs. Still, one of the main reasons for the popularity of assertion training is that its methods are extremely practical. Most people find it instantly applicable and have a high degree of success using it.

This chapter defines what is meant by both the defensive and impacting aspects of assertion, distinguishes assertion from both submission and aggression, and notes the payoffs and penalties of each of those approaches to living. The chapter concludes by highlighting the importance of responsible choice as a desired outcome of A.T. People who have a firm grasp of the materials in this chapter usually find it easier to learn the skills of assertive communication which are presented in subsequent chapters of this part of the book.

THE NEED TO PROTECT ONE'S PERSONAL SPACE

Each individual has a unique personal space—a physical, psychological, and values territory which is hers. The space varies in size and in many other ways from one person to another. Within our life space, we exercise the prerogatives of our own individuality. Outside of this personal space we move in a common area where the rights of others need to be considered and where adaptability is required. Occasionally (or perhaps even frequently), an individual becomes an aggressor encroaching on our territorial rights or infringing on our intimate concerns.

The life space concept is easier to understand than to describe. The easiest part to portray is the territorial aspect. "Territory" includes a person's possessions—her clothes, particular pieces of furniture, and so on. Beyond that, a person's physical or territorial space includes an area that extends beyond the body and is surrounded by an invisible boundary. The poet W. H. Auden described his territory this way:

Some thirty inches from my nose
The frontier of my Person goes,

> *And all the untilled air between*
> *Is private pagus or demesne.*
> *Stranger, unless with bedroom eyes*
> *I beckon you to fraternize,*
> *Beware of rudely crossing it:*
> *I have no gun but I can spit.* [5]

Georg Simmel, the German sociologist, noted that the personal space of a famous person is larger than that of an average person. He said people typically show deference to important figures by remaining twenty-five or more feet away from them.[6] The journalist Theodore White's *The Making of The President 1960* provides an interesting example of the large personal space accorded to important figures. The setting is a "hideaway cottage" used by John F. Kennedy and his staff:

> Kennedy loped into the cottage with his light, dancing step, as young and lithe as springtime, and called a greeting to those who stood in his way. Then he seemed to slip from them as he descended the steps of the split level cottage to a corner where his brother-in-law Sargent Shriver and brother Bobby were chatting, waiting for him. The others in the room surged forward on impulse to join him. Then they halted. A distance of perhaps 30 feet separated them from him. . . . They stood apart, these older men of long-established power, and watched him. He turned after a few minutes, saw them watching him, and whispered to his brother-in-law. Shriver now crossed the separating space to invite them over. First Averell Harriman; then Dick Haley; then Mike DiSalle. Then, one by one, let them all congratulate him. Yet no one could pass the little open distance between him and them uninvited, because there was this thin separation about him, and the knowledge they were not as his patrons but as his clients. They could come by invitation only, for this might be a President of the United States.[7]

Some scholars claim that our territorial concerns are genetic—inborn, and "ineradicable." Others say they are culturally determined and that in some rare societies, territorial concerns are absent.[8] Though there is controversy over some of the fine points of this theory, it is generally established that a sense of territoriality is a powerful force in contemporary life. As Albert Scheflen and Norman Ashcroft note in their book *Human Territories: How We Behave in Space-Time*, we humans "have now marked off most of the planet's surface, some of its waters, and the surface of the moon as well."[9]

Just as respect for someone's personal space means keeping a fitting spatial distance from the other, it also involves maintaining an *appropriate emotional distance*. Other persons can keep off our psychological or emotional turf by refusing to make put-down comments, ask nosy questions, offer unwarranted advice, endeavor to manipulate us into doing their will, overwhelm us with their affection, attempt to submerge our own identity in theirs, and so on. Respect for our personal space *allows us the right to our own values*. People often attempt to push their values on us. Teachers commonly try to impose values on their students, coaches on their players, employers on their workers, and spouses on their mates. For many people, it is extremely difficult to avoid intruding on another's space in values issues.

Undoubtedly there are other factors that constitute one's personal space, but by now I think you have a feel for what I mean by that term. Let me sum it up in one sentence: *Respect for my personal space involves honoring my physical territory and possessions and allowing me to be my own person.*

When two or more people are together in a vital way, they form a *social space* that belongs exclusively to them. People honoring their social space will respond in a variety of ways. They will walk around rather than between a pair or, when there is no alternate route, they may duck their heads as they walk between them. They will refrain from interrupting the pair when their interaction is most intense and will ask if they may join them when that seems appropriate.

Maintaining an appropriate emotional and values distance from other people's social space is often difficult. Frequently when children grow up and marry, their parents intrude on the young couple's social space to the detriment of the fledgling marriage.

It also takes some effort for a spouse to figure out the relationship between one's personal space and the social space of the marriage. Healthy relationships will keep inviolate each partner's physical, emotional, and values "space." Each party in the relationships needs to maintain a separate life space apart from the loved one. A husband and wife need to allow each other emotional space which is separate and unique. A parent also needs to respect her child's emotional space.

We live in a crowded world of imperfect people. It is inevitable that some of them will, knowingly or unknowingly, intrude on your space unless you vigorously defend it.

You have undoubtedly watched animals defend their territory. I see it daily on my walks with Misty, our Brittany Spaniel. As she approaches a house where the owner's dog is in the yard, the other dog clearly indicates through ruffled neck fur, bared fangs, and surly growls just where the boundaries of her territory lie. Even a small and seemingly weak dog utilizes enormous energies to defend her territory against trespass by dogs of virtually any size or strength. Away from their home turf, the behavior of these dogs toward each other is far different than when they are in or near one of the canine's territory.[10] Fortunately, assertion skills enable human beings to defend their personal space with more finesse than occurs in the animal world.

Lois Timmons summarizes the concept of life space in these words:

> Life space is acquired through birth, kept through determination, and lost through weakness. . . . When I have life space I either occupy it or lose it. . . . When I have life space I feel a purpose in life, self-confidence, assured, satisfied, well-adjusted, full, responsible, self-controlled, powerful and aware.[11]

IMPACTING

To learn to successfully defend one's space is important, but if that is all a person does, she will have a bleak, narrow, and dismal existence. Assertive people enjoy a personal venturesomeness that launches them into nourishing relationships, ennobling work, creative leisure, and/or causes worthy of their devotion. I use the word *impacting* to describe this nonaggressive spiritual adventuresomeness that takes a person outside herself.

An impacting individual reaches out to other people, establishing vital relationships. She also influences institutions and society. She uses the raw materials of nature while following sound ecological practice. Impacting provides the assertive person with constructive ways of meeting her needs, exercising her abilities, doing her truth, utilizing her creativity, and developing powerful relationships of equals.

Each of us has a psychological need to give and receive love—to be caught up in a few significant and powerful relationships. We also need to devote ourselves to a worthy purpose. As George Bernard Shaw says, the true joy of life is "being used for a purpose recognized by yourself as a mighty one; . . . the being a force of nature instead of a feverish, selfish little clod of ailments and grievances complaining that the world will not devote itself to making you happy."[12]

The psychologist Abraham Maslow, who devoted much of his life to the study of psychologically healthy people, found these were the people who lived their lives to the full. Calling them "self-actualizing" people, Maslow concluded from his research that they "were, without one single exception, involved in a cause outside their own skin, in something outside of themselves."[13]

I think of impacting as a responsibility as well as an opportunity because we live in a society that, like other societies, is encumbered with social malfunctions and grave injustices. When others suffer because of the injustices of our society, I am unavoidably involved. I feel some obligation to try to have some impact on my society even though I recognize my influence will be slight.

THE SUBMISSION-ASSERTION-AGGRESSION CONTINUUM

One way of understanding assertion is to see it as a way of defending one's space and impacting on other people and society in nondestructive ways. A useful and more common way of defining assertion is to place it on a continuum between submission and aggression and contrast it with them (see Figure 8.2). For the sake of contrast, some of the descriptions of submission and aggression that follow come from fairly extreme positions on the continuum.

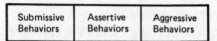

Submissive Behaviors	Assertive Behaviors	Aggressive Behaviors

Figure 8.2. The submission-assertion-aggression continuum.

Submissive Behaviors

People who typically behave submissively demonstrate a lack of respect for their own needs and rights.* They do this in many ways.

Many submissive people do not express their honest feelings, needs, values, and concerns. They allow others to violate their space, deny their rights, and ignore their needs. These people rarely state their desires when in many instances that's all it would take to have them met.

Other submissive people do express their needs but do it in such an apologetic and diffident manner that they are not taken seriously. They add qualifying phrases like " . . . but it really doesn't matter that much to me" or ". . . but do whatever you want." Sometimes they think they have spoken clearly, when unwittingly their message was coded to such an extent that the other person doesn't understand what they mean. Nonverbals like a shrug of the shoulder, lack of eye contact, an excessively soft voice, hesitating speech, and other factors may undercut their expression of a need or the defense of their space.

For example, at a family conference everyone agreed to put their dishes and silverware into the dishwasher so the mother would spend less time in the kitchen at night. When anyone forgot his plate, mother took care of them. Within a month, mother was regularly cleaning the table for everyone. Though the mother was not even aware of it, she was systematically training her family to ignore their agreements.

---

*Most books on assertion use the word *nonassertive* rather than *submissive*. *Nonassertive behavior* implies a lack of action. It conveys a rather neutral meaning. *Submissive behavior* indicates a choice. The person has selected a way of relating. She not only refrains from asserting herself, she submits. Submission usually involves collaboration with the aggressor. Although this point of view can be pushed too far, I believe the distinction is useful.

Some people habitually invite others to take advantage of them. They offer to do things that make their relationships very lopsided, thus insuring that others will violate their rights and ignore their needs.

The submissive person communicates: "I don't matter. You can take advantage of me. I'll put up with just about anything from you. My needs are insignificant—yours are important. My feelings are irrelevant; yours matter. My ideas are worthless; only yours are significant. I have no rights, but of course you do. Pardon me for living."

The submissive person lacks self-respect, but her behavior indicates lack of respect for the other person, too. It implies the other is too fragile to handle confrontation and shoulder her share of the responsibilities.

Submissive behavior is incredibly common in our society. Thomas Moriarity conducted several studies to determine the level of "assertive resistance" in various groups of subjects (who were unaware they were being observed). Moriarity found that college students were reluctant to ask another student to turn off loud music that annoyed them when they worked on an important and involved mental task. Eighty percent of the students did not voice their needs to the noisemaker. They simply tolerated what they later admitted was a bothersome distraction. Fifteen percent asked the other person to turn down the music, but when she did not comply, they did not repeat the request. Only 5 percent of the students asked twice and had their needs met.

A similar pattern was observed in numerous other situations involving various age groups, including adults. Typically, 80 percent or more of the people would not say even one word to defend their personal rights or to get their needs met. Moriarity concluded that we are a "nation of willing victims."[14] Submissive behavior seems to have become a way of life for the majority of the population.

Aggressive Behaviors

The word *aggression* is somewhat confusing because two dissimilar meanings derive from its Latin root, *aggredi* (to "go forward, approach"). On the one hand, the word means to approach someone for counsel or advice. The other, more common definition of *aggression* is the one I use: to "move against" or to "move with the intent to hurt."

An aggressive person expresses her feelings, needs, and ideas at the expense of others. She almost always wins arguments. The aggressive person sometimes seems to carry a "chip on her shoulder." She may speak loudly and may be abusive, rude, and sarcastic. She may berate clerks and waitresses for poor service, dominate subordinates and family members, and insist on having the final word on topics of conversation important to her.

An aggressive person tends to overpower other people. Her point of view is:

"This is what I want; what you want is of lesser importance—or of no importance at all." Carolina Maria de Jesus was a woman trapped in poverty in a Brazilian slum. She wrote a moving book in which she raged against the aggression of many wealthy people: "What I revolt against is the greed of men who squeeze other men as if they were oranges."[15]

Assertive Behaviors

The assertive person utilizes methods of communication which enable her to maintain self-respect, pursue happiness and the satisfaction of her needs, and defend her rights and personal space *without* abusing or dominating other people. True assertiveness is a way of being in the world which confirms one's own individual worth and dignity while simultaneously confirming and maintaining the worth of others.[16]

The assertive person stands up for her own rights and expresses her personal needs, values, concerns, and ideas in direct and appropriate ways. While meeting her own needs, she does not violate the needs of others or trespass on their personal space.

People sometimes say that a given person has become "too assertive." By my definition, that is impossible. If assertive behavior is action that considers the rights of ourselves and others* and is appropriate to the situation, there is no such thing as behavior that can be too assertive.

Examples of Three
Styles of Relating

One of the most helpful ways to distinguish between submissive, aggressive, and assertive responses is to look at each type of response in specific situations.

After reading the following situations and each of the responses, classify each response according to whether it is basically submissive, assertive, or aggressive. For the first situation, I will indicate the appropriate category. In the following situations you can categorize the responses. The answers are found on page 128.

---

*Leaders in the field of assertion training have rarely dealt in depth with some of the relevant ethical issues that have engrossed philosophers for centuries. For many such thinkers, *the* basic ethical issue is how one deals with situations in which there is a definite conflict of interest between two or more people—that is, in the very issues we will be examining for the remainder of the book. One of the assets of assertion training is that it provides laymen with practical methods to change behavior without a detailed course in ethical or psychological theory. At its worst, however, assertion training merely provides lip service to heeding the rights of others and becomes, in part, a series of methods of counteraggression or even of aggression. Though the theoretical sections in this book do not delve into basic ethical dilemmas, I believe a strong and consistent case is made for trying to behave in ways that respect the rights and fulfill the needs of all parties in a transaction. Where that is not possible, conflict resolution methods and sound ethical judgment are required.

	Submissive	Assertive	Aggressive
EXAMPLE In a packed theater, the people behind you keep talking in a fairly loud voice, distracting you from the plot and detracting from your enjoyment of the movie. The theater is so crowded that you cannot change seats.			
Response A You say nothing and suffer in silence.	×		
Response B You turn around and snarl at them, "Don't you have any respect for others? If you don't shut up immediately, I'll call the manager and have him throw you out of the theater."			×
Response C You turn around, look directly at the talkers, and say, "Your talking is distracting from my enjoyment of the movie."		×	
SITUATION #1 A school principal makes frequent announcements over the loudspeaker system and interrupts Mr. Jones's classroom unnecessarily.			
Response A Mr. Jones says, "When you make announcements over the loudspeaker system in the midst of the period when I am teaching, I feel frustrated because my lessons are interrupted."			
Response B Mr. Jones is furious, thinking how insensitive the principal is. But Jones keeps his feelings to himself.			
Response C Mr. Jones says to the principal, "What kind of jerk are you sending			

	Submissive	Assertive	Aggressive

messages over the speaker system at all times of the day? Can't you get organized enough to do them at one time? If you were much of an educator, you'd mimeograph the stupid announcements!"

SITUATION #2
Carlos Santos is often physically and emotionally drained when he returns home from his day at work. As soon as he comes into the house, his wife tells him about all the trouble she's had during the day. Carlos needs a breather. He doesn't want to listen to anyone for a few minutes. He needs to center himself first.

Response A
Carlos is seething inside while he half-listens to her words. Sometimes he glances at the newspaper while she is talking, hoping she will take the hint. All the time he thinks, "Boy, is she selfish. If she loved me, she would know how I feel right now."

Response B
Carlos storms around the room screaming at her, "You are the most selfish person I've ever known. All I want is a few minutes peace and quiet when I get home from work. But what do I get? Your depressing babble. I'm sick of it and I'm sick of you."

Response C
Carlos immediately tells Mrs. Santos how tired he is and how much he needs a period of quiet before dinner. He says that unless there is something very pressing, he would like to wait until after dinner to hear about the events of her day, adding that he would also like to tell her about his day.

These examples may seem like caricatures. They were described in extreme terms to make recognition easier. Many people do behave in extreme ways, however.

I rate the responses this way:

Situation #1
Response A—Assertive
Response B—Submissive
Response C—Aggressive

Situation #2
Response A—Submissive
Response B—Aggressive
Response C—Assertive

The Swing to the Opposite Style

Whenever a person's rights are persistently trampled on, or her needs go consistently unmet, she accumulates resentment and anger.

People who typically behave in submissive ways often accumulate enormous amounts of anger that finally spill over in a "Mount Vesuvius" response. This volcanic eruption, often over a trivial incident, spews the lava of aggressive anger on whomever happens to be nearby. Following the aggressive outburst, the normally submissive person feels very guilty and returns to her submissive behavior pattern. After a time, the pressure builds to the explosion point again and another Vesuvius is unleashed upon a victim who may be quite innocent—or whose current behavior did not warrant such a vigorous response.

Though it is usually less obvious, people who are primarily aggressive are apt to become submissive when they reach a certain level of inner stress or tension. As tension begins to climb, their aggression mounts and they become more autocratic or more attacking. At some point of increased tension, however, the aggressive person is apt to withdraw or acquiesce. But only temporarily. Like people who are primarily submissive, those who are basically aggressive swing from one end of the continuum to the other and then back again. They do not seem to realize that assertive options may better meet their needs.

Placing Yourself on the Continuum

Most people tend to rely on one style of behavior more than others even though they are not completely consistent. A *situationally submissive person* normally behaves submissively. However, with some persons and in some situations, she is assertive or even aggressive. Likewise, a *situationally aggressive person* is one whose behavior is typically aggressive but who may use an assertive or submissive style, depending on the situation and persons involved. Persons who are situationally submissive or aggressive are most comfortable using their dominant style in the majority of situations. But there are occasions when they will rely on other responses.

Some people are *generally submissive*. In most situations and with virtually all persons, they behave submissively. Similarly, other people are *generally aggressive*. They tend to behave aggressively in nearly all situations and with nearly everyone they meet.

Take a few minutes to figure out where you belong on the submission-assertion-aggression continuum. Which style is most comfortable for you? When, and with whom, are you most likely to behave differently. Your responses to those questions can make the following pages more relevant to you.

PAYOFFS AND PENALTIES
OF THREE WAYS OF RELATING

There are benefits and there are liabilities for submissive, assertive, and aggressive behavior. Let's take a look first at the rewards, then at the disadvantages of each of these three approaches to relating.

Payoffs for Submissive Behavior

Submissive behavior is appealing to many people because it is a method of avoiding conflict. Just as "it takes two to tango," it takes two to tangle. Submission is a way of avoiding, postponing, or at least hiding the conflict that is so fearful to many submissive people.

The person who behaves submissively also has the comfort and security of maintaining a familiar pattern of behavior. Most people have been trained for submission by parents, schools, and other agencies of our society. To break these established patterns of behavior is often quite stress-producing.

Submission is often a way of trying to purchase the approval of others. People who behave submissively are often praised for being selfless, for being a good sport, for going the second mile, and so on.

The submissive person carries a much smaller load of responsibility than does the assertive or aggressive person. If things go wrong, people rarely blame the person who merely followed someone else's leadership. If the movie we attend turns out to be one of the poorest we've ever seen, the submissive person cannot be criticized for the selection. After all, he said, "Anything's OK with me—you choose."

Again, some submissive people seem so helpless that other people take it upon themselves to look after and protect them. They do not have to stand on their own two feet; they entice others to help them in a world that sometimes seems too overwhelming to them.

Finally, people often control others by means of their submissive behavior. Fritz Perls notes that when the top dog (aggressive person) and the underdog (submissive person) strive for control, ironically, the underdog usually wins.[17] You can probably think of persons whose wheedling, crybaby, or martyrdom methods ultimately proved stronger than the power methods of the aggressor. I've heard many men say, "I can stand anything but a woman's tears."

What's in it for the person who behaves submissively? Lots. She can control others while avoiding conflict and responsibility. And at the same time, because of her weakness, she can be protected by those she controls. She relies on familiar behavior patterns and is praised for her selflessness. No wonder it is hard for people to give up their submissive behaviors!

"The Price of 'Nice' "

In our culture, people who behave submissively are often termed "nice" guys. Nice children sit quietly and obediently for six hours a day in the classroom. Nice adults are people who "go along" with the wishes of others. The "price of 'nice,' "[18] however, is extremely high. And as we shall see, "nice" seldom is nice at all—it is usually only a façade covering a sordid interior.

The first price of "nice" submissive behavior is that the person lives an unlived life. The submissive person does not call her own plays. She goes along. Her course is chosen by others. Created to enjoy a unique and fulfilling destiny, she squanders her years by kowtowing to the desires and commands of others.[19]

Another price paid by the submissive person is that her relationships tend to be less satisfying and intimate than she desires. Any worthwhile relationship involves two real people. But the submissive person forfeits herself, crowding herself into what she thinks is another person's picture of what is lovable. She has very little real self left to love with or to be loved. Though she may have many acquaintances, the submissive person lacks deep and enduring friendships.

The affection others have for the submissive person soon grows cold. Psychologists have discovered that when a person is repeatedly submissive in her interactions with another person, the other tends to feel guilty about getting her own way so much. This feeling generates pity, irritation, and finally disgust toward the submissive person.[20]

The submissive person's affection for others also tends to wane over time. This is partly because she represses much of her anger, and when that happens, much affection is automatically repressed with it. Also, excessive sacrifice for or giving in to other people breeds resentment. George Bernard Shaw says, "If you begin by sacrificing yourself to those you love, you will end by hating those to whom you have sacrificed yourself.[21]

Perhaps the most frequently enacted tragedy of all times is that in which people give up being themselves and living their own lives so that they will be loved, only to find the ultimate consequence of their sacrifice is an inability to have the fulfilling relationships they sought.

A third consequence of submissive behavior is the inability to control one's own emotions. This, too, is ironic because one of the main reasons people choose to be submissive is to be able to "handle" their emotions. Submissive people tend to repress their "negative" emotions.* As we have already noted, pent-up emotions often cause relationships to wither because affection seems to be automatically repressed with the repression of anger. Or emotions that are held in may suddenly pour forth in a big explosion. Another likelihood is that when people try to hold back their emotions, they get expressed indirectly. When this happens, submissive people become masters of the put-down. In the guise of being "helpful," they may become occupied in extensive fault finding. Or withhold sex. They can subtly and perhaps unconsciously try to ruin the good times others are having. They become saboteurs, undermining the efforts of others. They make cutting remarks. Or they may avoid others or silently terminate a relationship. These approaches are indirectly hostile, alienating, and destructive. When anger is expressed through these disguises, it adds to the interpersonal problem rather than contributing to its solution.

If the repressed emotion does not escape in one of the above ways (or is only partially vented by those means), it remains to wreak destruction on the mind and/or body of the "nice" person. Diseases sometimes caused or aggravated by submissive behavior include migraine headaches, asthma attacks, many skin diseases, ulcers, arthritis, chronic fatigue, hypertension, and high blood pressure. In one study, victims of cancer were described as "inhibited individuals with repressed anger, hatred and jealousy."[22] Psychological problems associated with submission include low self-esteem, high anxiety, depression, and inhibition, with their attendant results. Extremely inhibited people may become compulsive, paranoid, impotent or frigid, and even suicidal.[23] In its extreme manifestations, the wages of submission can be literally neurosis, psychosis, or death. Of course, the typical reader of this book will not be nearly so submissive as to experience the worst effects described above. All submissive people do well to note, however, that in general the more submissive the behavior and the more covert the communication, the less healthy the person.

The Benefits of Aggressive Behavior

An aggressor is one who tries to get her needs met, even at the expense of others. A sizeable proportion of the population is aggressive. Why? At least partly because their aggression pays off for them. Three primary payoffs for aggressive-

---

*When using the popular phrase "negative" emotions, I put the word negative in quotation marks because no emotion or category of emotions (like anger or grief) is any "better" or "worse" than any other (such as joy or excitement).

ness are somewhat related. Aggressors are likely to secure the material needs and objects they desire. They tend to be able to protect themselves and their own space. And they seem to retain considerable control over their own lives and the lives of others.

In our society, the aggressive person is apt to seek and secure what she wants. She often gains a larger store of worldly wealth than does the submissive person. She sees to it that her material needs get met. For those of us who are struggling to make ends meet, that benefit is certainly not without appeal.

The aggressive person seems to have greater capability for protecting herself than does the more docile person. Through the centuries, aggressiveness has been linked to physical survival. The aggressive are less vulnerable in a society characterized by struggle, hostility, and unbridled competition. Thomas Henry Huxley, a nineteenth-century English biologist who popularized (and somewhat distorted) Charles Darwin's theory of evolution, commented that destructive fighting is pervasive in the animal world and that "the strongest, the swiftest, and the cunningest live to fight another day."[24]

In our welfare state, people tend to survive until disease kills them off, often in old age. But in the competition between companies or among persons for leadership positions in industry, government, and even nonprofit organizations like the church, the aggressives tend to succeed and survive far better—at least in the short run. And aggression seems to be paid far more handsomely than does submission.

The aggressive person is usually very controlling. Through charisma or the naked use of power, she controls others. She gets others to do her bidding. Things tend to go her way. She is very active in shaping her own destiny. This control is usually highly valued by aggressive people.

The Penalties of Aggression

The potential negative consequences of aggression are numerous. They include fear, the provocation of counteraggression, loss of control, guilt, dehumanization, alienation from people, ill health, and the creation of a society that is too dangerous even for the aggressive to live in comfortably and safely.

One consequence of aggression is increased fear. Many people behave aggressively not because they are strong but because they feel weak. Their aggressive behavior tends to make enemies, and their aggression ultimately makes them more vulnerable and fearful.

Former President Richard Nixon and his closest advisors often acted aggressively. The roots of Watergate and the other "White House horrors," as former Attorney-General John Mitchell characterized them, stemmed not so much from a confidence in power as from fear that ultimately things would get way out of hand. "The thing that is completely misunderstood about Watergate," said former White House special counsel Charles Colson, "is that everybody thinks the people surrounding the President were drunk with power. . . . But it . . . was insecurity. That insecurity began to breed a form of paranoia. We overreacted to the attacks against us and to a lot of other things."[25]

A second negative consequence of aggression is related to the first. Aggression creates its own opposition and fosters its own destruction. "Uneasy rests the head that wears the crown" is a truth applicable to most aggressors. We often ask participants in our communications skills workshops how they have coped when people behaved in an authoritarian (aggressive) manner toward them. The methods that they (and other people) generally use to cope with aggressive behavior include resistance, blaming others, defiance, sabotaging, striking back, forming alliances, lying, and covering up.

For centuries, wise men have commented on the tendency of aggression to bring about the aggressor's destruction. The ancient book of Esther tells the story of a very aggressive and powerful Persian courtier, Haman. At one point in Haman's life, his chief goal was to kill Mordecai, whose only offense was that he did not grovel sufficiently before Haman. Haman commanded that a huge gallows be built for the execution of the object of his displeasure. In the end, however, "they hanged Haman on the gallows which he had erected for Mordecai."[26]

A third liability of aggressive behavior is that it often results in a loss of control. This, like many of the other drawbacks of aggressive and submissive behavior, is paradoxical since aggressive behavior provides a measure of control over one's life and the lives of other people. We have already noted that the underdog often controls the top dog in subtle ways. In another way, however, control over other people's lives limits one's own freedom. If through my aggressiveness I control what you do, it takes my time and energy to supervise you. This creates a kind of self-imposed servitude. Too much control over others can be about as bad as falling into the clutches of people who attempt to run your life. In the sixteenth century, Francis Bacon commented on this paradox: "It is a strange desire to seek power and lose liberty."[27]

Guilt feelings which come from an aggressor's abuse of power are another unpleasant outcome of aggression. Though her sensitivity to the plight of others may be more blunted than that of the typical person, the aggressive person is rarely so deficient in conscience and compassion that she does not suffer pangs of guilt from many of her overbearing acts.

Then, too, aggression tends to dehumanize the aggressor. Each of us was created to love people and use things. In aggressors, there is a strong tendency to love things and use people. When a person *uses* another person, she treats that person as a thing and is said to be "thinging" him. "When someone 'things' another," say George Bach and Ronald Deutsch, "he also automatically things himself."[28] The aggressor's personhood shrinks with every aggressive act. When she does violence to another's selfhood, she diminishes herself.

A sixth outcome of aggressiveness is alienation from other people. Aggressive persons create for themselves a double bind: they do not respect anyone they can dominate, yet they fear an equal relationship. Frederick the Great, the militant king of eighteenth-century Prussia, illustrates this point. He said to his subjects, "Obey." Ironically, just before he died, he commented, "I am tired of ruling slaves."[29] Like Frederick, many a dominating spouse, authoritarian parent, controlling teacher, and aggressive manager learn how frustrating and unfulfilling it is to relate to and work with those who have capitulated to their authority.

Aggression undermines love at the other end of the relationship, too. Ultimately, the person being dominated will experience alienation from the aggressor as a result of being controlled. Like other aggressors, Adolf Hitler was a lonely man. Though millions cheered him at the height of his power, Hitler was aware of his complete loneliness. Albert Speer, one of Hitler's top associates, reports the *Führer's* telling him that after his (Hitler's) eventual retirement, he would soon be forgotten. Speer summarizes Hitler's words:

> People would turn to his successor quickly enough once it became evident that power was now in those hands. . . . Everyone would forsake him. Playing with this idea, with a good measure of self-pity, he continued: "Perhaps one of my former associates will visit me occasionally. But I don't count on it. Aside from Fräulein Braun, I'll take no one with me. Fräulein Braun and my dog. I'll be lonely. For why should anyone voluntarily stay with me for any length of time? Nobody will take notice of me any more. They'll all go running after my successor. Perhaps once a year they'll show up for my birthday."[30]

Not all aggressors perpetrate the kinds of evils associated with Hitler. Some people are aggressive for good causes, but they pay too high a price in human relationships. As someone put it, "I love reforms but I hate reformers."

Aggression can also do serious injury to one's health. Coronary thrombosis, one of the deadliest diseases of our time, takes its heaviest toll on aggressive people.

Another negative consequence of aggressive behavior is that it creates an unsafe society for everyone. The widespread aggression in our society has made it increasingly dangerous to casually enjoy simple pleasures we once took for granted. The evening stroll in the park, the freedom to leave one's possessions momentarily unattended in a public place or one's home vacant during a holiday, the fun of seeking treats on Halloween—these are a few of the "routine personal pleasures" that can no longer be enjoyed without carefully premeditated self-protection. A growing distrust and fear hamper the pleasure and freedom of aggressive, submissive, and assertive people alike.

War is the most devastating problem we face. Today the incredible horrors of thermonuclear, chemical, and bacteriological warfare threaten the very survival of all life on earth. While we face many other serious problems in the twentieth century, unless we learn to cope with our human aggressiveness, we may not be here long enough to solve them.

The Advantages of Assertion

One of the most striking things about assertive people is that they like themselves. They are in a much better position to feel good about themselves than are submissive or aggressive individuals. Although assertiveness isn't the only factor in building a sense of self-worth, there is much truth in therapist Herbert Fensterheim's claim that "the extent to which you assert yourself determines the level of your self-esteem."[31]

A second benefit of assertion is that it fosters fulfilling relationships. Assertion releases much positive energy toward others. Less preoccupied by self-consciousness and anxiety and less driven by the needs for self-protection or control, the assertive person can "see," "hear," and love others more easily. Assertion makes you more comfortable with yourself, and therefore others find it more comfortable to be with you. The richest and most wholesome intimate relationships are between two assertive people. Intimacy has been defined as "the ability to express my deepest aspirations, hopes, fears, anxieties, and guilts to another significant person repeatedly." That kind of disclosure is assertive behavior. There is another important dimension to intimacy, however, which is frequently overlooked. In their book *The Intimate Marriage*, Howard and Charlotte Clinebell point out that intimacy is "the degree of mutual need-satisfaction within the relationship."[32] Healthy, mutual need-satisfaction can only occur between mutually assertive people. The finest marriages, friendships, and parent–child relationships are the fruit of assertive living.

Then, too, assertive behavior greatly reduces a person's fear and anxiety. Research has proven conclusively that learning to make assertive responses definitely weakens the anxiety and tension previously experienced in specific situations. As the increasingly assertive person realizes she can and will gain her needs and defend herself, she does not approach others with fears about being hurt or controlled.

One of the biggest plusses of assertive behavior is living one's own life. Your chances of getting what you want out of life improve greatly when you let others know what you want and stand up for your own rights and needs. Assertion, as we teach it, is results-oriented. My observation of others and my personal experience leads me to believe that *more of a person's needs will be satisfied by being consistently assertive than by submissive or aggressive behavior.* There are times, of course, when effective assertion does not succeed in obtaining its goal. But I believe that in most circumstances assertive behavior is the most appropriate, effective, constructive way of defending one's space and fulfilling one's needs.

On those occasions when assertion does not obtain the results sought, it may still be a preferable way of relating. As John Ruskin said, "It is better to prefer honorable defeat to a mean victory."

The Price of Assertive Behavior

Assertive behavior has many plusses, but assertive people will also pay a price. That price includes disruptions in one's life, the pain associated with honest and caring confrontation, and the arduous personal struggle involved in altering one's own habitual behaviors (for those persons who are changing from submissive or aggressive life styles).

Though submissive people tend to exaggerate the number, the extent, and the probability of mishaps occuring as a result of being assertive, negative results may occur. In the realm of work there have been occasions when people asserted constructively and were fired for it. One's family life can be upset and one's spouse even seek a divorce in extreme situations. I think it important to underscore the fact that these drastic results rarely occur as a result of *effective* assertion. Rather, when one becomes skilled at assertion, human relations tend to improve and the assertive person tends to become more impactful and successful at work. Still, even with the best assertion, some disruption may occur.

Another price of assertion stems from the fact that being authentically oneself can sometimes be a painful experience. While authenticity in a relationship makes possible joy and intimacy, it also leads to some conflict. To be assertive involves a willingness to risk dissension knowing that some conflict is necessary to build a significant relationship of equals. To be assertive also involves becoming vulnerable in significant relationships. Without that vulnerability, one cannot experience the joy of enduring love. (One may experience infatuation without authenticity, but not the fulfillment of a rooted relationship.) Still, when we dare to be vulnerable, even with trusted friends, we sometimes get hurt.

Assertion training often forces reappraisal of one's basic values. People find themselves trying to understand conflicting values in a new light. If one has always valued "peace at any price" and then sees how assertion training demonstrates the negative effect which that stance can have on both parties, the difficult task of reshaping values is at hand. The reexamination of values held since childhood is scary stuff for many people.

The greatest price of all probably is the exercise of willpower required to forego overreliance on submissive or aggressive habits and to develop new and effective ways of relating. Most of us have struggled to give up some bad habits. Even when our sense of identity is consistent with the behavioral change we seek, and our values reinforce the need to change, it is still very difficult to alter ingrained habits.

A major contribution of assertion training is that it deals with each of these negative factors. It helps people learn to make more realistic appraisals of the possible consequences of their assertion. It helps many see some of the values issues in a different and helpful perspective. Drawing on learning theory and other sources, it helps people learn how to break dysfunctional habits as they develop more fulfilling ways of living and relating.

CHOOSE FOR YOURSELF

A major goal of assertion training is to enable people to take charge of their own lives. It helps them break out of ruts and away from stereotyped or compulsive behaviors. At its best, assertion helps people develop the *power of choice* over their actions.

Because of early conditioning, some people automatically behave submissively. Others are habitually aggressive. Most people are predictably submissive or aggressive at least in some specific situations. The proper goal of assertion training is to help individuals choose their behaviors effectively, not to have them behave assertively in every situation.

Henry Emerson Fosdick wrote, "Submissiveness . . . is an inescapable element in our make-up, and something good or evil must be done with it."[33] There are times in every person's life when submissive behavior is appropriate. I believe that the same is true of aggressiveness. There are moments when aggressive behavior is the most fitting response. To make people compulsively assertive is not the goal of this book.

Sometimes it is wise for me to give in to others. Sometimes it may be necessary for me to aggressively defend my rights. One day I may choose to do my own thing. The next day I may suppress my own needs and give way to another's concerns. Though I may choose to be submissive on some occasions and aggressive at some other times, *I strongly believe that behaviors in the assertion range of the continuum will be most appropriate most of the time.*

SUMMARY

Listening and assertion are the *yin* and *yang* of communication—the very different but complementary and interdependent parts of relationships. Just as there are skills for developing one's ability at listening, so there are skills for increasing one's assertiveness.

Each individual has a personal space which needs defending. Likewise, each of us has a psychological need to impact on others and the world. Assertion training teaches constructive methods of defending one's space and impacting on others.

One way of understanding assertion is to see it in contrast with submission and aggression. There are payoffs and penalties for each of those ways of relating. A primary goal of assertion training is to enable people to take charge of their own lives. It helps them avoid repeating dysfunctional and stereotyped behaviors so that they make a fitting response in the situation in which they find themselves. In the next chapter the focus is on how to use one of the most effective of the assertion methods available.

CHAPTER NINE

Developing Three-Part Assertion Messages

When people won't let you alone, it's because you
haven't learned how to make them do it. [1]
—David Seabury, psychologist

You can defend your personal space. This chapter tells you how to do it. Most animals defend their space—and their lives—by fight or flight. Only humans have the third option of verbal confrontation. Some ways of verbal confrontation are much more effective than others. One of the most productive ways of asserting involves the use of a message which contains three parts:

- a nonjudgmental description of the behavior to be changed;
- a disclosure of the asserter's feelings; and
- a clarification of the concrete and tangible effect of the other person's behavior on the asserter.

In the process of framing these messages, the asserter unexpectedly finds himself on a voyage of self-discovery, learning much about himself.

VERBAL ASSERTION: THE THIRD OPTION

Every creature of every species on earth has the problem of defending its space, its life, from invasion and attack. Likewise, every creature has inherited certain coping mechanisms for self-preservation.

Fight or flight are the primary coping behaviors of the subhuman species, especially the vertebrates. These responses are nearly automatic, preprogrammed behaviors of significant survival value for the lower animals. Human beings use these methods, too, sometimes openly and sometimes in veiled ways. But unlike other species, we humans have a third important option for defending our space. The feature that most distinguishes us from other species is the "new" verbal and problem-solving brain which evolution added to our more primitive animal brain.

About a million years ago, according to Dr. Manuel Smith, evolution seems to have weeded out our ancestral cousins who did not incorporate this third option into their primitive coping behaviors of fight and flight. At the same time, evolution improved the verbal and problem-solving abilities of our ancestors who survived and produced us as their descendants. When our space is about to be invaded, this portion of our human brain makes it possible for us to communicate and work out our problems. These skills are the major survival difference between humans and those species which have already died, face extinction, or survive only by mankind's sufferance.

The coping mechanisms of fight and flight inherited from our prehuman ancestors correspond roughly to aggression and submission. While occasionally helpful to people in our day, these ways of coping are often inadequate. Excessive dependence on either of these approaches is undesirable.

Smith writes:

> The patients I see in therapy get angry and aggressive toward other people too often for their own liking, or continually fear and then retreat from other people, or are fed up with losing and being depressed most of the time. Most people seen by therapists are seeking help as a result of over-reliance on fight or flight in various . . . forms.[2]

While we have inherited the ability to fight or run for survival, we alone of the earth's species are not limited to those options. Instead, we have the human option to resolve our differences by talking things out with others.

A most important and often difficult aspect of utilizing this third option is learning to use language precisely and effectively.[3] Assertion, like surgery, requires accuracy—not rash statements or rambling comments. As one of our students put it, "When you have a right to beef, there's a right way to word it."

Even under normal circumstances, people often find it difficult to speak with precision. When asserting, a person is usually angry, frustrated, or afraid, and in that condition of emotional stress it is even more difficult to convey one's meanings accurately and succinctly. Concerning moments when assertion is appropriate, people have told me: "When he does that, it just gets to me. It touches off my temper and I can't control myself." Others say, "Something seems to come over me, and I can't do a thing about it. I just crawl into my shell and suffer in silence."

When someone violates our space, the working of our bodies usually impedes our verbal capacity. Stress causes the lower brain centers to interfere with much of the operation of the higher brain. A large proportion of the blood is automatically routed away from the brain to the skeletal muscles during these emotional states. These factors inhibit the verbal and problem-solving brain, and so it does not perform with usual efficiency.

Though it is difficult to speak accurately while under stress, it is not impossible. Even when we are very scared or furiously angry, our behavior can be selected, not compelled, and our words can be chosen, not triggered.

THREE-PART
ASSERTION MESSAGES

When a person invades my life space, I want him out of it. To accomplish that purpose, I will send an assertion message with the goal of changing the behavior which is intruding on my personal territory.

People in our classes often believe it is unethical to try to change another person's behavior. I agree with them in large measure. One of the major interpersonal problems is that too many people are trying to shape and control other people's lives. However, *when someone is violating my space, I want THAT behavior changed.*

This issue needs to be faced squarely at the outset of our discussion of learning to use assertion messages. When another person trespasses on my space, it is in my best interest, in his best interest, and in society's best interest for me to confront him in such a way that the behavior is altered and he respects the legitimate boundaries of my space. It is neither manipulative nor controlling for me to utilize the most effective and humane means available to defend myself.

Effective assertion is characterized by *firmness without domination.* It vigorously defends one's own space while steadfastly refusing to violate the trespasser's turf. That is why the three-part message contains no solution. It is up to the other person to figure out how he can best evacuate my space. The recipient of these messages can usually come up with a resolution of the problem that preserves his self-respect and meets my needs.

When I want another person to modify a behavior that is intrusive on my space, the method I use must meet the following criteria:

1. *There is a high probability that the other will alter the troublesome behavior.* That is, the method needs to be effective in protecting my space.
2. *There is a low probability that I will violate the other person's space.*
3. *There is little likelihood of diminishing the other person's self-esteem.* While I cannot control how another person will react to what I say, I can discipline myself not to use blaming, put-down, or other derogatory kinds of language.
4. *There is low risk of damaging the relationship.* Of course, if a relationship is very fragile, even the most tactful assertion may be the final act that severs it. In fragile relationships, however, submission is often as dangerous to the relationship as assertion, or even more dangerous. In most healthy relationships, effective assertion strengthens the relationship over the long haul. It is normally a bonding factor between mature people.
5. *There is a low risk of diminishing motivation.*
6. *There is little likelihood that defensiveness will escalate to destructive levels.* An assertion message can be phrased in ways that are less likely to provoke excessive defensiveness in the other person. And defensiveness-reducing methods can be used when the other person does experience greater stress.

The three-part assertion message meets the above criteria. It begins with a description of the offending behavior and includes a description of the consequences on your life and how you feel about those consequences. Each part of the message is important to the success of the assertion. Beginners at assertion usually send more effective messages when they use the formula: "When you [state the behavior nonjudgmentally], *I feel* [disclose your feelings] *because* [clarify the effect on your life]." The three parts of the assertion message are stated as succinctly as possible and are contained in one sentence. For example, in one family, two children frequently made snacks and did not clean up the kitchen counters when they were finished. The mother sent this message:

Behavior   When you don't clean the counter
                    after making snacks,
       +
Feelings   I feel very annoyed
       +
Effects   because it makes more work for me.

EFFECTIVE AND INEFFECTIVE WAYS OF CONFRONTATION

When participants in our communication skills courses learn about three-part assertion messages, they often contrast the way they recently handled confrontations with the way they would do it after having learned assertion skills. With virtual unanimity people had previously used "shaming or blaming" or some of the other roadblocks described in Chapter 2. Dr. Thomas Gordon's experience is similar; "It is no exaggeration that ninety-nine out of a hundred parents in our classes use ineffective methods of communicating when their children's behavior is interfering with the parent's lives."[4]

Brenda Judson said that five minutes before the school bus was scheduled to arrive, and seven minutes before she had to leave for work, her nine-year-old son, Brad, said he couldn't find his shoes. Brenda said, "How can you do this to me? If you would only put your clothes away, you'd know where they are now. How can you possibly expect me to find them in your messy room? If you don't find them right away you'll be punished."

As Brenda thought about what happened, she said, "In that situation I used the following roadblocks: moralizing, judging, and threatening. While this was happening the clock was ticking away and neither of our needs was being met. Because of our argument the shoes were not found on time and we now had another problem—he missed the bus. I was under even more pressure. Brad went to school in a bad frame of mind and I allowed my whole day to be ruined by that incident."

Brenda then stated how she would have related differently with Brad that day using some of the skills learned in class. "In the first place," she said, "I wouldn't have confronted him when neither of us had the time to talk about it. I would have said something like, 'You look in your room and I'll look downstairs.' Later, after school I would have used the following assertion message: 'Brad, I'd like to talk with you about what happened this morning. When you can't find your shoes in the morning, I feel very irritated because I am under a lot of pressure trying to get to work on time myself.' " Within a few days, the situation occurred again and Brenda followed the plan she outlined to the class. "It really worked," she said later. "The missing clothes hassle occurred about once a week until I sent the assertion message. In the nine months since then it has only happened once."

WRITING THREE-PART ASSERTION MESSAGES

Three-part assertion messages look deceptively easy to write; in actuality, most people find that it is hard, time-consuming work to make up an effective message. For that reason we will examine each part of the message in some detail.

Nonjudgmental Descriptions of Behavior

When a person violates your space, the behavior to be altered must be described very accurately and objectively. Otherwise, the other person may not clearly understand what behavior you find offensive.

People often find it hard to believe that the trespasser may not know what behavior you want modified. They repeatedly tell us, "Don't be ridiculous. He knows it bugs me. He just doesn't care enough to stop doing it." Sometimes, of course, the offending party was well aware of his actions and the negative effects those behaviors had on the other person. Even in those circumstances, a well-executed assertion message will often prevent a repetition of that behavior. Frequently, however, people who were certain that the intruder was aware of how a specific behavior violated their space learned differently when they sent an assertion message. Many are surprised to find that the trespasser had no idea that he had intruded on their space and stressed them. People often report to us that after asserting, the trespasser says: "Gee, I didn't know that bothered you" or "I guess you've tried to tell me about this before, but I never really understood until now."

If you are to protect your personal space, you must communicate what the other does that violates your space. This is not easy. People seldom describe behavior accurately enough so that the other has no problem understanding what he is doing to bother us. These guides will help you develop an effective behavior description:

First, *describe the behavior in specific rather than fuzzy terms.* Some assertion messages are inexact. The language is general rather than specific; the other person does not know precisely what you mean. If your assertion message does not accurately describe the other's behavior, it is unlikely that your needs will be met.

Specific Behavior Description	Fuzzy Behavior Description
When you don't shovel the snow from the driveway before going to school . . .	When you don't do your part around the house . . .
When you arrive late for work three times this week . . .	When you ignore company policies . . .
Situation: A husband and wife drive to work together. The wife is a slow eater. They have been arriving late for work because the wife is not ready on time.	
When you are not ready to leave for work by 7:30 . . .	When you dawdle over your breakfast . . .

In each of the three cases, in the left-hand column the person receiving the assertion knows exactly what behavior needed to be altered. In the examples in the right-hand column, the asserter might have had specific behaviors in mind but did not state his message accurately. The person receiving could easily be confused about what behavior was troublesome.

Second, *limit yourself to behavioral descriptions. Do not draw inferences about the other person's motives, attitudes, character, and so on.* [5] When people try to describe another's behavior they frequently state what they think the other intended rather than describe what he actually did. Compare the differences between the behavior descriptions in the left-hand column with the inferences in the column at the right:

Behavior Description	Inferences
Situation: I am a committee chairman. When you talked more than any of the others at the meeting today and cut off several people before they were finished . . .	When you behaved so rudely at the meeting . . .
Situation: I am a committee chairman and the person receiving my assertion promised to stay until the end of the meeting to give a report.	When you were so bored during the meeting that you left early . . .
When you left the meeting twenty minutes before your report was to be given . . .	When you left the meeting early just because Frank criticized you . . .

The behavior in the left-hand column is *observable*. Anyone present who had sound hearing and sight could have noticed the same behaviors. The behaviors in the right-hand column represent guesses at what was going on inside the other person. I can know for a fact that a person left a meeting twenty minutes early without having given his report, but since that is the only data I have, I can't be sure whether he was bored, annoyed, had another appointment to keep, became sick, or left early for still another reason. Assertions are weakened by inferences because we often guess wrongly about the internal state of another—and even when we are right, the other probably won't admit it. Assertion theory tells us that an individual's feelings are part of his personal space. We have no right to try to control someone else's feelings (since that is meddling in their space), but we can try to alter behaviors that intrude on our space.

Third, *make your behavior description an objective statement rather than a judgment.* An assertion statement does not imply that the other person's behavior was immoral, stupid, naughty, bad, or wrong. It does not include "loaded" words, caricatures, sarcasm, generalizations, absolutes, exaggerations, or profanity. In fact, a unique factor in sound assertion messages is the avoidance of "attacking" and "evaluative" elements that often contaminate interpersonal confrontations.

Assertion messages avoid character assassinations:

Behavior Description	Character Assassination
When you say women are incapable of being effective managers . . .	When you behave like a male chauvinist pig . . .
When you repeatedly talk more than others in the class . . .	When you have constipation of the brain and diarrhea of the mouth . . .

Assertion messages avoid absolutes. They do not use words like "never," "always," and "constantly."

Behavior Description	Use of Absolutes
When you are frequently late in picking me up . . .	When you are *never* on time . . .
When you interrupt me before I have completed my statement . . .	When you *constantly* interrupt me . . .
When you park so that my car is blocked in at noon . . .	When you *always* park so that my car is blocked in at noon . . .

Assertion messages avoid profanity. Swearing during confrontations often triggers extra emotion and defensiveness in the other person.

Behavior Description	Use of Profanity
When you do not call to let me know you will be late for supper . . .	When you drag your ass in here late for supper night after night . . .
When you do not have my car repaired at the time promised . . .	You lying son of a bitch, you promised that my car would be ready by four.

Even when we try to be objective and avoid character assassination, absolutes, and profanity, we are apt, perhaps subconsicously, to insert partially veiled judgments and innuendos into our speech. It has been said that we typically use language in this manner: *"I am firm, you are stubborn, he is pigheaded. I am shrewd, you are a sharp operator, he is crooked."*

After you try to describe a behavior objectively, examine it carefully to be sure that no subtle judgmental words have crept in.

Behavior Description	Descriptions with Judgmental Words that "Creep In"
When you don't return the can opener to the same place after you are through with it . . .	When you *hide* the can opener on me . . .
When you overspend our clothing budget . . .	When you *waste* our *hard-earned* money on *unnecessary* clothing . . .

Sometimes people want to retain the judgmental and attack elements of their message. Then we ask them, "Do you want to have maximum likelihood of changing the other person's behavior and maintaining the relationship through an assertive message; or would you rather tell off the other person even though you will have less chance to change the behavior and maintain a good relationship? People occasionally choose the path of aggression. Our goal is not to tell others how to behave but to help them distinguish between submissive, assertive, and aggressive behaviors and to predict with some accuracy the probable consequences of each type of behavior.

Fourth, *behavioral descriptions should be as brief as possible*. The assertion message should be sufficient without sacrificing accuracy in describing the behavior that needs to be changed.

Many people use needless words in their assertions. I try to keep the assertion as trim as possible so that the person sees my need in stark clarity. Some people try to give reasons and extraneous data with their assertion. Mine is pared down to its essentials. Some people lump several behaviors in one assertion. I typically concentrate on one behavior at a time.

Brief Behavior Description	Lengthy Description
When you are frequently late for supper . . .	When you get all involved in your football game and forget about the family and come home late and all dirty for dinner . . .

What behavior does the parent in the right-hand column want changed? Does he prefer that the child not be involved when he is participating in athletic events? Or doesn't he want the child to play football? Does he want the child to remember the family? What does it mean to "remember the family"? Is it more important for the child to be on time for supper or to be clean? *What is not said is as important in an assertion message as what is said.* Don't add peripheral data to your bare-bones assertion. Relinquish side issues and explanations. *The entire assertion message should be compressed into one sentence.*

Fifth, *be sure that you assert about the real issues.* Many people send *displaced assertions.* They confront on a topic other than the one that really troubles them.

Sometimes people are afraid to tackle the big issues in their relationship and so assert on a series of less threatening matters. A husband, for example, may assert about the amount of money his wife spends for clothes when his real concern is that she has taken a full-time job while the children are still pre-schoolers. Even if the wife changes her behavior about the purchase of clothes, the man's deepest concerns will not be addressed. He probably won't appreciate her gift of behavioral change and will simply shift to another topic on which to "assert."

At the opposite extreme, people are often reluctant to assert about the "little things" in life. They say, "I shouldn't be so 'small' and 'picky' to be bothered by such an insignificant thing." Sometimes we can truly develop more acceptance of another person's behavior, but often a pseudoacceptance develops in the top of our mind while the irritation continues to grow in the depth of our gut.

Little things often become the major irritants of life. A man who walked across this continent from the Atlantic Ocean to the Pacific was besieged by reporters at the end of his journey. One journalist wanted to know, "What was the most difficult part of your trip—the Rocky Mountains, the heat of the desert, or the large crowded cities like Chicago?" "None of these things," said the hiker. "The biggest problem was sand in my shoes."

In relationships, too, the "little things" are often more serious than they seem. Hazen Werner writes, "Most marriage bonds are not broken on the rocks in a great storm; they are worn away by the endless battering of pebbles, . . . the tiny conflicts and seemingly petty irritations of daily life."[6] Judge Joseph Sabath, commenting on the 100,000 divorce cases he has heard, reflected, "Usually it isn't the big arguments or even physical blows, but the constant hammering and chiseling in a thousand different ways that signal the lethal warrant of their union." In other relationships—parent-child, boss-subordinate, friend-friend, colleague-colleague—the same principle is often true: *seemingly minor irritants can create major problems* unless they are dealt with assertively.

If you are frequently unable to locate the newspaper at night when you want to read it, if someone is playing his hi-fi so loud you cannot concentrate even when you are in your room with the door closed, if dirty dishes and empty food packages are left about the house from other people's snacks and you are the one who eventually cleans them up—if these things happen to you, chances are that you will feel your space has been invaded. Unfortunately, many people tell themselves, "These are such small things. They shouldn't bother me." Or they may even say, "I don't want to go through the hassle of confronting him on this."

Our experience of assertion training with thousands of people leads us to conclude that repeated small irritants often grow until they loom large in our feeling world. When people do not get their needs met in the commonplace trivialities of life, they build up reservoirs of resentment that diminish their acceptance of the other person, undermine the enjoyment of the relationship, and make it far more difficult to solve the "big" problems when they arise.

This built-up resentment often eventually becomes focused on a "larger" issue about which it seems more "reasonable" to be upset. On a subconscious level, people frequently transfer their irritations from many small issues to a larger one. Their assertion is displaced from the actual troublesome behavior to a target that seems more "legitimate." When handled by assertion, these displaced confrontations do not bring the kind of resolution that normally accompanies assertion.

Another form of displaced assertion takes place when a person wants "love" from his spouse, friend, or child or "respect" from his boss or subordinate. He may become angry over some behavior, feeling that if the other really loved him, he wouldn't do that. He may even attempt assertion to alter the behavior, but if what he really wants is assurance of love or respect, he will still be unhappy even if the other alters his troublesome behavior. This process can continue indefinitely because people seeking love or respect are rarely convinced when another person changes his behavior following an assertion. "If he loved me, I wouldn't have had to assert for him to change that behavior" is the way the reasoning goes. Asserting for behavior change when one really wants reassurance of being loved and respected is always fruitless.

Displaced assertions keep a relationship in such frequent disharmony and offer such little possibility for improvement that the whole relationship often goes sour. These pseudoassertions that do not deal with the real issues rarely if ever help and often hinder a friendship, marriage, or work relationship.

Sixth, *be sure to assert to the right person.* People commonly confront the wrong person. This is known as a *misattributed assertion.* When there is trouble at work, a person may become more confrontative at home. Or confrontations at work may be directed at subordinates rather than the superior when the assertion should be directed at the boss. Some people find a scapegoat—one person who takes the brunt for everyone. You undoubtedly recall some teachers who unfairly singled out a particular child for confrontation. It does not solve your problem to assert to the wrong person, and it probably will increase your interpersonal difficulties with the person who is unfairly confronted and usually with others in the group as well.

Disclosure of Feelings

The second part of the three-part assertion message communicates how the asserter feels about the effect the other's behavior has on him. For example, a working wife had an agreement with her husband that when she was out of town he would be responsible for seeing that the household cleaning tasks were kept current so that she did not face a big accumulation when she returned home. When she returned from a tiring week-long business trip, she discovered that no housecleaning and laundry had been done and that dirty dishes from several meals were stacked in the sink. She had strong feelings and said to her husband, "When you don't do the household cleaning and laundry as agreed, *I feel very angry . . .*"

The genuine disclosure of emotion underscores the importance the assertion has for the person sending the message. When you begin to send this kind of assertion message you will see how the expression of your own feelings contributes greatly to the other person's willingness to change his behavior to meet your needs.

The beginning of assertion training in modern psychology is often traced to Andrew Salter's innovative approach to psychotherapy and his influential book *Conditioned Reflex Therapy*.[7] One of Salter's major contributions was his emphasis on the direct expression of feeling.

Salter was the first of a long line of modern assertiveness trainers to discover that the average person in assertion training has a difficult time identifying and communicating his emotions. Many people are like the college professor in one of our workshops who was trying to express his feelings in an assertion message. After several struggling attempts he said, "I have smart brains but a dumb gut. It is hard for me to know what I am feeling—and when I do get in touch with my emotions it is even more difficult to express them."

People tend to have three problems with the expression of emotion. First, they may substitute one emotion for another. Some people express anger when their primary feeling is that of fright. For example, if a child surprises a parent with a loud noise, the parent may respond very angrily without even mentioning the fear—yet it was the fearful feeling that led to the anger. We call that substituting a *secondary emotion* for a *primary one*.

Substitution of one emotion for another needs to be overcome if a person is to assert effectively. Fortunately, most people can accomplish this by asking themselves, "When I experienced the negative effect of the other's behavior, what was the *first* feeling I experienced?" Often the first feeling is the primary feeling—the one which belongs in the assertion message.

Another method of tuning into the primary feeling is to recognize some of your patterns of emotional substitution. If, for example, you usually become angry when you feel vulnerable or sad, the next time you find yourself becoming angry check to see if it is possible that you are really stressed by feelings of vulnerability or sadness. Or if you tend to cry as a substitute for expressing anger, begin to search for possible traces or causes for anger as soon as you feel sadness welling up inside you.

People also find it difficult to accurately state the *degree* of feeling they are experiencing. It is not unusual for someone to say, "I'm angry" when he is merely annoyed, or "I'm irritated" when he is seething with rage.

The asserter can increase the emotional accuracy of his statement by selecting from several words of varying intensity to see which best matches his inner feeling. For example, he might try such words as "nervous," "worried," "afraid," or "petrified." It is better to select the word carefully so that one word will communicate the feeling. Sometimes, however, additional, modifying adjectives are helpful. A person may feel "*somewhat* worried." Greater anxiety could be expressed by "*very* worried."

Genuine disclosure of feeling is the only appropriate expression of emotion in an assertion message. Sometimes people feign stronger emotions, thinking that that will be more convincing. I find that pretense distasteful because it is manipulative. It is also counterproductive. People who are likely to respond to genuine emotion often disbelieve the magnified emotion and tend to be less responsive to that kind of message. When a person understates his feelings, it deprives the other of some important data that will motivate him to alter his behavior. So the assertion loses much of its strength.

Another problem experienced by people trying to phrase the feeling part of an assertion message is that they may choose a word that is laden with judgment. The word selected provides more of a slur on the other's character than a disclosure of the asserter's feelings. One person's assertion message came out like this: "When you smoke in our small office I feel *abused* because my eyes smart and my throat becomes irritated." The message can be improved by the substitution of another feeling word. "When you smoke in this small room, I feel *annoyed* because my eyes smart and my throat becomes irritated."

People often ask, "How do I get in touch with what I am feeling?" Three things prove helpful. First, try to listen to your emotions without distorting or censoring them. John Powell says, "Whenever you are ready to stop telling your emotions what they should be, they will tell you what they really are."[8]

Another way to increase your sensitivity to your emotions is to listen to your body. When you have a headache your body is usually telling you about some emotions. When you have muscular tension, your emotions are trying to speak through their primary channel of communication—your body. When I began listening to my body, I was amazed both at what my body tells me and how constantly it informs me about my inner feeling world. Sometimes I don't like what I hear and I will ignore the signals for weeks at a time. My body continues to transmit its message, however, and whenever I am ready to receive again, I can regain contact with my rich emotional life. Unfortunately, if one ignores the body's messages too long, the ability to hear them atrophies.

A third way to increase your emotional awareness is to express the feelings that you do experience. You can acknowledge your feelings silently to yourself, talk about them with others, or express them vigorously through laughter, crying, shouting, dancing, or lovemaking. The more we express our feelings, the more we sharpen our emotional awareness.

The benefits gained by constructive expression of emotions in assertion messages are impressive. As we have already seen, the disclosure of feelings provides the receiver with important emotional data that can significantly influence his decision to alter troublesome behavior. Constructive expression of emotion also releases positive feelings for the other person. It is a psychological rule of thumb that once a person is able to express "negative" emotions to another person, he becomes liberated to discover and express the "positive" feelings that may have been hidden for a long time.

Those who give expression to their feelings constructively are stimulated to greater mental and physical health. Andrew Salter noted that most people suffer from "constipation of the emotions."[9] We are all aware of the harmful effects of constipation on one's physical condition. In a similar way, "negative" emotions need to be disposed of continually or our physical and mental health and interpersonal relationships will suffer.

Clarification of the Tangible Effect on the Asserter

A major reason the three-part assertion works is because it describes how the other person's behavior affects the sender of the message. If I want you to voluntarily alter a specific behavior, it certainly helps if I provide you with a convincing reason to change. My experience is that people are usually willing to modify their behavior if they can see that they are trespassing on my space or interfering with my efforts to secure my legitimate needs.

The effectiveness of this part of the message depends on whether or not the person intruding on my space believes that his behavior does indeed have negative consequences on my life. *"Concrete or tangible effects"*[10] seem to be most convincing to people. By *concrete or tangible effects* we mean those things that unnecessarily cost the asserter money, harm his possessions, consume his time, cause him extra work, endanger his job, and/or interfere with his effectiveness at work. These results negatively affect the asserter in what may be described as a *materialistic* way. A well-delivered assertion message that cites a concrete and tangible effect usually persuades the other person to change his behavior to meet the asserter's needs. I estimate that by using this type of assertion I have been able to satisfy my needs about 90 to 95 percent of the time.

Let's look at some examples of tangible effects from the assertions made by some of our workshop participants.

	Behavior Description	Disclosure of Feeling	Tangible Effect
Costs money	When you use my car and don't refill the gas tank . . .	I feel unfairly treated . . .	because I have *to pay more money* for gasoline.
Harms possessions	When you borrow my tools and leave them out in the rain . . .	I feel annoyed . . .	because they *become rusty and don't work well.*
Consumes time	When you are frequently late to pick me up after work . . .	I feel frustrated . . .	because *my time is wasted* while I wait for you.
Interferes with effectiveness at work	When you call me at work and talk at length . . .	I feel tense . . .	because *I don't get all my work done on schedule.*
Causes extra work	When you do not put your dirty clothes in the hamper . . .	I feel irritated . . .	because it *makes extra work* for me when I do the wash.

There are five common difficulties that people have in writing this part of an assertion message. First, *a fairly large number of people say they cannot think of a single situation in which someone is intruding on their space in a tangible way.* This, of course, does not mean that they are exempt from this kind of intrusion on their space. In most ordinary relationships and in every significant relationship, people trespass on one another's turf in tangible ways. If a person cannot specify occasions when this has happened, he has simply banished them from his awareness. Our trainers have found that most people can increase their ability to identify behaviors with tangible negative effects on their lives once they have made the decision that this is worth doing.

A second, very common difficulty people have with this part of the assertion message is that *they think these materialistic intrusions are insignificant compared to other behaviors.* One father told me, "Sure, I get mad about the tools being left out in the rain. But what really bugs me is that my son doesn't treat me civilly ninety percent of the time." A young adult had a similar point of view. "It bothers me when my fiancé returns my records with scratches and dirt all over them. But what I really dislike is the way he takes me for granted."

Like many others in assertion training, these people didn't want to bother with assertions that seemed insignificant. They wanted to deal with "more important" things. While situations with tangible effects may *seem* less important than situations that are primarily values issues, we've often found that this is not true.

The assertion message that cites tangible effects often influences the intangible areas of a relationship. Not leaving tools outside is one specific behavior that constitutes "more civil treatment" of the boy toward his father. Moreover, when the father's needs begin to be satisfied by the son's response to an assertion message, the father's reservoir of resentment is often diminished—which further strengthens the relationship. Usually the very process of effective assertion improves the communication between two people. They tend to respect and like each other more as a result.

A third problem when trying to send an assertion message is that people often discover that *they can find no effect on their physical or psychological space.* They have lots of strong feelings, but no concrete effects. A parent told his teenager, "When you wear jeans to the school play it annoys me [a feeling] and I feel irritated [another feeling]." This kind of a message is often *an attempt by the sender to impose his values on the other person, and hence is an intrusion on the other's space.* When one person tries to change another person's behavior about values issues, he often ends up aggressing against the other person rather than asserting. [11]

One controversial parent-child issue raised frequently by parents in our classes is the anger and frustration they feel in reaction to how their children keep their rooms. Many parents value neatness, orderliness, and maintenance of clothes and other possessions. In contrast, many children rank these values much lower than others they hold, such as having an active play or social life, spending time with friends, or playing sports.

The central question to help clarify these values issues is: "Whose space is the child's bedroom?"

In our family we have satisfied ourselves and the children by saying that the child's room is his own space to be managed in the way he chooses. In the common areas of the house—the living room, dining room, and kitchen—which all of us use, our values for order, lack of clutter, and esthetics are met.

An elementary classroom teacher faces a similar dilemma when her values hold that students' desks should be well organized. Many children see their desks as their personal space and jam into them whatever they wish in as disorderly way as they choose. Again the clarifying question, "Whose space is the desk?" needs to be addressed.

Assertion training does *not* teach that we should avoid trying to influence other people's values. It does teach that a *three-part assertion on values issues is never appropriate* (in fact, you can never complete the third part—citing a concrete effect of the other's behavior on your life space).

Another difficulty people have in writing assertions is *when the effect is on someone other than the asserter.* It is the effect on you that is important. *Don't try to send an assertion for a third party.* Let him send his own. If the offending person is not trespassing on your space, you cannot send a valid three-part assertion.

Finally, *people sometimes state an effect that isn't the real reason.* Sean and Molly Molloy were newlyweds. Each Friday after work he went to the bar to drink with the boys for several hours. Molly didn't like the behavior and sent this message: "When you stay late at the Clover Club I feel frustrated *because things are not getting done at home."* Later Molly told me, "This was a very unsuccessful assertion. The message was incorrect. I was not frustrated because things were not getting done but because I was not with him. Thus, the message was not an honest one. Because the message was incorrect I kept getting off the track. We started talking about drinking, which really wasn't the issue. Then we used a lot of roadblocks. It became real bad."

Effective assertion is open and honest communication. Substitution of a more plausible effect for the effect that most concerns you is both inappropriate and ineffective in an assertion message.

We have focused on assertions with tangible effects because they are so important and because many people try to bypass them. Other varieties of assertion are also significant, and we will discuss many of them in a later chapter.

There are some assertions that fall into a "borderline" category. While certain people say the effect is tangible, others are not convinced that it is. Most people, however, believe that in these situations the person to whom the assertion is addressed would "buy" the effect on the other's life. Here are some "borderline category" behaviors and effects:

Behavior Description	Disclosure of Feeling	Effect
When you make plans with me and then cancel at the last minute . . .	I feel irritated . . .	*because it is too late to make plans with my other friends.*
When you make loud noises when I am watching TV . . .	I feel annoyed . . .	*because I can't concentrate on the show.*
When you don't take accurate telephone messages . . .	I feel upset . . .	*because I lack information and can't return calls that may be very important.*
When you don't give me an answer on my request for a vacation during the last two weeks of July . .	I feel frustrated . . .	*because I can't plan my summer.*
When you eat early on weekends and don't prepare your breakfasts quietly . . .	I feel angry . . .	*because I wake up an hour or two earlier than I planned to get up.*

A VOYAGE OF SELF-DISCOVERY AND GROWTH

One of the things that has fascinated our teaching staff and students alike is the amount of self-discovery involved in framing assertion messages. When we are concentrating on altering another person's intrusive behavior, we can learn a lot about ourselves.

Probably the biggest insight comes when the asserter tries to phrase the concrete effect that another's behavior has on his life. One assertion after another is discarded—as many as half to three-quarters of them—because they fall into the values area and constitute an intrusion on the other person's space rather than a defense of the asserter's space. As he learns to defend his own space, the typical person tends to develop a greater sensitivity to other people's territorial boundaries and a much greater acceptance of the other person's right to his own space, his own values, his own life. As one person said, "Learning to write these assertion messages has enabled me to be more 'me,' and at the same time I let other people be more themselves."

The voyage of self-discovery that accompanies the writing of assertion messages is exciting and productive. At the same time, it can be very difficult. It is hard to toil over words until they describe behavior accurately. It is tough to tune into one's emotions, and even harder to make oneself vulnerable by expressing feelings to others in the midst of stress. It is also frustrating to discover that one message after another that we wanted to send has no tangible effect and may well mean we want to invade the other person's turf.

Fortunately, the few assertions that withstand this winnowing process have a high probability of altering the behavior of others. Equally important, the relationships of genuinely assertive persons are stronger, more nearly equal, and more fulfilling. Virtually all our students who discipline themselves to use this kind of assertion find that this journey of self-discovery and growth is well worth the effort.

SUMMARY

Virtually all creatures defend their space using a variety of tactics which fall into one of the two basic categories—fight or flight. Only humans have a third option—verbal assertion. There are effective and ineffective ways of verbally confronting others. One of the most effective methods of confrontation is the three-part assertion message with its nonblaming description of behavior, disclosure of feelings, and clarification of the tangible effect the other's behavior has on the asserter's life. In the process of developing a message to change another person's behavior, the asserter often learns a great deal about himself.

CHAPTER TEN

Handling The Push-Push Back Phenomenon

Crisis in dialogue occurs when the participants . . . fail really to address each other but
turn away defensively, each within himself, for
the purposes of self-justification.[1]
                    —Reuel Howe, theologian

SURPRISE ATTACK

Picture this scene. Someone has trespassed on your space, causing an adverse tangible effect on your life. Instead of responding with the inflammatory words so common in such situations, you use the skills learned in the preceding chapter to phrase an assertion message. All elements of sarcasm, put-down, blame, or exaggeration have been deleted. Because you have discharged some of your "negative" emotions while writing the message in private and because you are confident that the other person will ultimately meet your needs, you state your assertion without any "edge" in your voice and without hostile body language. Despite all your efforts to treat the other with respect, she becomes very abusive and verbally attacks you.

Beth had learned how to *write* three-part assertion messages but had not yet learned the full process of sending the message. Though the class had been warned not to try using the messages until they learned the whole process, Beth thought she would give it a try. Here is her description of what happened:

> Three friends and I were eating in a crowded restaurant. The lady at the next table started smoking and the smoke kept drifting toward me. I am allergic to cigarette smoke and my eyes smarted and my throat and nose were affected. I decided to assert myself.
>
> I was very calm and nonabrasive as I said, "When you smoke, it bothers me because I am allergic to cigarette smoke and it causes unpleasant physical reactions that last for hours."
>
> I anticipated that she would simply stop smoking since I had sent such a nonblameful message. What happened next was unbelievable. The woman said I had incredible gall to ask her to stop smoking. She insisted she had the right to smoke. She said there were no signs in the restaurant prohibiting smoking.
>
> Then I countered that nonsmokers also have their rights.
>
> This seemed to infuriate her even more. She said that all long-haired youths (I'm in my early thirties but I do have long hair) were the same and hated the United States and what it stands for.
>
> I said, "All I asked was that you stop smoking because the smoke is bothering my allergy."
>
> She countered with a barrage saying that I was uncouth, discourteous, and a shameful person. She continued smoking.

For beginning asserters, this kind of response is totally unexpected. After all, it was the other person who trespassed on Beth's space. Many people in her situation would have hurled invectives, but she spoke in a reasonable and objective manner. Instead of appreciating Beth's restraint and consideration, the receiver of her assertion turned on her venomously.

Novices at assertion typically experience this kind of reaction as a surprise attack. They are about as prepared for it as the United States was for Pearl

Harbor. Yet this is "par for the course" in human behavior. People usually respond defensively to an assertion.

The skill of sending assertion messages effectively involves learning to expect and deal with people's defensive responses. For this purpose it is advisable to follow the six-step assertion process described later in the chapter. If an assertion does not work, a checklist can help you determine what went wrong.

THE HUMAN TENDENCY
TO BE DEFENSIVE

Defensiveness is a major factor in every person's life.[2] A person's defensiveness often blocks her constructive decisions and actions. Even with one's best friends a person's defensiveness makes her feel somewhat vulnerable, so that she guards much of what she says. Since defensiveness is so pervasive in our lives, it is not surprising that people usually respond defensively to assertion messages. Gregory Baum writes:

> Strength is needed in every truly human conversation. But, it is especially necessary in the dialogue in which the special word is addressed to us, the word that makes us face who we are, that reveals to us the destructive and superficial in us. . . . This special word . . . is always a threat to us. We are tempted to draw up our defenses against it. We tend to feel that if we listen to it we may not survive the judgment contained in it. . . . [Whenever] man is called . . . to open himself to the truth, then the power to respond is not something that can be taken for granted. . . . On the contrary, a man finds present in himself a hundred hesitations to respond, to act, and to be in a new way.[3]

We have a special phrase that we use to describe an assertion and the predictable defensive response to it. We call it the "push–push back phenomenon." Virtually every assertion message is experienced as a "push." Even when the assertion is only attempting to remove the other person from the asserter's territory, the confrontation is experienced as a "push." In response to that push there is an almost inevitable "push back."

No matter how well we phrase assertion messages, people seldom like to receive them. Who wants to find out that she trespassed on another's space and made a tangible and negative impact on that individual? It is uncomfortable to learn that you have adversely affected another's life. That's why even the best assertion messages tend to trigger defensive responses from the receiver. We warn our students: "When you send a well-worded assertion message, don't expect an accolade. Anticipate an attack or some other form of defensive response."

THE UPWARD SPIRAL
OF INCREASING DEFENSIVENESS

Dr. Jack Gibb, a social psychologist, studied defensiveness by listening to recorded conversations in many different settings over an eight-year period. He discovered that defensiveness in one person tends to trigger defensiveness in the other person(s) in the interaction.[4] As the conversation proceeds, an upward spiral of increasing defensiveness often occurs, causing an escalation of aggressiveness and destructiveness in both parties.

This spiral is very evident when one person asserts to another. The person receiving the assertion is apt to become very defensive. What she actually hears is often a distortion of what was said and her response is typically hostile. This response triggers the other person's defensiveness and she counters with inflammatory remarks. The vicious cycle of mutual recrimination has begun. After much heat and heartache, the asserter's needs are still unmet, the relationship suffers, and each person's self-esteem tends to be diminished.

Not long ago, I heard an assertion get sidetracked by the spiral of increasing defensiveness. The conversation went like this:

Everett: When you leave my tools outside, I feel angry because they get rusty.

Charlene: Well, if you'd do the man's work around this place, I wouldn't have to use your damn tools.

Everett: You know as well as I that I've had no time to do any repairs this week. I brought work home from the office every night.

Charlene: (*sarcastically*): You seemed to have lots of time to watch football all Sunday afternoon and on Monday night, too.

Everett: Well, at least I don't watch those stupid soap operas all afternoon while the house goes to seed around me. Only an imbecile would watch those things.

What I've reported here was just round one. The argument soon became even more heated. Everett made some comments about Charlene's mother and Charlene put down Everett's ability to satisfy her sexually. Before they were through, they had "thrown in everything but the kitchen sink."

Everett said, "That night lasted a long time. Two days later there was an uneasy truce between Charlene and I. For a long time we wouldn't even remember how the fight started."

A SIX-STEP
ASSERTION PROCESS

In the face of people's *predictable* defensive responses, the simple statement of an assertion message rarely achieves results. My colleagues, students, and I have a high degree of success using an assertion process with these six steps: (1) preparation, (2) sending the message, (3) silence, (4) reflective listening to the other's defensive response, (5) recycling steps 2 through 4 as often as necessary, and (6) focusing on a solution.

Preparation

The preparation for sending an assertion message can make the difference between whether an assertion is successful or not. The first stage of preparation is *writing the assertion message* before sending it. Writing the message serves two important functions. First, the process of developing the message in advance helps to diffuse some of the asserter's pent-up feelings. The other advantage of writing your message is that when it is appropriately formulated, you will be confident that it is appropriate, brief, nonblameful, and capable of getting your needs met. When beginners at assertion ad lib, they usually formulate less effective messages.

Part of the preparation before asserting involves *testing the appropriateness of the message*. There are four tests that I use. First, I ask myself: Am I *refraining from trespassing* on the other person's space? If the message has a concrete and tangible effect, I am fairly certain that I am not intruding on someone else's turf. Next I ask myself whether I am asserting about something that is a *persistent concern*.[5] Though there will be some occasions when it is appropriate to assert the first time that someone trespasses on my space, these situations will be fairly infrequent. This test helps prevent that curse of interpersonal relations—nagging. Then I ask whether I have built a *base of trust* with the other person. Though there will be occasions when it is appropriate to assert before rapport has been established, an assertion that is sent before trust develops is more likely to have severe repercussions on the relationship and on motivation. The final test is an assessment of whether I am likely to get my needs met through an assertion. *It is a firm law of assertion training to send your first assertions to those persons and in those situations where there is a high likelihood of getting your needs met.* With this success and experience behind you, you can slowly work your way up to more difficult assertions.

These four tests of the appropriateness of the assertion message will weed out many of them. The ones that remain, however, will have a high likelihood of changing the other person's behavior *and* strengthening the relationship.

Many times the preparation for an assertion includes a *rehearsal* of the interaction. Before a press conference, the president of the United States meets with his press secretary and major policy advisors. These people ply the president with all the questions they expect media representatives to ask during the press conference. This dress rehearsal helps the president to shape and practice his responses to the difficult issues that may be raised, and thus to do a more competent job at the actual reportorial confrontation. Presidents Truman, Kennedy, Johnson, Nixon, Ford, and Carter all used this preparation at times. Though they did not use this label, they were employing *behavioral rehearsal,* one of the most successful assertiveness training techniques.

For a behavioral rehearsal, select a quiet place and arrange to be uninterrupted. Write your message before you send it. Instruct the person role-playing the other's part to respond defensively at first. Demonstrate some examples of defensiveness. For the first "dry run," allow the other to be defensive in whatever ways she chooses. The key is for you to remember to alternate between assertion and reflective listening. Later, you may wish to tell or show your practice partner how the recipient of your message is apt to respond. If she can role-play that type of defensiveness, all the better. But it is not necessary. Instruct your practice partner not to be "harder than life." In the practice session, you should achieve your assertive goal if you follow the assertion process.

Securing an appointment to converse with the the other can be very important for the success of your assertion. If you have not agreed to talk for at least ten minutes to half an hour, the other can make the defensive response of breaking the session off in the middle, saying she has other things to do right now. That's a very frustrating and needless way to have an assertion session aborted.

Select the place carefully. If at all possible, avoid confronting the other person in public. (In some classes, families and other groups, where there is a high level of trust established and when the behavior to be asserted about is relevant to the whole group, and when the asserter is experienced, it may be preferable to assert in the presence of the group.) Determine whether the confrontation should take place in a location comfortable to the other, comfortable to you, or on "neutral" ground. When first asserting, it may be helpful to you to do it on "your ground." Later, if you can be sure you will be free of interruptions, you may choose to assert on the other's ground or in a neutral territory.

Timing is important. In family situations, try to avoid asserting during the "arsenic hour"—the time just before dinner when everyone is tired, hungry, and irritable and when they may also be rushed.

Sending the Assertion Message

Once the assertion message is prepared, the appointment made, and the time is at hand, the message can be delivered. The *way* the message is sent helps determine the successfulness of the assertion.

I don't begin the interaction with "small talk." I get down to business quickly. I'm very serious and want to communicate that without being heavyhanded. I may preface my assertion message with a few sentences like this:

Bob: Thanks for setting aside time to see me today. (*Pause for other to speak if she chooses.*)

Sally: It's a busy day, but I wanted to make the time.

Bob: I appreciate it because I'd like to work out something that is bothering me. Sally, when you . . . I feel . . . because. . . .

In contrast with this direct approach, beginning with small talk tends to undermine the seriousness of my intent. If I talk about Sally's son pitching a winning game in the Little League, she may not take my assertion quite as seriously or as soon as when I plunge right into my message within the first few sentences.

How the assertion is sent is as important as the phrasing of the assertion message. During a well-delivered assertion message, one's body language enhances one's verbal message. When you send an assertion, your body language should demonstrate that you mean what you say, that you are not ambivalent about it, and that you expect to get your needs met. At the same time, assertive body language communicates respect for the other person.

Body language can transform speaking the same sentence into a submissive, aggressive, or assertive act. For example, Clara and her boyfriend Don had a date for dinner and a show. He was to pick her up at 7:00 P.M. at her house. He arrived at 8:15. There was no phone call saying he would be late and no explanation at the door. Using identically worded messages, Clara's body language could have made her confrontation submissive, aggressive, or assertive.

Clara's Verbal Message	Clara's Body Language
When we . . . uh . . . set our date for . . . uh . . . seven o'clock and . . . er . . . you come at eight-fifteen I feel . . . uh . . . frustrated because I couldn't continue painting my room once I got dressed up.	Voice soft. Hesitant speech. Lots of "uhs" and "ers." Didn't look Don in the eye. Slumped posture. Fidgeted with jewelry. Stood at a distance of five feet.

With such submissive body language it is unlikely that Clara would have been taken seriously enough to get her needs met.

Had Clara been aggressive in getting her needs met, the same message could have been spoken with very different nonverbals:

Clara's Verbal Message	Clara's Body Language
When we set our date for seven o'clock and *you* come in at *e-i-g-h-t-f-i-f-t-e-e-n*, I feel frustrated because I couldn't complete painting my room once I got dressed up.	Clara's voice was loud and shrill. Her speech was rapid. She emphasized the word "you" and spit it out like an accusation. She emphasized the time of arrival and dragged out the pronunciation of that time as her lips curled in a sneer. She stood two feet from Don, pumping her forefinger at his

chest as she talked. Her hostile stare was
directed unwaveringly at his eyes. She
rolled her eyes in disbelief when Don
apologized and explained why he was late.

Obviously, this type of body language does not foster a cooperative spirit. It
defeats the purpose of an assertion message. Don may continue to arrive late for
dates just to get back at Clara. Or he may come unreasonably early—for spite. Or
he may submit but increase the distance in the relationship.

Had Clara been assertive, the body language might have been something
like this:

Clara's Verbal Message	Clara's Body Language
When we set our date for seven o'clock and you come in at eight-fifteen, I feel frustrated because I couldn't complete painting my room once I got dressed up.	Clara's voice was calm yet serious. She was about a yard away from Don, with both feet planted flat and firmly on the floor. Her eye contact was steady and firm but not hostile. She leaned slightly forward, demonstrating the energy she had on this issue.

When you send an assertion message effectively, your body language and
your verbal language are harmonious, reinforcing each other.

Let's examine some of the elements of assertive body language:

Posture. Face the other person squarely. Stand or sit erectly, leaning slightly
forward at an appropriately close distance. Keep your head erect. Place your feet
firmly on the ground (even if you are sitting). Maintain an "open" position, with
arms and legs uncrossed.

Eye contact. Look directly at the other person's eyes when you are asserting.
This helps convey the fact that you mean what you say. Your goal is not to
overpower the other with an aggressive stare. A serious, steady look into the
other's eyes, sometimes relieved by an occasional glance away, helps communicate your intensity of purpose without being aggressive.

Facial expressions. Your facial expression should match your message.
People commonly smile or even laugh nervously when they are telling another
person they are angry about something the other did. This results in a double
message, with the smile and/or laughter undermining the verbal message. Many
people are not aware that they are smiling at such times. Practicing before a
mirror or receiving feedback from a role-playing session can help you know
whether you engage in inappropriate smiles or other facial expressions that
undermine your assertions.

Gestures. Some people are rigid and statuelike when asserting. Their physical rigidity impedes their assertion. A message that is emphasized with appropri-

ate gestures acquires added emphasis. Some gestures, however, undercut assertions. Especially emphatic gestures or excessive use of gestures of any kind are likely to distract from the message. Pounding the table and pointing one's forefinger at the other are likely to increase her defensiveness. On the other hand, shrugging one's shoulders, covering one's mouth while speaking, fidgeting, tinkering with jewelry, shifting from one foot to another, pacing, and similar movements significantly diminish the impact of an assertion.

Voice. A whispery monotone or a singsong voice will seldom convince another to vacate your personal space. Robert Alberti and Michel Emmons, two of the pioneers in assertion training, write:

> Voice is one of our most valuable resources for communication. . . . Does your inflection really emphasize what you want to? . . . How about volume? Do you ordinarily speak so softly that others can barely hear? Can you bring out a shout when you *want* to? Or is your conversational volume always so loud that people think you're always angry? Get control of your voice, and you'll have harnessed a powerful element of your developing assertiveness. [6]

I almost always begin an assertion in a calm yet firm voice. People often ask how I can be so calm. There are two reasons. I did a lot of venting of emotion when I wrote out the assertion—thus, much of my feeling has already been discharged. Then, too, I have asserted successfully so often that I expect that the other person will find a way of meeting my needs.

Breath. Having sufficient breath is more important to an effective assertion than most people realize. When you have little air in your lungs, your chest cage sinks and you look less assertive. Also, the diminished air in your lungs leads to diminished energy—and you want all the energy you can have for your assertion. Inadequate amounts of air in the lungs may lead to increased anxiety, which blocks your assertive power. Finally, a full chest of air is needed to produce the vocal quality desired for your assertion.

When people become anxious, as most do when asserting, they tend to hold their breath to some degree. Many people's assertive body language increases enormously when they learn to plant their feet firmly on the floor, refrain from slouching (which makes breathing more difficult), and fill their lungs with air before asserting.

While the asserter's body language affects the other person, it affects the asserter, too. I find that by squaring my shoulders, straightening my back, placing my feet flat on the floor and filling my lungs with air, I develop more inner assertive resources. I tend to be less anxious and depressed and become more determined and confident.

Being Silent

After sending your brief assertion message with appropriate body language—*stop*. Be silent. Your silence allows the other to think about what you said or speak whatever is on her mind. The other person's first response is usually defensive. Sometimes the other offers excuses, sometimes she attacks, sometimes she withdraws. A defensive response is to be expected. It is an unusual situation when it does not come. The silence allows the confronted person to express her defensiveness, which normally needs to be vented before she willingly tries to meet the needs of the asserter.

Later on in an assertive interaction, silence enables the other person to arrive at a solution that meets both persons needs. In one of our workshops, a Canadian college president commented, "The theory you gave us stated that the other person should come up with a solution that is satisfactory to the asserter. But that never happens to me." I suggested he role-play the situation. In the role playing, he never allowed enough silence for the other person to volunteer a solution. I pointed this out, and the situation was role-played again. This time, when silence was provided, the other person suggested a satisfactory solution. In subsequent dealings in real life, the college administrator reported how valuable he found the silence which followed an assertion message.

Reflectively Listening to the Defensive Response

Once an assertion message has been sent and silence has been provided, it is almost certain that the person to whom the assertion was addressed will make a defensive response. Instead of reasserting or explaining your assertion or becoming aggressive at that point, as commonly happens, *it is most important to "shift gears" and listen reflectively to the predictable defensive response*. As Figure 10.1 indicates, this shifting back and forth between assertion and listening normally takes place several times before the assertion is completed.

Reflective listening at this time can accomplish one or more of four things. First, it helps diminish the other person's defensiveness. As the recipient of the assertion expresses her defensiveness and that is reflected back with respect, her defensiveness subsides. The vicious cycle of increasing defensiveness is broken and constructive conversation can begin again.

The defensiveness-reducing power of effective listening responses is truly remarkable. For many people, it must be seen to be believed. In our courses, people can watch the dramatic effects on videotape and hear other participants tell of their experiences. Readers of this book may not find the printed page convincing. They will have to rely on their own experiments with these skills.

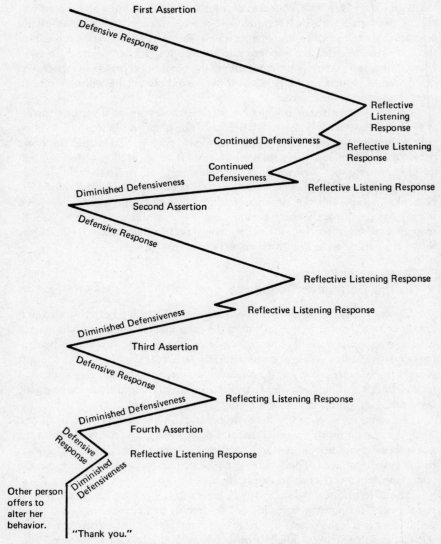

LOW   **DEFENSIVENESS**   **HIGH**

First Assertion

Defensive Response

Reflective Listening Response

Continued Defensiveness

Reflective Listening Response

Continued Defensiveness

Reflective Listening Response

Diminished Defensiveness

Second Assertion

Defensive Response

Reflective Listening Response

Reflective Listening Response

Diminished Defensiveness

Third Assertion

Defensive Response

Reflecting Listening Response

Diminished Defensiveness

Fourth Assertion

Reflective Listening Response

Defensive Response

Diminished Defensiveness

Other person offers to alter her behavior.

"Thank you."

Figure 10.1. The increase and decrease of defensiveness in the assertion process as the asserter "shifts gears" between asserting and reflective listening responses. (Adapted from a similar chart by Thomas Gordon, Ph.D.)

Then, too, there are times when the data we receive from our listening modifies our need to continue the assertion. For example, my son had a junior driver's license and was required to be home with the car by 9:00 P.M. When he returned from high school basketball practice at 9:30 P.M., I confronted him. He informed me that the law states that students with junior driver's licenses could not drive after 9:00 P.M. except when returning from school activities. Since his arrival home at 9:30 was OK with me as long as it was legal, I had no further reason to assert.

A third value of listening to the other's response after an assertion is that you sometimes discover a strong need of the other person which conflicts with your need. You may decide to switch to collaborative problem solving. That is what occurred when a dormitory counselor sent this assertion to the custodian of his building: "When you leave the floors and sinks dirty, I become irritated because I have to work in an unclean environment." In listening to the custodian's response, the counselor discovered that because of cutbacks in the college budget, the janitor had to clean twice as many square feet as he had previously. He also had a need not to work overtime. The counselor realized that collaborative problem solving (a skill described in Chapter 14) was more appropriate than assertion in this case. Together, she and the janitor found a way to meet both of their needs.

Finally, when you assert to someone you are likely to receive a lot of data about how that person perceives you and your relationship. Because the words are spoken from a defensive stance, they may seem much more extreme than the other person actually feels. Still, they are important clues and too valuable to ignore. Much of this data would probably go unspoken if it were not for the assertion that you sent. If you reflect rather than defend yourself, you will be alerted to many ways the relationship can be improved. (During an assertion, however, do not respond to these issues except by means of reflective listening. Once the assertion is over, probably on another day, the two of you may wish to look at some of the issues that cascaded out of the other's mouth when she was most defensive.)

While you will find some occasions when your need to assert is modified by data that you receive from the other person, and though you will sometimes discover that the other person has a strong need that makes problem solving appropriate, most of the time the key result of your reflective listening will result in the diminishment of the other person's defensiveness.

Handling hostile responses. The finest assertion message is often received as a hostile blow. Instead of really listening to the assertion, "most people are searching for a counterblow at the time the information is being presented to them."[7] The counterblow contains words designed to put you "on the defensive and inflict damage." The person usually does not deal with the subject matter of your assertion but picks an issue selected for its ability to inflict high damage on you with relatively low risk for herself.[8]

Joan, a first-line supervisor, confronted Mike about his performance on the assembly line which affected the output of several people. He reacted with hostility and she listened reflectively to his defensive responses.

Joan:	When you produce thirty percent less this month than in previous months, I feel annoyed because it lowers the productivity of our unit and I get less pay.
Mike:	The others sure were right. You are just a castrating female who is hostile to all males.
Joan:	You think that what I said about your productivity is a smokescreen for my anger toward you because you are a man.
Mike:	You said it! You women libbers are nothing more than a bunch of aggressive bitches.
Joan:	*(Who does not consider herself a women's libber):* Women today are really pushy and you are sick of it.
Mike:	Yeah. Why don't you stay home and take care of your kids like a mother should.
Joan:	You feel I should be taking care of my kids and not be working.
Mike:	I sure do. What's going to become of these kids who have no mother to come home to after school?
Joan:	Mike, when you produce thirty percent less this month than in previous months, I feel annoyed because that lowers the productivity of our unit, and I receive less pay.

Let's examine Joan's responses in this interaction.

First, *she reflected Mike's content and feelings, with special emphasis on his feelings.* She made three consecutive reflections. There is no magic to the number three. Sometimes, one reflection is all that is necessary before reasserting. Sometimes, five or six are required before a person's defensiveness is lowered sufficiently to make another try at communicating the assertion message.

Second, *Joan did not allow herself to get sidetracked* into a discussion of her femininity, her character, women's liberation, or the care of her children. She knew she would get into a "go-nowhere" argument if she took up any of the gauntlets he flung down. She also knew that commenting on any of these topics would divert the conversation from her assertion, so that her needs would go unmet. She steadfastly refused to be drawn into a discussion of the topics Mike initiated. *Her interaction was limited to an assertion message and reflective listening responses.*

Thirdly, *she treated Mike with respect.* She didn't use judgmental words, even when she was being attacked personally. Her tone of voice was free of condescension and sarcasm. Her posture and facial expression assertively indicated that she was serious, but it was definitely not aggressive. Though it was difficult for her, Joan really tried to understand Mike's frame of reference.

Finally, *Joan reasserted*. She repeated virtually the same words that she used in her opening assertion. She realized that Mike, like most people, wouldn't really listen to her first assertion message. He might *hear* the words but not really *listen* to her concerns. So she was prepared to send the message again. As she planned this assertion, Joan had guessed that Mike would give her a hard time at first. She also realized that she might let some judgmental words slip into her assertion message, so she memorized it and disciplined herself to say exactly the same message again.

After Joan restated her assertion, Mike became defensive again. She reflected his resistant statements and then sent the same assertion message once more. After several more cycles through this process, Mike came up with a solution that met Joan's needs. She thanked him and suggested that they meet in a week to see if Mike's solution worked as well as they both thought it would. When Joan met with him a week later, Mike's production was the highest it had been all year.

Some people hearing about this interaction said Joan "should never have let Mike get away with saying all those things." Joan, however, was elated. She asserted, got her needs met, and improved a working relationship with one of her most difficult employees. "One of the biggest payoffs," she added, "is that I feel so good about myself. I've felt kinda high all week."

Dealing with questions. In addition to showing hostility there are many other ways in which people react to an assertion message.[9] Some defend themselves by means of *questions*. A person may not consciously know what she is doing, but her subconscious probably knows that the use of questions is a way of derailing assertions in a nonconfrontative way. After all, while you are answering questions, you aren't asserting and the other person is not coming up with solutions about how to vacate your space and meet your needs. I follow a rule (which occasionally has to be broken): Don't answer a question when you are asserting; reply with a reflective listening response instead. Every question can be converted into a statement and reflected back to the other person. For instance.

> Gail: Did you always do the dishes when you were a girl?
>
> Mother: You doubt that I lived up to the standards I expect of you.

Further information is rarely needed in assertion situations. When more data is appropriate, it should be given nonjudgmentally, specifically, and succinctly. Then provide silence for the other to take the next step in the conversation.

Sidestepping debates. Some people respond to an assertion by *debating*. A person relying on this defensive approach often uses mental quickness and verbal ability to win arguments even when they "don't have a leg to stand on." They give the impression that they are very objective, striving only for a clearer understanding when all the while they are avoiding the action that will terminate their trespass on your space. Debates are win/lose affairs: if she wins, you lose; if you win, she loses. In either case, the assertion usually gets sidetracked, so your needs are not met and the relationship suffers because no one likes to lose. By refusing to engage in a debate and by using reflective listening responses, you can get your needs met and probably strengthen the relationship at the same time.

Coping with tears. For some people *tears* are the major coping mechanism when confronted with an assertion. Crying is often a manipulative way to avoid confrontations and dodge any behavioral change even though the individual is trespassing on another person's space. Unfortunately, this method can be highly effective. When I assert to a person who typically cries when confronted, I vow not to let her tears control me. I believe that the tears are real and that the person is genuinely sad. I reflect the fact that she is sad about being confronted (or having failed to meet the deadline, or whatever she is sad about) and then I gently but firmly reassert. If she gets too upset, I suggest we continue the conversation at a specific time that day or the next day, and at the appointed time I reassert. Unless the person has been subjected to unusual emotional stress in this period, I stick with the second assertion until the problem is resolved.

Overcoming withdrawal. Some people respond to assertion by withdrawal—like the turtle who pulls into its shell whenever it feels threatened. This person may sit in total silence following an assertion. Sometimes the body language is disapproving; sometimes it is despondent. Often the individual puts on a poker face, making it difficult to read her feelings. Inappropriate silence, however, communicates that the person is feeling uncomfortable and defensive. In these situations I provide a lot of silence, reflect what I think the body language is saying, and then reassert. If the other person continues to say nothing, I say, "I take your silence to mean that you don't want to talk about it and that you will meet my needs by getting the car home at the agreed-upon time. I'll touch bases with you next Sunday to make sure this is working out OK." In these and many other situations it is important to realize that the goal of this kind of an assertion is for the other person to change her behavior. She doesn't have to be joyful about it.

We have looked at some of the most prevalent ways of expressing defensiveness and how to deal with them. There are, of course, many other ways of being defensive. Fortunately, *the general strategy for dealing with defensive responses is always the same: listen reflectively (especially to the feelings) and reassert.*

Helping the other express understanding of your predicament and/or a solution to the problem. Sometimes we are so busy trying to reflect the other person's defensive responses that we overlook statements they eventually make which tell us they are beginning to acknowledge the validity of our assertion. The recipient of an assertion message is often very indirect and vague when she begins to move from a defensive posture to a problem-solving role. She may drop a hint in the midst of highly defensive remarks. If you can note it and reflect it back, you will shorten that process and decrease the stressfulness that both parties may be experiencing.

It helps to realize how difficult it is for most people to say, "Boy, I really hurt you when I did that. This is what I will do to correct the situation. . . ." People are often quite guarded when they acknowledge your discomfort or offer a solution. The concern they express or solution they offer may be so camouflaged that you can miss it altogether. An important assertion skill is to catch the slightest nuance of an offered solution or concern for your predicament—and reflect that back to the other. Then offer silence so the person can further explore that. When you become skilled at doing this, you can achieve desirable results much more quickly.

Recycling the Process

Once you have sent your assertion message, provided the other with silence in which to think or respond, and reflectively listened to the predictable defensive response, you are ready to begin this process all over again. *Because the other was defensive, she probably was unable to understand the situation from your point of view.* You send the identical message again. Follow it with silence. Then reflect the expected defensive response. In many situations it will take five to ten recyclings of the process before the other really understands and suggests a way of meeting your needs.

Effective assertion hinges on a rhythm of asserting and reflecting. Shifting between these two different roles is the most demanding interpersonal skill we teach. After asserting, most people forget to listen. When the other person makes her defensive response, they clobber her with another confrontative statement and a battle ensues. Their interaction becomes aggressive even when they intended to assert. Other people get stuck in the listening role and neglect to reassert. They may end up consoling the other person while their own needs continue to go unmet. Their interaction becomes submissive even though they meant to assert.

Persistence is one of the keys to effective assertion. One of the main reasons why people do not get their needs met when they assert is because they give up after the first defensive response of the other person. *Typically it takes three to ten repetitions of the assertion message* (interspersed by silence for the other's solution or defense and the asserter's reflective listening responses) *to change the other's behavior.*

After sending several well-phrased messages and listening reflectively to the other's defensive responses, you may reach a temporary stalemate. Though the other person may be able to repeat your assertion word for word, she probably hasn't understood you yet. You need to *increase the affect*—the level of feeling communicated by your tone of voice and body language. As some trainers put it, "You can't send a boy to do a man's work."

Increasing the affect isn't a calculated manipulation. After a few defensive responses by the other, the asserter's emotional temperature will probably rise spontaneously. As the asserter's anger or frustration increases, she often expresses these feelings to the other person. *When increasing the affect, use the same words you used before* (to protect your assertion messages from being contaminated by blame, put-downs, or irrelevant statements). The higher your emotional temperature rises, the greater the tendency to contaminate the message and the greater the need to discipline yourself to use the message you formed in moments of clearer objectivity.

Even when you are very angry, you can be genuine without being hostile or aggressive. It is important not to fake—to express neither more nor less emotion than you feel.

As the affect in the interaction increases, it is more difficult to listen reflectively. As the emotional impact of your assertion is heightened, however, effective listening responses are even more necessary than when lower-octane assertions were sent.

Allan Frank says, "One of the marks of adult maturity is a balanced relationship between the emotions and rational control systems, which allows for emotional responses without permitting them to overwhelm reason."[10] The assertion process enables a person to maintain this mature balance between rational control systems and genuine expression of emotion. This system permits the expression of much emotionality at the same time that it offers protection to both parties and to the relationship.

You will not always work the assertion process perfectly. You will forget to listen. Or you will state the message poorly. Or you will forget to concentrate on feelings when you reflect. Keep going. Unless you make too many mistakes, your assertion will probably be effective.

Once in a while, the other person will agree to meet your needs immediately. There is no defensive response—just an instant solution. People who are conditioned by training to expect a defensive response often do not know what to do. Simply reflect the solution and say, "Thanks."

Focusing on the Solution

One of the reasons assertion messages work so well is that they do not back the other person into a corner. The other does not have to say yes or no to a solution that I suggest. She may think of something that meets her needs, too. And when she arrives at a solution, she can offer it as a gift. It is not a concession that is grudgingly wrested from her. This allows the other to regain her dignity. When she offers me the gift of a satisfactory solution, even after what may have been a heated exchange, we both feel better. The process of reconciliation makes our relationship stronger.

When the other comes up with a solution, make sure it meets your needs. It is important to be flexible and open to a broad range of possible options that could meet your needs. But if your needs are not met by the other's proposal, it is important to say so. After turning down an offered solution, it is well to allow for a lot of silence. In that time, a person may come up with another solution. Or she may become defensive again. One needs to allow the silence that encourages either of these responses if the assertion is to reach a successful conclusion.

Don't insist that the other person be cheerful about meeting your needs. All you can ask from an assertion is that the other's behavior be changed. You cannot count on an attitude change (though that may come) or a conversion experience. Whether the other grumbles or smiles, you can rejoice that she has removed herself from your life space.

Paraphrase the solution back to the other. That way, you can be sure you both have the same understanding. The paraphrase also reinforces the solution on the other's mind.

Say "Thanks." The process you will have just completed may have been so arduous that you forget the elementary courtesies.

Arrange a time when you will check with each other to make sure the solution is working. Sometimes a solution proposed with the best of intentions does not work out well and a new arrangement needs to be devised. Or occasionally the receiver of the assertion will come up with a solution he doesn't intend to implement. The proposed solution may merely be a cagey defensive response designed to get you "off her back." We call this ploy being "kissed out the door." When you arrange to check back to see how well the solution is working, the other realizes you mean business and her games will not work with you.

SUMMARY

Whenever you send an assertion message, there is a high likelihood that the other person will respond defensively. Defensiveness in one party in an interaction tends to trigger defensiveness in response. The result is frequently an escalating spiral of defensiveness which results in aggression or alienation. An assertion process designed to help the asserter get her needs met while responding constructively to the expected defensiveness of the other person follows these six steps:

1. Preparation
2. Sending the Assertion Message
3. Being Silent
4. Reflectively Listening to the Defensive Response
5. Recycling the Process
6. Focusing on the Solution

CHAPTER ELEVEN

Increasing Your Assertive Options

The assertive education process can be compared with learning a foreign language. At first you master words, phrases, ground rules. Suddenly, you can communicate with a child's vocabulary. You continue to learn until you acquire fluency. With the mastery of your new skill, you feel the freedom to be more creative in what has become your second tongue.[1]

—Herbert Fensterheim, psychiatrist, and Jean Baer, writer

MANY VARIETIES
OF ASSERTIVE BEHAVIOR

There are many ways of being assertive. The preceding three chapters were devoted to a fairly detailed presentation of the three-part assertion method. Once you have mastered the principles and practices of that method, other ways of asserting can be learned more easily.

This chapter outlines twelve additional ways of being assertive. I refer to them as methods, but that is a much more formal designation than they deserve. The way most of these "methods" developed was by someone observing something in his own or others' behavior which achieved desirable interpersonal outcomes. The behavior being noted may have been spontaneous—following no conscious pattern. In trying to find out what made that spontaneous behavior work effectively, the observer noted specific patterns of behavior that occurred again and again. In writing them down, they became guidelines. In teaching them, they became methods which could be used by a larger number of people.

The methods in this chapter were observed and recorded by a number of people. The treatment here is brief, but the footnotes will help the reader find more extensive explanations when available.

Once one has learned these methods well and practiced them frequently, one can become less conscious of the guidelines and freer in his expression.

"NATURAL" ASSERTIONS

"Natural" assertions are nonaggressive ways of getting one's needs met without following any particular method. They are most appropriate when neither you nor the other person is experiencing much stress and when the assertion is unlikely to trigger much tension in the other.

Most of the assertion messages I send are "natural" assertions:

- Jim, since we're having company on Sunday, I'd appreciate your mowing the lawn on Saturday this week.
- I don't like it when you leave your jacket over the railing in the front hall.
- I need the workshop registration report each Friday in order to do adequate planning.
- Give me a hand, will ya? This is too heavy for me to move alone.
- I don't want my workbench used as a storage area. When would be a convenient time to get your things off it? . . . Tonight? Great Then I want the top free and clear for my work projects.

These assertions do not follow a formula. They are spontaneous ways of letting others know my needs and the boundaries of my space. Even though the assertions were "natural," some negative things were avoided. There were no put-downs, there was no swearing, and there were few roadblocks.

Our trainers find that people's "natural" assertions become more constructive and yield better results after thorough training in the consequences of roadblocks, methods of listening, the concept of life space, the implications of the assertion message. Without the person even thinking about it, some of that training influences what is said and increases the likelihood that the "natural" assertion will be effective.

As people practice the other assertion "methods" over a long period of time, they find themselves using these other methods at appropriate times without consciously thinking about it. Thus, with practice, you can have much more variety and richness in your "natural" assertions.

SELF-DISCLOSURE

Sidney Jourard writes:

> A choice that confronts everyone at every moment is this: Shall we permit our fellows to know us as we now are, or shall we remain enigmas, wishing to be seen as persons we are not?
>
> This choice has always been available, but throughout history we have chosen to conceal our authentic being behind masks. . . .
>
> We camouflage our true being before others to protect ourselves against criticism or rejection. This protection comes at a steep price. When we are not truly known by the other people in our lives, we are misunderstood. When we are misunderstood, especially by family and friends, we join the "lonely crowd." Worse, when we succeed in hiding our being from others, we tend to lose touch with our real selves.[2]

Self-disclosure occurs when you are your real self in the presence of others. It is intellectual and emotional honesty—a refusal to veil one's inner self from the other people. All true assertion involves some degree of self-disclosure, but there are higher levels of interpersonal transparency which are both intimate and redemptive. T. S. Eliot says:

> *If a man has one person, just one in his life,*
> *To whom he is willing to confess everything—*
> *And that includes, mind you, not only things criminal,*
> *Not only turpitude, meanness and cowardice,*
> *But also situations which are simply ridiculous,*
> *When he has played the fool (as who has not?)—*
> *Then he loves that person, and his love will save him.*[3]

Self-disclosure includes the expression of my true opinions and values, but is far more than that. It is basically *feeling-talk*—or even more accurately, the direct expression of my feelings through words and body language. It is *being my feelings*. Self-disclosure is King David dancing jubilantly before his victorious soldiers as they return home from battle. It is Job shaking his clenched fist at the heavens and shouting his anger and hurt to God because of the incredible tragedies that befell him. It is Butch Cassidy and the Sundance Kid openly expressing their affection for each other.

This kind of emotional directness between people is both rare and difficult. Rollo May says, "The act which requires the most courage is . . . simple truthful communication."[4] The goal of the assertive person is not emotional nudity, but appropriate authenticity. In the fifth century, Basil of Caesarea offered a guideline which is still sound today: no one should keep secret, or declare incautiously, any agitation of his soul, but confess it to "trust-worthy brethren."[5] Self disclosure is best when it is:

- *to the right person*—often one who is capable of empathic understanding;
- *to the right degree*—you may decide to disclose all or part of your experience;
- *for the right reasons*—be sure your goal is to disclose yourself rather than to burden the other or "show off";
- *at the right time*—in hours that are appropriate and when the other is not heavily burdened with his own needs; and
- *in the right place*—in a location conducive to this kind of communication.

While too close an adherence to these guidelines can inhibit spontaneity, to ignore them totally would probably make a person too vulnerable to survive in this world.

Though a small percentage of people may be overly transparent, most of us have too many barriers between our hearts and our tongues. So often we talk about the weather and how things are going at school or work, but the really important things—like how we feel about each other—go unspoken. John Powell demonstrates the tragic deprivation that occurs when we needlessly shield our emotions from other people:

> It was the day my father died. It was a bleak, cold and blustery day in January. In the small hospital room, I was supporting him in my arms when his eyes suddenly widened with a look of awe I had never seen before. I was certain that the angel of death had entered the room. Then my father slumped back and I lowered his head gently onto the pillow. I closed his eyes and told my mother, who was seated by the bedside praying: "It's all over, Mom. Dad is dead."

> She startled me. I will never know why these were her first words to me after his death. My mother said: "Oh, he was so proud of you. He loved you so much."

Somehow I knew from my own reaction that these words were saying something very important to me. They were like a sudden shaft of light, like a startling thought I had never before absorbed. Yet there was a definite edge of pain, as though I were going to know my father better in death than I had ever known him in life.

Later, while a doctor was verifying death, I was leaning against the wall in the far corner of the room, crying softly. A nurse came over to me and put a comforting arm around me. I couldn't talk through my tears. I wanted to tell her:

"I'm not crying because my father is dead. I'm crying because my father never told me that he was proud of me. He never told me that he loved me. Of course, I was expected to know these things. I was expected to know the great part I played in his life and the great part I occupied in his heart, but he never told me."[6]

DESCRIPTIVE RECOGNITION

Many people think of assertion as being solely concerned with the confrontation of people or groups who are thwarting one's needs or restricting one's rights. Not so! The truly assertive person expresses his appreciation freely and constructively.

When people want to be verbally supporting, three ways are often used. *Flattery* is saying something you don't really mean. It is insincere. Most people share a distaste for those who "talk with flattering lips and double minds."[7]

Evaluative praise is the expression of favorable judgment about another person or his behaviors: "Eric, you are such a good boy." Evaluative praise often utilizes superlatives like "wonderful," "marvelous," "superb," and so on. This kind of praise, especially when it constitutes a favorable global evaluation of the person, is rarely constructive. It is one of the roadblocks described in Chapter 2. (You may want to review the material on page 20.) Dr. Haim Ginott summarizes the reasons for avoiding evaluative praise:

> Evaluative praise . . . creates anxiety, invites dependency, and evokes defensiveness. It is nonconducive to self-reliance, self-direction and self-control. These qualities demand freedom from outside judgment. They require reliance on inner motivation and evaluation.[8]

Descriptive recognition is a way of letting another person know that you value his *specific behavior*. A descriptive recognition does not contain superlatives. Unlike evaluative praise, descriptive recognitions typically positively affect the person and enhance the relationship.

An incident in the life of Pablo Casals, the famous cellist, demonstrates the difference between evaluative praise and descriptive recognition. When a young cellist named Gregor Piatigorsky first met Casals, Piatigorsky was asked to play. He was nervous and gave what he believed a terrible performance—so bad that he stopped in the middle of the sonata. "Bravo! Wonderful!" Casals applauded. Piatigorsky said, "Bewildered, I left. I knew how badly I had played. Why did he, the master, have to praise and embarrass me?"

Years later, when the two great cellists were together again, Piatigorsky told Casals how he felt about the praise a few years before. Casals rushed to the cello angrily. "Listen!" he said as he played a phrase from the Beethoven sonata. "Didn't you play this fingering? It was novel to me. . . . And didn't you attack that passage with up-bow, like this?" The master went through all the music, emphasizing all he liked that Piatigorsky had done. The younger cellist said of that evening, "I left with the feeling of having been with a great artist and a friend."[9]

On both evenings, Casals had the same *goal*—to acknowledge the great skill of the younger musician. But the *methods* and the *results* were different. On the first occasion, he used evaluative praise. He said it was "wonderful" and "magnificent." Piatigorsky was bewildered and embarrassed and, it would seem, he was angry, too. At their next gathering, Casals provided a descriptive recognition of the behaviors. Piatigorsky was deeply moved by these explicit statements about his artistry.

Descriptive recognitions contain one or more of the ingredients of the three-part assertion message. First, they always have a clear description of the other person's behavior or the results of that behavior. What is the other doing or has he done that deserves recognition? The goal is to accurately describe the actual work, behaviors, or accomplishments of the other—rather than evaluate his personality or character. "The windows you just cleaned look spotless."

Also tell the other person how you *feel* about or *value* those behaviors. Don't just say the words but *demonstrate* them in your voice. "When you straighten up your room before your grandparents come to visit I feel relieved because the neatness of the house has been a source of unpleasant arguments in the past." In descriptive-recognition statements some people use the words "appreciative" or "grateful" almost exclusively. Try to use some of the other feeling words when possible.

Then, if there has been a positive *effect* of the other's behavior on your life, mention it. Let him know the good things that have happened to you as a result of his actions. "When you did the grocery shopping for me today I felt much less tense because I could spend more time preparing for my presentation at the meeting tonight."

State the elements of the descriptive-recognition message in a single sentence. That way it has more impact, and evaluative words are less apt to encumber the statement. The formula "When you . . . I feel . . . because . . ." can be helpful when you first send descriptive recognition statements with two or three parts.

> "When you worked overtime to type that report, I felt very appreciative because the proposal might not have been considered if it arrived late."
> "When you wrote letters to me each week during my sickness, I felt less lonely."
> "When you make a special breakfast for me each Sunday, I feel very cared for."

The formula may seem stilted, but it can be useful in two ways: first, it helps break the pattern of evaluative praise that is so common in our society, and second, it makes explicit certain thoughts that might not be spoken and that help a person think more clearly about another's behavior and his response to it. With the principles of the formula clearly in their minds, many people prefer to use more natural phrasing, such as:

> "I'm so happy with the new tie you bought me."
> "I like the way you did the layout on that report."
> "I'm very touched that you would come to visit me in the hospital."
> "I'm excited about the production record this group established last month."

Descriptive recognitions are sometimes responses to the big things in life or to ongoing activities. Many times, however, we are touched by little things that a person does. The English poet William Wordsworth noted that "the best portion of a good man's life" consists of "his little, nameless, unremembered acts of kindness and of love."[10] These tremendous trifles deserve more attention than they usually receive. Nothing is too insignificant for a descriptive-recognition message if you have strong positive feelings about it.

Once you have stated your descriptive-recognition message, *be silent* so that the other can think about your words and/or respond to them.

When the descriptive recognition is well-phrased, the recipient may accept the message immediately. Often, however, people ward off even the most carefully constructed statements. They discount the positive feedback, saying things like, "It was nothing, really" or "I was just lucky." One of my friends, Ed Lisbe, says, "It is such an overwhelming thought that even a well-worded compliment is apt to stimulate a defensive reaction."

To help the recipient receive our descriptive-recognition message, we must be prepared to listen to his defensive comments, reflect back the meanings, and then state the message again. This rhythm between sending the descriptive-recognition message and reflectively listening to a defensive response is similar to the confrontative assertion process except that the sending/reflecting process is only recycled once or twice.

These "matchless units of life sustaining recognition"[11] build self-esteem, foster improved motivation, reinforce behaviors we appreciate, and strenghten relationships.

RELATIONSHIP ASSERTIONS

Sometimes there is a need to make an assertion about another person's behavior which has a negative impact on the *relationship* between the two of you. In these cases it is appropriate to use what we call a *relationship-assertion message*. This kind of assertion has many similarities to the three-part assertion message discussed in the previous three chapters. The differences, however, are also significant.

As in the three-part assertion message, the other person's *behavior* is described accurately. One also discloses one's *feelings*.

A major difference between the two types of messages is that there is *no concrete or tangible effect* in the relationship-assertion message. There is often an effect, but it is not something tangible (the effect doesn't harm your property, cost you money, etc.). Becky, a young woman whose relationship with her husband was largely healthy and happy, was troubled about one aspect of their interaction. When she brought up some facet of their relationship that displeased her, he would seldom discuss the matter. Instead, he usually diverted with humor. Because there was no materialistic effect, Becky couldn't find any reason to use a regular three-part assertion message. She decided the best way to tell him how she felt was through the use of a relationship assertion. She wrote the message out so that she would be prepared the next time he tried to divert her from discussing their relationship. Then a few weeks later, when he tried to divert her, she said:

> When you distract with humor when I am trying to discuss something very important to me, I become furious *because that often results in my needs not being discussed or met.*

After sending such a message, reflective listening is required. Then reassertion followed by more listening.

Because there is no concrete or tangible effect, there is less likelihood that the other person will meet the asserter's needs than when there is a concrete or tangible effect. People are often angered by this. They say, "If he really loved me, he would change a behavior that is frustrating to me whether or not there is a concrete or tangible effect. It is the intangible things that are most important to me." Though many people agree with this point of view, my observation of human interactions for many years suggests that the average person will more readily change his behavior when it has a concrete negative effect on the other person's life than when less tangible effects result. You may not like this tendency of human beings, but it helps to know that when someone is behaving this way, it is probably not a sign that he doesn't love you. Instead he is reacting in what for human beings is a predictable fashion.

After several reassertions interspersed with reflective listening, the other may or may not offer to meet my needs. If the other does not meet my needs, I may say something like this: "It is very important for me that you understand what I am trying to say *and* how I *feel* about it. Let me say it once more and you just repeat back to me what I said and how I feel. Once I'm sure I've communicated accurately, we can drop the subject, at least for now. OK?" Then I repeat the relationship-assertion message. Once he demonstrates understanding of my concern I say, "Thanks. That's what I said and those are my feelings." Then I try to be alone for a while to think about the interaction, and I hope he will have some alone time to ponder what I told him.

Here are some other examples of relationship-assertion messages:

(*Twelve-year-old child to parents*): "When you don't include me in the planning for family vacations, I feel 'unfaired against' because I have no say in what we do."

(*Husband to wife*): "When you don't talk to me for hours after I have done something that annoys you, I feel despondent because we don't work through our conflicts and disagreements."

Many people think they are sending a relationship assertion when in fact they are intruding on the other person's space. There is a fine line between a relationship assertion and an attempt to impose one's values on the other person.

While it is appropriate at times to try to influence another person's values, I believe it is never appropriate to try to *impose* one's values on another person—even one's children.[12] That is invading their space and is, in my eyes, an act of spiritual aggression. Therefore, I do not use relationship-assertion messages regarding matters like my children's grades in school, their companions, whether or not they go to church, their political activities or lack of them, the formality or informality of their dress, and so on. On those occasions when I want to discuss a values issue in my child's, spouse's, or friend's life, I rely on self-disclosure or the conflict resolution method outlined in Chapter 13. When a person tries to impose his values on another it tends to damage the relationship and/or the other's selfhood.

The relationship assertion can be the most difficult kind of an assertion to send. Before trying it, you may wish to review the parts of Chapters 9 and 10 that are relevant to this skill (pp. 144–152 and 158–176). Since this type of assertion often evolves into a discussion requiring the use of conflict resolution skills, you may also want to read pages 216–231 before sending a relationship assertion.

SELECTIVE INATTENTION

People in our classes sometimes raise the question: "How can I deal assertively with someone who is making aggressive and abusive remarks to me?" Alfie complained that his wife, Peg, called him "Fatty" much of the time. Instead of using his name, she would say, "Hey, Fatty, how did work go today?" "What will we watch on TV tonight, Fatty?" "Wow, Fatty, look at you go after that dessert."

It is important not to allow oneself to be the repeated butt of someone's abusive remarks. *While the other person's remarks cannot hurt me, my continued submissiveness in the face of persistently abusive remarks by another can be injurious to me.* When I do not respond assertively to attacks, my self-esteem suffers and with it many other things that can include my health, my relationships, and the regard of others for me.

To allow another to repeatedly put me down is bad for the other, too. We have already noted how harmful aggression can be to the aggressor. For the sake of the other, as well as for my own sake, and for the sake of any actual or potential relationship between us, it is important for me not to tolerate continued abusive remarks.

Several of the methods described in this book may be effective in preventing others from repeatedly speaking abusively to you. Here is one approach that is often successful.

Begin by telling the other person that you will not participate in any conversation in which he speaks abusively to you. Describe the behavior specifically, phrasing it succinctly.

Next, use *selective inattention*. That is, ignore any comments from the other that contain abusive remarks. Don't answer questions, refute charges, attack the other, and so on. Do not use good attending skills when the other is speaking abusively. Don't nod or maintain eye contact, don't smile, don't stop what you are doing. Refuse to reward or reinforce the other by your participation in the conversation. If the other asks you why you aren't talking, say your succinct message again, but not if the other uses abusive language when he asks you. Provide lots of silence.

When the other person speaks to you without being abusive, pay attention and participate in the conversation. Make every effort to be civil and reasonable during these exchanges.

Here's how Alfie used this approach:

Peg: Hey, Fatty, how did work go today?
Alfie: I feel angry when you call me "Fatty," so I won't talk with you when you use that word.

Peg: Well, you've got to admit you've put on a lot of weight in the last six months, Fatty.

Alfie: *(Selective inattention: silence; keeps busy with what he is doing.)*

Peg: Boy, are you supersensitive to constructive criticism. I am only trying to help you.

Alfie: *(repeating succinct assertion statement)* I feel angry when you call me "Fatty," so I won't talk with you when you use words like that.

Peg: *(Long silence.)*

Alfie: *(changing the subject)* Sam is very excited about making the basketball team. I enjoy his enthusiasm for whatever he's in.

Peg: Yes, he sure enjoys his basketball.

Several hours later:

Peg: What will we watch on TV tonight, Fatty?

Alfie: *(Selective inattention: silence.)*

Peg: I'm interested in that new series on the Public Broadcasting System. The one about the people who made some of the greatest medical breakthroughs. I think it starts at eight-thirty.

Alfie: I'd like to see that, too.

Next morning at breakfast:

Peg: What time shall we leave for the Smythes' party tonight, Fatty?

Alfie: *(Selective inattention: silence.)*

Peg: Oh—are you still into that?

Alfie: *(repeating succinct assertion statement)* Yes, I've said, I feel angry when you call me "Fatty," so I won't talk with you when you use words like that.

Peg: All right, I'm sorry. I'm sorry! How many times do I have to say it?

Alfie: You're saying you won't call me "Fatty" anymore.

Peg: Yes, but I worry about where your weight will end up if I don't keep reminding you.

Alfie: *(changing the subject)* Well, I've got to go to work now. Let's leave for the Smythes' at seven-thirty.

Peg: Okay.

That last interchange did it. Peg has not spoken abusively to Alfie since. Selective inattention combined with one or two broken-record statements changed a behavior that the couple had fought and argued over for years.

We told Alfie that psychologists have a word for what he did. They call it *extinction*, which simply involves not rewarding or reinforcing a behavior. Alfie laughed and said, "I'd call it plain old common sense. No, wait a minute," he said. "It's *uncommon* common sense."

WITHDRAWAL

Sometimes temporary or permanent withdrawal is the most fitting thing that can be done in a relationship.

Temporary Withdrawal

When we were first married, there were several occasions in fairly rapid succession when my wife, Dot, and I were both under extreme stress coupled with fatigue. I would come home emotionally drained from a training session and look to Dot for the warmth and support I had learned to count on from her. When I needed her caring the most, she was so emotionally drained herself from her involvements that she had nothing to give. Not only was she unable to pour her energies into caring for me—she was looking desperately for my love and emotional nurturance, which I was unable to give. When we were unable to meet each other's needs, we became angry and fought with each other. We were so depleted that we didn't fight constructively, even though we knew how. With great anxiety about our young marriage, we sought out a therapist friend, Dr. Martin Seldman.

Marty taught us to withdraw from each other when we were emotionally depleted. In time our emotional reservoirs filled again just as he said they would. Our withdrawals from each other took a variety of forms. Often we were physically present to each other, sitting in the same room, but each doing our separate thing. It wasn't a hostile withdrawal from each other—just a recognition and verbal disclosure that we needed some creative solitude before we could be together in a positive way.

The art of temporary withdrawal has been a very important part of our lives since. Sometimes, we get "peopled out." Now we try to anticipate this before it happens and we preventatively schedule strategic withdrawals *before* we become totally depleted. When I retreat from people and demands before becoming depleted, my alone time is more fulfilling and my times with other people are richer.

Permanent Withdrawal

It is sometimes helpful to distinguish between five types of interpersonal relationships:

1. *Very nourishing relationships*—these contribute greatly to my life.
2. *Mildly nourishing relationships*—these make some contribution to my development and/or to my enjoyment of life.
3. *Noncontributing relationships*—these neutral encounters do nothing for me.

4. *Mildly toxic relationships*—these slightly diminish my selfhood and/or my enjoyment of life.
5. *Very toxic relationships*—these excessively demanding, hostile, or nerve-wracking relationships are very depleting to me.

Sometimes a given relationship will be both nourishing and toxic.

Each of us experiences many toxic relationships. Toxic relationship may be with a neighbor, an acquaintance, "good friend," òne's child, one's parent. It is tragic but not uncommon to see a husband and wife who deplete one another far more than they nurture one another.

What can be done about relationships that are very toxic and have depleted one or both parties for a long period of time? My approach has been to first determine if the relationship is important to me. If it is unimportant, I withdraw from the association immediately and permanently. There are too many good relationships on which to spend my time and energy. I wouldn't purposely choose to live in a physically toxic environment if I had a good alternative, so why should I poison myself interpersonally when I have other options?

If the relationship is an important one, I try to use self-modification methods and assertion skills to improve the interaction between us. With one person in particular, this has been a long and sometimes painful (but primarily growth-filled rather than toxically painful) process. In this particular case, and in some others, the effort was well spent. The relationship is now primarily nurturing and satisfying. In another situation, we struggled for years to improve the relationship which was important to both of us. Despite the fact that we both have considerable ability in communication skills, our efforts proved futile.

When I don't succeed in improving an important but toxic relationship, I choose to end it. Decisive withdrawal from relationships that are toxic is probably a wise move in most people's lives. While some relationships are more draining than others, I think that if I lack the courage to either improve or end the relationships that are toxic to me, all my relationships, and indeed my selfhood, will be diminished.

THE SPECTRUM RESPONSE

The spectrum response provides a way of *making honesty nondestructive* when you do not fully agree with another's idea, point of view or plan of action. George Prince and his colleagues at Synectics, Inc., noted that in meetings, ideas are typically "shot down" before they are fully developed and understood. When this happens, the proponent of the idea may suffer loss of self-esteem and the trust level and the creativity of the group decreases. Many managers have expressed a need to find a way of criticizing a subordinate without snuffing out initiative and

spirit. They wanted to know how to respond to a subordinate's seemingly impractical ideas without hurting the other person and discouraging him from bringing
up other ideas which might be beneficial. Synectics devised a three-step process
that is applicable in settings as diverse as homes, schools, businesses, and volunteer organizations.

The first step is to *hear and understand* the idea. This requires great discipline. Though most ideas that are put forth are neither all good nor all bad,
people typically speak about the faults of the idea and may totally ignore its
advantages. "It seems to be universal that the faults in an idea will take prece-
dence in your mind, so don't fight it; simply do not voice the faults then.
Temporarily focus the very best of you—your intellect, your feelings, your
intuitions—on that small portion of the idea that is worthwhile. . . . By holding
in abeyance your negative concerns about a new idea, you release a neglected
capacity to contribute, to advance, to add to the creative sum of an emerging
idea."[13]

Sometimes I have thought, "I can't find *anything* good in what the other
person is saying." In those cases, the spectrum approach suggests that I encourage the other to talk about his idea some more—and I listen to hear something
good. "We believe that the good is there," says Prince, "but it is difficult to hear
because of the interference caused by awareness of the faults. As you become
skillful, you will find that there really is good intent in every suggestion. You will
be able to hear it, pick it up, and use it. By reacting this way, you promote a
speculative discussion that can build rather than an airing of different points of
view that invite defensiveness and deadlock."[14]

Once you understand the full spectrum—the good as well as the faulty
aspects of the idea—you are ready for step 2: *share with the other(s) your view of
that part of the idea (or intention) that seems worthwhile.* Tell what you like
about it. Build on what the other has said, adding any data or ideas that might
strengthen the advantages you see in the proposal. In addition to any contributions you may make, you also make it clear that you do not intend to put down
the other person or his idea.

Finally, after having disclosed what you like about the notion, *express your
concerns.* Choose your words carefully so your concern is stated as precisely as
possible. Avoid judgmental words and sweeping generalizations. Moreover, says
Prince, try "not to prove a negative point but rather seek [to] help in finding a
solution. Cure the faults if you are able."[15]

When both positive statements and concerns about an idea are raised, the
person whose contribution is being discussed often discounts the affirmative
elements even when they are sincerely expressed. A friend of mine discovered
that this tendency of the contributor is diminished if *both* the plusses and the

concerns are stated at the outset so the other person doesn't feel "set up." He often says, "I really like the idea—at least most of it. I do have some concerns, too. I'd like to share all my thoughts with you."

The spirit and method of the spectrum response can alter the climate of business meetings, classroom sessions, and family interactions. It can foster more creativity in groups and one-to-one interactions. Though the method is simple to understand, I find that it requires considerable discipline on my part to use it as frequently as is appropriate.

OPTIONS

People commonly try to halt the troublesome behaviors of others by saying something like, "Stop that right now!" When no options are stated, the person has no way to "save face," feels driven into a corner, and is more apt to behave aggressively than when alternatives are offered.[16]

Rather than directing or ordering the other person's behavior, the asserter can offer some choices and invite the other to select whichever one he prefers. The asserter may only be able to think of two or three choices, and these may not seem highly desirable to the other person, but by offering even limited choices the asserter demonstrates that he recognizes the other as a person who can make decisions and control his own life. Providing alternatives helps to prevent the unnecessary aggressiveness that occurs when a person feels backed into a corner.

A small group of students working together on a project became noisy and were disturbing others in the class. The teacher might have said, "Be quiet!" or "Break it up and work separately." Instead, she stated a norm and gave them an alternative:

> We need to have it quiet in the room so others can work. You can work together and talk quietly, or you can work separately. What's your preference?

NATURAL AND LOGICAL CONSEQUENCES

The psychologist Rudolph Dreikurs has promoted a method of helping children develop self-discipline without the use of punishments or rewards or excessive reasoning.

Dreikurs makes a strong case against punishment (which you recall, is one of the twelve roadblocks). Punishment pummels some people into the half-life of submissiveness. A saying has it that the only people who will respond to punishment are the ones who don't need it. For those who do not become overly compliant, punishment often feeds a power struggle and a deliberate *increase* in misbehavior. Nietzsche, the German philosopher, summed it up in one sentence: "Punishment hardens and numbs, it sharpens the consciousness of alienation, it strengthens the power of resistance."[17]

According to Dreikurs, *rewards* are no more effective than punishment. He has two primary complaints about rewards: they tend to harm the recipient's personality, and in the long run they cease to be effective. Rewards demonstrate a lack of respect for the other person. We reward our inferiors for good deeds and favors. Rewards also signal a lack of trust—else why would we have to bribe a person for good behavior? Rewards undermine one's sense of responsibility and the satisfaction that comes from participation and contribution freely given. Finally, when the emphasis has been placed on "What's in it for me?" we soon run out of satisfying rewards. The pathetic truth is that the others' demands continually escalate, but there is no reward that totally satisfies. Dreikurs concludes, "The system of rewarding children for good behavior is detrimental to their outlook as the system of punishment. . . . In our mistaken efforts to win cooperation through rewards, we are actually denying our children the basic satisfactions of living."[18]

Many times people try to *reason* with a misbehaving child. Dreikurs points out that logic (another roadblock) is usually futile because it cannot engage the child at the level of his needs and the goals of his misbehavior. You have undoubtedly noticed how quickly children become immune to persistent parental reasoning; they become "mother-deaf."

Dreikurs's observations about the frequent inadequacy of words, rewards, and punishment apply to adult-adult relationships as well as to adult-child encounters. If reasoning does no good in these situations, and if reward and punishment don't work, what can be done? The use of natural and logical consequences is often a constructive option.

Natural consequences are based on the normal flow of events and take place without anyone's interference. They represent the pressure of reality. This method is based on *inaction*—simply allowing another person to experience the consequences of behavior without trying to cushion the blow.

Kathy received a ten-speed bike for her birthday. There were many bike thefts in that neighborhood and her parents explained that if the bike were left outside overnight, it might be stolen. If stolen, she would have to save her money for another one, or go without a bike. The parents would not buy another for her.

Kathy chose to leave her bike outside and soon it was stolen. Kathy pleaded for another bike. She wheedled and cajoled. One day she threw a tantrum. Her parents were tempted to give in and buy her another. But they were also convinced they should not shield her from reality, so no bike was forthcoming until she saved enough money to buy one. This required great self-discipline on the part of those particular parents.

Some people think the approach of Kathy's parents was a disguised form of punishment. This was not the case. Kathy knew the consequences ahead of time. Her parents' tone of voice and body language were matter-of-fact. The parents simply let events take their course. That is one of the best ways to enable a person to develop self-responsibility.

Parents can avoid the reasoning trap and still share their experience and knowledge with their child. Sometimes children learn this way, though, like most of us, children gain much of their learning from their own experiences.

In moments of real danger, a person should be protected from natural consequences—as when a child runs into the street in front of a car. When there is no acute danger, it is seldom helpful to shield a person from the natural consequence of his behavior.

Logical consequences are arranged or applied. They must be experienced as logical in nature and not as arbitrary or capricious actions. If a child spills milk, he must wipe it up. If a person repeatedly arrives late for an appointment, he only is given the remaining amount of time for the interview. If there is no time remaining for the interview, he must reschedule it. When several people do not arrive on time for a meeting, it is still begun at the stated time. In each case, the consequences were logically related to the behavior.

There is a significant difference between natural and logical consequences. Because natural consequences represent the pressure of reality without any specific action by you, they are always effective. By contrast, logical consequences cannot be applied when there is a power struggle (except in rare situations and then with great caution) because in that circumstance, they typically deteriorate into or are seen as acts of retaliation. Natural consequences are always beneficial, but logical consequences can backfire.

Here are some guidelines to help you use the consequences method effectively.

1. Ask yourself, "What would happen if I didn't interfere?" Look for natural consequences and allow them to occur. Otherwise, you are protecting the other from developing and exercising his sense of responsibility.

2. When relevant, use the formula "When you [description of behavior], then [statement of consequences]. You will have another chance [statement of when this can occur]." In the case of the ten-speed bike, Kathy's parents could have told her, "When you leave your bike outside all night, it may be stolen. If stolen, you can get another bicycle when you have saved enough money."

3. One of the keys to using this method is to detach yourself emotionally from the issue. If the parents aren't affected emotionally, the child begins to learn that it really is "his own ball game." Whether this is verbalized to the other person or not, it is important for the person to remain emotionally uninvolved with that *issue*. When that is the case, the nonverbals often let the other person know that there is nothing personal in this—it is just the other person's problem and it won't do either of us any good if I make it mine. Some people like to verbalize this to the other. The important thing however, is to achieve emotional neutrality in that area of the other's life.

The consequences must be put into operation consistently and with all people. Dreikurs says, "Natural and logical consequences must be applied so that the child becomes convinced that they will follow his misdemeanor, just as he is convinced that if he were to put his hand in water it would come out wet."[19]

People often expect miracles after they have applied consequences for a few days. It is important to remember that the other's behavior was probably years in the making. Because it usually takes longer than a couple of days for a person to alter a behavior which he has used for a long time, the person following this approach may be discouraged if there are no quick, drastic changes. The appropriate goal of consequences messages is not an instant miracle, but significant self-directed behavioral change.

STOP THE ACTION; ACCEPT THE FEELINGS

Sometimes a person feels very angry and expresses that anger through hostile behavior.[20] This frequently happens with children, but anyone who watches pro hockey is aware that it is not limited to children. When faced with an outburst of hostile behavior, the recommended assertion procedure is to act quickly to:

1. stop the action,
2. don't become emotionally embroiled yourself,
3. accept the feeling, and
4. (perhaps) suggest alternative behaviors.

Five-year-old Brad hit his little brother. His mother said, "Stop hitting your brother right now. You are real mad at him and want to smash him. Feeling mad is OK, but hitting him is not. Here, you can pound this pillow and get some of your anger out."

Brad stopped hitting his brother. He pounded the pillow and screamed out his rage at his brother, who had broken one of his toys. His mother stayed in the room and heard his rage without expressing either approval or disapproval. In fact, she didn't say a word. Having vented his anger, Brad was ready to play again.

Brad's mother told me, "A few months ago, I wouldn't have allowed Brad to 'own' his feelings. I would have stopped the hitting, all right, but I also would have moralized and ordered: 'Aren't you ashamed of yourself? Tell Albert that you are sorry.' I now realize that making Brad keep his anger in simply meant that it was stored inside him so the next time his brother bothered him, there was a greater accumulation of anger to pour out."

Let's take a more detailed look at each of the steps of this method. First, there are times when another person's actions must be halted. If words do not succeed, the person should be physically restrained. If Brad kept punching Albert after his mother told him to stop, she would have had to hold his hands firmly (but nonpunitively) while repeating her message.

It is especially difficult for young children to control their socially unacceptable feelings. Parents should be allies in the child's struggle to cope with these strong feelings. Parental limit-setting stops the destructive behaviors and conveys the unspoken message, "You don't have to fear your feelings; I won't let you express them harmfully."

The next step is to refrain from becoming emotionally embroiled yourself. Some people say, "That's just the trouble. I do get overinvolved. I can't seem to help it." Three things have helped many people attain emotional control. One is realizing that, at times, all of us have so-called negative feelings, like anger. If Jesus could express his anger both nonverbally and verbally, and if prophets like Hosea could speak of God's "fierce anger,"[21] does it not seem reasonable to expect angry feelings in all human beings? Many psychologists teach that feelings are not good or bad, they simply *are*. When I don't think my child's emotions are "bad," I am more able to attain detachment from the situation.

Next, it helps me to realize that the expression of emotions is the best way of getting rid of that emotion and makes it *less* likely that the other person will want to act out that feeling.

Finally, it is possible simply to decide not to get emotionally involved. That decision can be made instantly, at the beginning of an incident. Otherwise, the increasing emotional momentum will be too much to surmount. Like the willpower required for me not to eat hot fudge sundaes or for another person to give up smoking or excessive drinking, the act of will is difficult, but not impossible.

The second step is to demonstrate acceptance of the other person's feelings. "Discipline problems" typically consist of two parts—angry feelings and angry acts. Most people tend to treat the feelings and the acts in the same way. Permissive (submissive) parents may allow both the actions and the feelings.

They are reluctant to set firm limits. Authoritarian (aggressive) parents usually try to control both the child's behaviors and feelings.

The assertive approach to these difficult situations is to take one approach to the person's conduct and another approach to his feelings. While the angry acts may have to be limited, the angry feelings are best expressed and accepted. This helps the child to feel OK about himself and thereby be in a better position to deal constructively with the situation.

The third step is to help the other person find alternative ways of expressing his feelings. The feelings exist, they are probably very genuine, and it is often beneficial to vent them. It is important to try to find action outlets as well as verbal outlets when suggesting a substitute expression for the destructive actions that were taking place. When children become older and more experienced at this they can be encouraged to come up with their own ways of venting their feelings nondestructively.

SAY "NO!"

The road to a significant *"Yes!"* usually leads through a definite *"No!"* The founders of our country discovered that they could not preserve the freedoms they struggled to win without the support of some powerful *nos*. To preserve their hardwon freedoms, they drafted a magnificently negative document, the Bill of Rights. Out of the ten amendments in that cornerstone of our democracy, eight of them incorporate important *nos* into the law of our land:

"Congress shall make *no* law. . . .

"The right of the people to bear arms shall *not* be infringed. . . .

"*No* soldier shall be quartered. . . .

"The right of the people to be secure . . . shall *not* be violated. . . .

"*No* person shall be held to answer. . . .

"*No* fact tried by a jury shall be otherwise re-examined. . . .

"Excessive bail shall *not* be required. . . .

"The enumeration of certain rights shall *not* be construed. . . ."

To say *yes* to individual freedom, our country has had to say *no* to a whole series of acts of government.

In our individual lives, too, our most important *yeses* have to be protected by resolute *nos*. If I am to say *yes* to writing this book, I must say *no* to my loved ones, I must often say strong *nos* to other people who want my time. If I am to say *yes* to some solitude, I must say some difficult *nos* to my loved ones as well as to the others who make demands on my life.

The word *no* is so important and the inability to say it is so widespread that the best-seller lists once simultaneously featured two books written to help people say that two-letter word.[22] Most of us are surrounded by people who will make many requests and place many demands on us. If you don't say this simple word when you want to say it, you lose control of your life. Yet many people find that this is the hardest of all the words in the English language to say face-to-face.

People who have difficulty saying *no* seldom think of the variety of ways that message can be conveyed. Here are some of the many ways of saying *no*:

Your Natural "No." Many people develop their own individual ways of turning down invitations or stating refusals.

Reflective Listening, Then "No." A friend of mine commonly uses this approach. She reflects both the content and feeling of the request and then states her *no*: "You really need me to crew for you in the sailing races. I'd love to do it but I made a prior commitment. I just can't do it this weekend."

The Reasoned "No." The person says *no* and gives a very *succinct* explanation of his *reason*. The reason is sincere and is not an excuse. For example, when Bertha asked Marie to play bridge, Marie said, "No. Thanks anyway. I don't enjoy playing bridge."

The Raincheck "No." The person says *no* to this particular request, but suggests that he be asked again. Earl, who had been a hi-fi buff for years, told Tom, who was about to buy his first set, that he would help him shop for one if he wished. On a Saturday morning, just as Earl was getting started on some yard work he planned to do, Tom phoned and said: "You promised to help me pick out a hi-fi set. Today is the day! How about it?" Earl replied, "Gee, today isn't good for me. But I can be free next Saturday."

The Broken Record. This way of saying *no* involves using a one-sentence refusal statement and repeating that like a broken record no matter what the other person says. The broken record is helpful in dealing with very aggressive or manipulative people who "won't take no for an answer." Extremely submissive people who are likely to buy things they don't want from high-pressure sales-people often find this method helpful. It is also useful for those people at the other end of the continuum who are highly aggressive and are apt to lose control and become verbally or even physically abusive. The broken record method can be 100 percent effective in maintaining one's refusal while continuing to retain emotional self-control.

Six guidelines will help you use the broken-record response:

1. Select a succinct one-sentence refusal statement and use only that statement, no matter what the other person says or does.
2. After each statement by the other person, say your broken-record sentence. Don't allow yourself to get sidetracked by responding to any issues the other raises.

3. Say it in a soft, calm, unemotional voice.
4. Don't "attend" to the other person very well—yet avoid gross nonattending behaviors. (Attending will only encourage him to keep talking.)
5. Allow plenty of silence. (In the silence, the other person will realize that all his statements and manipulations will be futile.)
6. Persist. You must simply state your broken-record refusal one more time than the other person makes his request, questions, or statements. If he has six interactions, you need to last only seven broken-record statements to get your needs met. If he has three statements, you simply have to do four. After the first interaction or two, the other will become ill at ease (but seldom angry) and will be ready to stop even though his momentum may carry him through one or more statements.

Meg Noblock told the members of a communication skills class that she consistently allowed her beautician to "con me into getting my hair done in the latest style even when I wanted it done differently." Meg would say she wanted it done in a particular way, but the beautician always went into a long dialogue and Meg finally relented even though she remained unconvinced. She seldom liked the results. After learning the broken-record method, Meg reported this conversation:

Beautician:	Should we frost your hair this time?
Meg:	No, I'd rather keep my normal coloring. I really don't want it frosted. Just shape it a bit.
Beautician:	If I frost your hair, your face will have a much softer look.
Meg:	I really don't want it frosted.
Beautician:	I bet everyone will like it much better than your plain dark brown hair.
Meg:	I really don't want it frosted.
Beautician:	I was just at a hair show in New York and light frosting is the in thing right now.
Meg:	I really don't want it frosted.
Beautician:	How about just a halo of frosting around your face?
Meg:	I really don't want it frosted.
Beautician:	Are you sure you just want me to cut it and not frost it?
Meg:	I really don't want it frosted.
Beautician:	Okay. I'll just cut it and forget the frosting this time.

The broken-record method may be used appropriately with magazine, encyclopedia, and telephone salespersons. It can be very helpful in the beginning stages of defending one's space nonaggressively, but one of the things that makes it most effective—the refusal to even acknowledge that you have heard most of the other person's statements—is a serious drawback to the method. The broken record protects your space and preserves peace, but it does not foster dialogue as much as many of the other methods described. So whenever possible—and especially with intimates or with neighbors or ongoing work relationships—I recommend using another of the assertive methods.

The Flat-out "No." In this kind of a "no" statement the person does not choose to reflect, offer reasons, or extend a raincheck. You have a right not to give reasons for your refusal or answer any questions, although it is usually easier on the other person if you do. A flat-out "no," blunt as it is, is usually a more appropriate response than rationalizations or lengthy justifications. The flat-out "no" is rarely used by assertive persons. However, they have the inner freedom to make this kind of a response when it is fitting.

The Celebrative "No." Sometimes a *no* is a major declaration and can be enhanced by dramatizing it. Mahatma Gandhi's dramatic "salt march" was his way of saying, "No!" to the oppression of the British Empire's imperialism in India. Martin Luther's nailing his theses to the door of the cathedral church in Wittenberg, Germany was a dramatic way of saying a notable "No!" to what he believed were significant ecclesiastical errors and abuses.

Whatever form of *no* is decided upon, its effectiveness depends largely upon one's own inner determination. What Jonathan Weiss says about a parent's inner resolution—the *"absolute no,"* as he calls it—applies to adult-adult relationships as well:

> There is evidence that what stops a young child is whatever the parents' absolute no is. A psychologist I know told me the following fact. Psychologists say that as parents they are themselves practically always too permissive; they let their kids do too much. But the one thing a psychologist's child never does is break into a conference room where his father is seeing a patient, not really because he thinks his father would *do* anything to him, but because he knows that is where the parent has drawn an absolute line. Whenever the parent draws an absolute line and lets the child know what the absolute no is, there the child stops.[23]

Saying *no*, as Weiss points out, is one of the most effective ways of clearly and seriously indicating the boundaries of one's own space. When that is done with strong inner resolve, the other person will nearly always honor your space.

No is one of the great words in the English language. Of course, it can be overused as well as underused. Some people sink into nitpicking and negativity. Some suffer from the "neurosis of defiance." But if one avoids these pitfalls, his life will be richer because of the power of a positive *no*.[24] Two thousand years ago, Jesus of Nazareth stated it well: "Let your yes be a clear yes, and your no, no. Anything else spells trouble."[25]

MODIFY THE ENVIRONMENT

Some of the problems that develop between people result in part from the environment. Rather than asserting to the individuals involved, the psychologist Thomas Gordon says, it may be more appropriate to alter the environment.[26]

The environment can be *impoverished*. When young children are apt to break valuable possessions, they can be placed out of reach. When a group of secretaries spent what seemed like an excessive amount of time talking with one another, office landscaping was used to decrease their interpersonal contact and the time spent conversing diminished considerably.

The environment can also be *enriched*. Parents of young children do this when they provide toys and games for long car trips. Parents of twin boys who were fond of roughhousing put some wrestling mats on the basement floor and asked the boys to confine their pushing and shoving to that area. A husband who is president of an international operation frequently battled with his wife about putting the car keys in a certain spot when they were through driving so the other would have easy access to the keys. After a class session on environmental modification, they bought some extra sets of keys and the unpleasantness about that topic ceased.

Most environments can be modified to better meet people's needs and to reduce interpersonal friction. Some graduates from our courses make quarterly or annual lists of ways they can improve their environment at work and at home.

Sometimes you can modify the environment by yourself. At other times, it is important to secure the agreement and ideas of several people. Brainstorming (see pages 243–245) is a good method to use when two or more people generate the ideas.

THE DANGER
OF GOING OVERBOARD

When people who tend to be submissive learn to protect their space with asser-tion skills, they often go overboard. They frequently go past the assertive zone on the continuum and become aggressive.

The sudden change can be difficult for friends, family, and colleagues. It would be hard enough if the change occurred at a slow pace. When the change is quick and radical, relationships may become very stressed.

Some submissive people seem to need to become aggressive for a short while before they develop an assertive life style. The excesses are often shortlived, but can be traumatic for all involved. Many could avoid the excesses with effective coaching and self-discipline.

Some people use assertion methods but have an aggressive spirit. Their approach is not collaborative. It is not win/win. My colleagues and I once were discussing the fact that our relationships with some assertive people were largely hassle-free. In other relationships, the people *seemed* assertive because they were using assertive methods. But they confronted over many little things. They asserted at the "drop of a hat." We finally decided there was a fourth category on the assertion continuum. Besides people who are submissive, assertive, and aggressive, there are the "fussbudgets"! The fussbudgets in our lives were no pleasure to be with and work with. They were too consistently demanding. It finally dawned on me that the fussbudgets were really a subgrouping within the aggressive category.

THE AURA OF ASSERTIVENESS

Have you ever noticed how one teacher will step before a class and have its attention and respect before he says a word, while another teacher cannot secure or hold its attention even when he shouts? The first teacher has what we call "the aura of assertiveness." The second teacher lacks it.

The aura of assertiveness results primarily from the body language that one develops as he becomes more assertive. The assertive person looks and acts strong, confident, and fair. Even when he is not consciously trying, he telegraphs signals that define his space, communicates his healthy sense of self-esteem, and lets people know that he will defend his rights and dignity while respecting the rights and acknowledging the dignity of others.

At first, being assertive may require strenuous effort. In time, however, much of one's assertion can be accomplished through effortless influence.

SUMMARY

There are many ways of increasing one's assertiveness. This chapter described several methods:

- "Natural" Assertions
- Self-Disclosure
- Descriptive Recognitions
- Relationship Assertions
- Selective Inattention
- Withdrawal
- The Spectrum Response
- Options

- Natural and Logical Consequences
- Stop the Action, Accept the Feelings
- Say "No!"
- Modify the Environment

Life is easier for everyone involved if the person learning assertion methods does not overuse them and provides some "loving allowances" for those with whom he interacts. In time, one's increased assertiveness will demonstrate itself in an "aura of assertiveness" that enables a person to get many of his needs met without the conscious use of assertion methods.

PART FOUR

Conflict Management Skills

In a world of finite men, conflict is inevitably associated with creativity. Without conflict there is no major personal change or social progress. On the other hand, runaway conflict (as in modern war) can destroy what men intended to save by it. Conflict management then becomes crucially important. This involves accepting or even encouraging such conflict as is necessary, but at the same time doing everything possible to keep it to the minimum essential to change, to confine it to the least destructive forms, and to resolve it as rapidly and constructively as possible.[1]

—Harvey Seifert, social scientist, and Howard Clinebell, Jr., pastoral counselor

CHAPTER TWELVE

Conflict Prevention and Control

One can distinguish between resolution and control as different goals of conflict management. The principals themselves or a third party may attempt to gain *resolution*, so that the original differences or feelings of opposition no longer exist, or they may attempt to merely *control* conflict, so that the negative consequences of the conflict are decreased, even though the opposing preferences and antagonisms persist.[1]

—Richard Walton, organizational consultant

CONFLICT IS UNAVOIDABLE

To be human is to experience conflict. The other night my wife and I spent an evening recalling the conflicts we weathered in the past few years. Though our life style is rather quiet and peaceful, we were amazed at the amount and also at the intensity of the conflicts we encountered at work, at home, and in our small community of thirty-five hundred people.

Then we thought about the conflicts in society. One-third of all marriages end in divorce. In many families there seems to be a wedge between parents and children called "the generation gap." Teachers are out on strike, school budgets are voted down, local churches are torn by dissension.

At 6:30 P.M., when we turn on our television sets, the conflicts of the world enter our household. News stories detail the struggles of labor against management, the city against the suburbs, whites against blacks, pro-abortionists against "right to life" groups, heterosexuals against homosexuals, environmentalists against nuclear power companies, and so on. The international coverage tells of coups, invasions, kidnappings, assassinations, economic sanctions, arms build-ups, and breakdowns in negotiations—many of which have a direct or indirect effect on us.

Though I am frequently surprised by the amount of conflict in my life and in our society, my experience should have led me to anticipate it. After all, differences in opinions, values, desires, needs, and habits are the stuff of daily living. Long before Karl Marx, James Madison said, "The most common and durable source of faction has been the various and unequal distribution of property."[2] That basic source of social friction is still very evident in our society.

Perhaps even more causal in our everyday squabbles is the fact that we are human and not gods. It is impossible to rise completely above selfishness, betrayals, misrepresentations, anger, and other factors that strain and even break relationships. As Florence Allshorn said, "We can love for a time but then it breaks down."[3] The best we can hope for is to "establish the peace of a true kind *at the other side of conflict.*"[4]

CONFLICT IS DISRUPTIVE
AND/OR DESTRUCTIVE

I hate conflict. I wish I could find a healthy way to avoid it or transcend it. But there is no such path.

I detest conflict because at best it is disruptive, and at its worst it is destructive. Once it erupts, conflict is difficult to control. Destructive controversy has a tendency to expand. Often it becomes detached from its initial causes and may continue after these have become irrelevant or have long been forgotten. Conflict frequently escalates until it consumes all the things and people it touches.

THE BENEFITS OF CONFLICT

Conflict is a dangerous opportunity. On an emotional level at least, many of us are more aware of its perils than of its possibilities. It is not without important benefits, however.

Social scientists have discovered that love only endures when dissension is faced openly. In his book *Love and Conflict*, sociologist Gibson Winter writes, "Most families today need more honest conflict and less suppression of feeling. . . . There are obviously proper times and occasions for conflict. No one benefits from the random expression of hostile feelings. There are, however, occasions when these need to emerge. . . . *We cannot find personal intimacy without conflict. . . . Love and conflict are inseparable.*"[5]

Some fascinating experiments document this thesis. In one noted series, the University of Wisconsin's Dr. Harry Harlow reared several generations of monkeys and showed that those which were raised by nonfighting monkey mothers would not make love.[6] Another well-known researcher, Konrad Lorenz, found that birds and animals that did not hold back their aggression became "the staunchest friends."[7] Likewise, students of human relationships like Harvard's Erik Erikson blame the failure to achieve intimacy on "the inability to engage in controversy and useful combat."

Then, too, Stanley Coopersmith's research suggests that some kinds of dissension in the home is healthy for children. He found that families that tend to express open dissent and disagreement tend to raise children who have that priceless quality—high self-esteem.[8]

Another value of conflict is that it can prevent stagnation, stimulate interest and curiosity, and foster creativity. Philosopher John Dewey wrote, "Conflict is the gadfly of thought. It stirs us to observation and memory. It instigates to invention. It shocks us out of sheeplike passivity, and sets us at noting and contriving. . . . Conflict is a *sine qua non* of reflection and ingenuity."[9]

Economic historians have noted that much technological improvement has resulted from the conflict activity of unions which resulted in the increase of wage levels. A rise in wages often led to a substitution of capital investment for labor.[10] The high level of mechanization of the American coalmining industry in the 1930s and early '40s has been partly explained by the vigorous unionism in our coalfields during that period.[11]

Many of our institutions, including the Christian church and the United States of America, were forged in the heat of conflict. Then, too, confrontation is a necessary ingredient of organizational renewal. Professor Richard Walton of Harvard University's Graduate School of Business noted the positive impact that conflict can have on business and other organizations. According to Walton,

> a moderate level of interpersonal conflict may have the following constructive consequences: First, it may increase the motivation and energy available to do tasks required by the social system. Second, conflict may increase the innovativeness of individuals and the system because of the greater diversity of the viewpoints and a heightened sense of necessity. Third, each person may develop increased understanding of his own position, because the conflict forces him to articulate his views and to bring forth all supporting arguments. Fourth, each party may achieve greater awareness of his own identity. Fifth, interpersonal conflict may be a means for managing the participants' own internal conflicts. [12]

We have seen that conflict is unavoidable. At its best, it is disruptive, at its worst it is incredibly destructive. Conflict, however, can bring important benefits—especially when it is handled skillfully. It can foster intimacy, aid the development of children, encourage personal and intellectual growths, spur technological development, and help create and renew our social, religious, political, and business organizations.

Thus the question faced by this chapter and by Chapters 13 and 14 is how can we manage conflict in such a way as to minimize the risks and maximize the benefits?

REALISTIC AND NONREALISTIC CONFLICT

Several well-adjusted middle-class American boys who were eleven or twelve years old attended a two-week-long experimental camp in the summer of 1954. They participated in activities that seemed natural to them and were not aware that their behavior was under observation by behavioral scientists.

The experiment was conducted in three stages. The first, which lasted about a week, was designed to produce a sense of togetherness in each of two groups. Each group came to the camp in a separate bus, and besides living in the same cabin, the youngsters in each group engaged in numerous cooperative activities. They cooked, improved swimming places, camped out, and so forth. As a result, each group developed a "we feeling"—a sense of cohesiveness.

In the second stage of the experiment, conflict was produced between the two groups by creating a series of competitive situations in which one group could achieve its goal only at the expense of the other group. A tournament of competitive events was set up with desirable prizes only for the victorious group.

As they competed in baseball, touch football, tug-of-war, and other events, good sportsmanship eroded and hostility began to develop. Name-calling, threats, physical conflict, and raids on each other's cabins took place in the second period of their stay.

In the third stage, some strategies were developed for reducing the level of conflict and preventing the further development of unnecessary strife.

Mere social contact at pleasurable events did not reduce the conflict. The two groups were brought together for movies, eating in the dining room, shooting off fireworks, and so on, but these experiences, far from diminishing the conflict, provided opportunities for the rival groups to berate and attack each other.

The conflict was finally resolved when the two groups committed themselves to superordinate goals (goals that could not be achieved without the cooperation of both groups). Water came to the camp in pipes from a tank about a mile away. The behavioral scientists arranged to have the water system break down. The two groups cooperated in searching for and correcting the trouble. On another occasion they jointly raised funds to go to a highly desired movie. The camp truck broke down away from camp one time and both groups combined to pull it. The campers, of course, were not aware that these situations had been purposely manufactured by the researchers.

While the mutual hostility did not disappear immediately, there was a gradual decrease in conflict which led in time to pleasant interaction. The two groups began planning activities together, and friendships were formed across group lines. Members of both groups requested that they go home together on the same bus rather than on the separate buses in which they had arrived. At a rest stop on the way home, one group invited their former enemies to be their guests for malted milks.[13]

This experiment by Muzafer Sherif and his colleagues at the University of Oklahoma was followed by experiments by Robert Blake and Jane Mouton with more than 150 nearly identical groups of adults drawn from industrial organizations. These experiments with adults showed that certain conditions stimulated needless and counterproductive conflict, while other conditions tended to mitigate or prevent conflict.[14]

Anthropologist Ruth Benedict noted that some societies are characterized by more conflict than others. In a series of lectures at Bryn Mawr College in 1941, she spelled out specific characteristics of cultures that she believed caused high levels of conflict and those characteristics which she thought tended to prevent or control conflict.[15]

Where two or more people are together for any length of time, some conflict will be generated. That is inevitable. The experiments of Sherif, Blake and Mouton, and others and the analyses of scholars like Ruth Benedict and Abraham Maslow suggest, however, that certain conditions, behaviors, and organizational climates tend to produce needless conflict, while other climates and conditions do not tend to generate unnecessary disputes. *Social scientists now make an important distinction between realistic conflict and nonrealistic conflict.* In *realistic conflict* there are opposed needs, goals, means, values, or interests. Nonrealistic conflict, however, stems from ignorance, error, historical tradition and prejudice, dysfunctional organizational structure, win/lose types of competition, hostility, or the need for tension release.

Realistic conflict can be faced and resolved using methods like those described in the next two chapters. Unrealistic conflict, however, creates unwarranted tension between people and can cause much unnecessary destruction. Unrealistic conflict should and—to a significant degree—can be prevented or controlled. There are important actions that individuals can do, and significant steps that groups and organizations can take, to prevent the development of needless conflict.

PERSONAL CONFLICT PREVENTION AND CONTROL METHODS

Though it is impossible to totally eradicate conflict, much needless strife can be averted by personal conflict prevention and control methods.

One way of diminishing the amount of conflict you experience is to *use fewer roadblocks*, especially when one or more person in the interaction has a strong need. Ordering (dominating), threatening, judging, name-calling, and other roadblocks are conflict-promoting interactions.

Reflective listening to another person when she has a strong need or a problem can do wonders. It helps the other dissipate "negative" emotions and/or may help the other solve a problem, which, if unresolved, could develop into a major conflict.

Assertion skills enable a person to get her needs met with minimal strife. By asserting when needs arise, one can prevent the buildup of emotions that so often causes conflict. Potential problems can be avoided by preventive assertion messages such as, "I'm going to be writing a chapter of the book today, so I will appreciate it if you are fairly quiet around the house." Both the assertion and listening skills help to clear up two major sources of conflict—errors and lack of information.

Awareness of which behaviors are likely to start a needless conflict between you and others can help you eliminate many confrontations. Certain words, looks, or actions tend to "trigger" specific people into conflict. Often these triggering behaviors have little or nothing to do with present relationships. They may be rooted in early childhood experiences.

Observant people can "read" storm warnings in the sky. Just so, the aware person can look for the signs and patterns in her conduct and the conduct of her associates which indicate that a storm is brewing. Though there is little that can be done about the weather, these early warning signals in interpersonal relationships can provide both the time and the insights to take effective preventive action.

"Dumping one's bucket" of tension without filling the other's bucket is another important conflict prevention and control method. Often, in the normal course of life, tensions build. These can be released in ways that build tension in other people. If I swear and shout at you, I release my tension—but probably increase yours at the same time. However, I can shout in my room alone or spout off to a neutral third party who agrees to hear me vent my feelings. Strenuous exercise, competitive athletics, and sexual activities also can drain off one's tensions without adding to other people's stress. I am more and more convinced of the importance of this conflict-reducing method.

Increased emotional support from family and friends can decrease one's proneness to unnecessary conflict. Each of us knows ways to activate more caring and warmth in our interpersonal environment. By and large, the more we are loved and cared for, the less we need to fight.

Heightened tolerance and acceptance of others also tends to diminish unrealistic conflict. To some degree our levels of tolerance and acceptance are conditioned by our upbringing and possibly even by genetic factors. But each of us can become more tolerant and accepting than we now are. Greater assertiveness, increased emotional support in our lives, effective courses in communication skills, and incorporating some of the wisdom of Rational Emotive Therapy[16] are some ways of increasing one's tolerance and acceptance.

"Issues control" is another important way of managing conflicts. In his book *International Conflict and Behavioral Sciences*, Roger Fisher points out that "issues control" may be as important as "arms control" in creating world peace.[17] This guideline is as valuable in controlling the conflicts between individuals as it is in regulating strife between nations. Factors in issues control include the following:

- It is often preferable to begin by establishing procedures for handling disputes rather than dealing immediately with substantive issues.
- It is often preferable to deal with one issue at a time.
- It is often preferable to break issues down into smaller units rather than deal with enormous problems with many parts.
- It is often preferable to start with issues that you believe can be most easily resolved to the satisfaction of all parties.

- It is important to eventually get down to the basic issues. When there is one fight after another, George Bach says, someone should have the sense to take the needle off the broken record and demand, "Will the real problem please stand up?"
- It is usually preferable to define the dispute in terms that do not pit the principles of one person against the principles of another. When possible, define the dispute in nonideological terms. Try to find out how your *needs* and the other's *needs* can be satisfied. To the extent that values issues are involved, Roger Fisher points out, it is wise to say that "the solution we seek is not only consistent with our principles but is also consistent with those of our adversary—at least if properly construed and applied. By insisting that our adversary can come along without abandoning his principles, we make it easier for him to do so."[18]

If the other person has a difficult time expressing her feelings or opinions during conflict, offer an *invitation* for her to talk about her beliefs and feelings and assure her of *protection* once she has spoken. During conflict, many of us want to have the last word—and most of the words that went before it! So it isn't always easy to encourage the other to talk by saying something like, "I'd like to know how it seems to you." When the other person tells you her differing point of view on a tense topic, there is a strong tendency in many of us to argumentatively disagree, put the other person down, or angrily denounce them. It is not enough to invite the other to open up, you must protect them from your potentially angry attack. I find that this is incredibly difficult to do, but very important—especially when the other person is underassertive.

Finally, *a careful appraisal of the full consequences and cost of a conflict* may deter you from involving yourself in needless disputes. It is difficult to estimate the cost of a conflict, because emotional interactions are unpredictable and frequently get out of hand. Nonetheless, it is a dumb fighter who hasn't tried to estimate the consequences of engaging in an unnecessary dispute.

GROUP/ORGANIZATIONAL CONFLICT PREVENTION AND CONTROL METHODS

Certain kinds of social arrangements breed needless conflict, other procedures and structures keep unrealistic conflict at a minimum, while still other social arrangements block facing and hence resolving realistic conflict. Let's look at some types of social arrangements for families, groups, businesses, individual relationships, and so on that help to prevent the development of needless controversy.

The way an organization (or a relationship) is *structured* has a bearing on the amount of conflict generated in it. For example, Eugene Litwak claims that the potential for conflict tends to be greater in centralized, bureaucratic organizations than in organizations where there is less centralized control.[19] Rensis Likert's extensive research enables him to place organizations on a continuum from fairly rigid to fairly flexible institutions. The more rigid institutions, according to Likert, have less effective communication and are less adept at managing conflict constructively than are the organizations at the other end of the continuum.[20]

The personality and methods of the *leader* are also important. Managers who have low levels of defensiveness[21] and who are supportive[22] tend to help people in their organizations avert unnecessary strife. Though it is possible for a "weaker party" to inaugurate the use of constructive conflict resolution and conflict prevention methods, a person in a position of power, one who has great charisma, or one who has developed effective communication skills tends to have the greatest influence on the way conflict is handled.

The *climate* of a group also influences the amount of conflict it generates. Though some kinds of competition can be healthy, research evidence suggests that win/lose competition fosters needless conflict and diminishes the ability to resolve disputes effectively. On the other hand, cooperating to achieve goals that could not be accomplished without joint effort promotes more genuine harmony.[23]

Well-conceived and clearly stated *policies and procedures* which have the understanding and support of the relevant persons create orderly processes which can help mitigate unnecessary chaos and conflict. Think of the vastly increased number of accidents and disputes that would occur on our highways if there were no rules of the road! Some people would be driving on the left-hand side of the road and some on the right-hand side, and incidents of strife would multiply enormously.

Polygamous marriages, though they are uncommon in our society, graphically demonstrate the need for clear-cut policies and procedures to prevent a surplus of conflict. Robert Blood writes:

> Whenever there are several wives but only one husband, the danger of jealousy and conflict among the wives is very acute. It is not surprising, therefore, that polygamous societies have devised . . . measures for preventing the outbreak of conflict. (1) Avoidance is achieved by placing each wife and her children in a separate hut. (2) Authority over subsequent wives is usually allocated to the first wife—her position is thereby less threatened and the loss of exclusive wifehood is offset by the addition of maid service. (3) More important for our present purposes is that the man treat his wives equally, that he not play favorites among them. This often takes the form of requiring the husband to follow a strict schedule of rotation among his wives, spending an equal number of nights with each in turn.[23]

Robert Blood goes on to say that in the contemporary American household the presence of certain policies and procedures are essential to conflict management. This, of course, is true of business and other organizations. On the other hand, when policies and procedures do not meet the needs of the organization or its members, when they are arrived at arbitrarily and administered highhandedly, they can add to the level of unrealistic conflict in the organization.

The *degree of change and the methods by which change is introduced* into a family or other organization influences the amount and severity of disputes in that institution. In a rapidly changing society, families and other organizations must change to some degree, sometimes significantly, or experience the tension of being unresponsive to the surrounding culture. At the same time, too rapid a change, or change utilizing inadequate methods of communication, can create significant and needless conflict.

Mechanisms to settle grievances need to be established. Kenneth Boulding says that the major factor in the negotiation of conflicts between organized groups is not the establishment of an agreement so much as the setting up of machinery for the adjudication of subsequent grievances and claims. According to him, labor and management made little progress when they focused exclusively on obtaining settlement of an issue. They made great progress, however, when there was an emphasis on the inclusion of machinery for the fair settlement of grievances that might arise thereafter.[24]

"Emotional plague" is a source of much unnecessary conflict. Psychotherapist Wilhelm Reich coined this term, which I use somewhat more broadly than he did. It is the affliction of people who behave in destructive ways to those who pose no threat to them. "Plague" individuals may be attractive, intelligent, and active. When they come in contact with a healthy, loving life or someone intensely involved in constructive work, they often do whatever they can to block or destroy the other's fulfillment. Nineteen hundred years ago when the crowd insisted that Barabbas' life be spared instead of Jesus', "emotional plague" was at work.[25]

"Emotional plague," like some other diseases, should be treated by isolation. I choose not to hire these persons into our organization or admit them into my relationships. The trouble is that emotional plague may be difficult or even impossible to spot at first. When these persons are finally discovered they need to be fired from the organization or decisively terminated from personal relationships. If someone with emotional plague is in one's family, the choices are indeed difficult.

Training for conflict management is necessary both for the prevention of needless conflict and for the resolution of the conflicts that are inevitable in any relationship or organization. My bias is that presentations alone are virtually useless. To be able to use sound methods in stressful conflict situations requires skill development. Further conflict management skills should be taught as part of a training program that includes listening, assertion, and collaborative problem-solving skills. Finally, the training should be but one aspect of the family or organization's effort to utilize conflict better. Agreed-upon ways of preventing and resolving conflict, adequate channels of communication, mechanisms for handling grievances—these and other methods when combined with effective training are parts of a comprehensive program of conflict management.

THE DANGERS
OF CONFLICT PREVENTION
AND CONTROL

Some conflict can be prevented constructively. Some conflict can be judiciously controlled to the benefit of all concerned. But much conflict needs to be faced and resolved at the earliest possible moment. When prevention and control strategies are used unwisely, they merely postpone the inevitable. The final result is worse than an early, direct resolution of the strife.

When some people want to dodge conflict altogether, they tend to misuse the prevention and control strategies listed above. Others use denial, avoidance, capitulation, or domination as mechanisms for keeping their lives free of the unpleasantness of strife.

SUMMARY

Conflict, which is unavoidable in human life, is disruptive at best and horribly destructive at worst—yet some forms of conflicts have important benefits. There are two very different kinds of conflict. In *realistic conflict* there are opposing needs, goals, or values. *Nonrealistic conflict*, on the other hand, stems from ignorance, error, historical tradition and prejudice, poor organizational structure, displaced hostility, or the need for tension release. To a large degree, nonrealistic conflict can be prevented or controlled utilizing the personal and group prevention and control methods outlined in this chapter. Efforts to repress conflict by denial, avoidance, capitulation, or domination only postpone the conflict and make the rupture more difficult to mend.

The next chapter presents a tested method for resolving the emotional dimensions of realistic conflict. Chapter 14 goes on to teach how the substantive differences of most realistic conflicts can be settled in such a way that the needs of both parties are satisfied.

CHAPTER THIRTEEN

Handling the Emotional Components of Conflict

The point here is that, while my emotions are throbbing with these fears, angers, and self-defensive urges, I am in no condition to have an open-minded, honest and loving discussion with you or with anyone else. I will need . . . emotional clearance and ventilation . . . before I will be ready for this discussion.[1]

—John Powell, theologian

FOCUS
ON THE EMOTIONS FIRST

A useful distinction can be made between the emotional and the substantive aspects of conflict. The emotional components include anger, distrust, defensiveness, scorn, resentment, fear, and rejection. When feelings are strong it is usually a sound strategy to *deal with the emotional aspects of conflict first*. Substantive issues can be handled more constructively once the emotions have subsided.

The substantive issues involve conflicting needs, disagreements over policies and practices, and differing conceptions of roles and uses of resources.

These two aspects of conflict interact with one another. Substantive conflict often generates emotional conflict—anger, distrust, and so on. And emotional conflict may multiply the substantive issues. These two dimensions are often intertwined and difficult to separate.

Many approaches to conflict resolution stress the importance of *rationally* examining specific issues at the outset. My experience suggests that this should usually be the second step. *When feelings run high, rational problem solving needs to be preceded by a structured exchange of the emotional aspects of the controversy.* After this has been accomplished and the emotions recede, the persons or group may proceed to the next stage—a rational and creative examination of the substantive issues (if any) that divide them.

There is a reason why the rational approach rarely works when the emotions are strongly engaged. Emotional arousal actually makes us different people than we are in moments of greater calmness. When we are angry or fearful, our adrenaline flows faster and our strength increases by about 20 percent. The liver, pumping sugar into the bloodstream, demands more oxygen from the heart and lungs. The veins become enlarged and the cortical centers where thinking takes place do not perform nearly as well. As we've noted previously, the blood supply to the problem-solving part of the brain is severely decreased because, under stress, a greater portion of blood is diverted to the body's extremities. George Odiorne, a management consultant, says, "This is an emotional condition that the person is in, and it means that, while he's beautifully equipped for a brawl, he's very poorly equipped to get a problem solved."[2]

In conflict resolution, then, the first goal is to deal constructively with the emotions. That is the purpose of what I call "the conflict resolution method."*

---

*When we call this *"the* conflict resolution method," it doesn't mean that we think it is the only effective approach to dealing with the emotional tension of conflict. Someone on our staff started calling it this, and the label has stuck through the years.

THE CONFLICT
RESOLUTION METHOD

The conflict resolution method can be thought of as a set of simple *rules* that govern conflict. We have learned through the centuries that conflict can be too dangerous if it is not governed by regulations. Thus, when burly wrestlers attack each other on the mat, they know they will be protected from certain types of violence by the rules which govern that sport. When the heavyweight boxer climbs into the ring, he has the security of knowing that there are certain things his opponent cannot attempt because the rules forbid it and the referee will enforce the rules. When political parties battle for the privilege of ruling the country, they agree to obey specific laws. Even when nations go to war there are some agreed-upon rules of conduct. But in some of the most important areas of life our conflicts are largely unregulated. For example, when a husband and wife pitch into each other, there are usually no agreed-upon rules designed to protect them or their marriage. The conflict resolution method described in this chapter provides a simple but practical set of rules that enable conflict to be more constructive.

While this conflict resolution method can be thought of as a set of rules to govern interpersonal strife, it can also be viewed as a constructive *process* for handling emotion-laden disagreements. This process encourages assertive communication and the expression of feeling, but it does not permit the typical verbal free-for-all which blocks creative resolution of conflict and which tends to be very destructive of relationships. The three-step process of conflict resolution helps people fight constructively—in a systematic, noninjurious, growth-producing way.

Step 1: Treat the Other Person
with Respect

What does it mean to treat the other person with respect in the midst of a controversy? Clark Moustakas, a psychologist, says:

> In the creative dispute, the persons involved are aware of the other's full legitimacy. Neither loses sight of the fact that they are seeking . . . to express the truth as they see it. In no way is either person reduced by this. Such a confrontation, within a healthy atmosphere of love and genuine relatedness, enables each individual to maintain a unique sense of self, to grow authentically through real communication with other persons, and to realize the worth of simplicity and directness in relationships.[3]

Martin Buber, one of the modern world's finest philosophers, tried to put his philosophy of dialogue into operation in the social, religious, and political turmoil of the Middle East. In his book *The Knowledge of Man*, he portrayed the respectful way of relating to others which he tried to embody amid the turbulent conflicts within which he was enmeshed:

> When two men inform one another of their basically different views about an object, each aiming to convince the other of the rightness of his own way of looking at the matter, everything depends, so far as human life is concerned, on whether each thinks of the other as the one he is, whether each, that is, with all his desire to influence the other, nevertheless unreservedly accepts and confirms him in his being this man and in his being made in this particular way. The strictness and depth of human individuation, the elemental otherness of the other, is then not merely noted as the necessary starting point, but is affirmed from the one being to the other. The desire to influence the other then does not mean the effort to change the other, to inject one's own "rightness" into him; but it means the effort to let that which is recognized as right, as just, as true (and for that very reason must also be established there, in the substance of the other) through one's influence, take seed and grow in the form suited to individuation.[4]

Respect for another person is an attitude conveyed by specific behaviors. The way I listen to the other, look at him, my tone of voice, my selection of words, the type of reasoning I use—these either convey my respect or they communicate disrespect.

Unfortunately, a disagreement with another person's beliefs or values or a conflict of needs often degenerates into disrespect for both the other person's ideas and his personhood. Even when I greatly respect another person, I am apt, in the heat of conflict, to disparage him. I may speak in put-down vocabulary: "What a dope! That's the dumbest idea I've heard in years!" Or I may turn sarcastic: "That's a marvelous idea, but it will take all the gold in Fort Knox to pay for it." Or I may attack the person and undermine his sense of self-worth. These words of disrespect are often spoken carelessly, but they block the current of communication and create wounds that may never fully heal.

After an angry outburst I have said, "You know I didn't mean that. I was just mad and wasn't thinking of what I was saying." But the other person tends to think, "The fact that you said it shows that it was on your mind. It took a burst of anger for me to find out what you really feel about me."

Some people think their disrespectful thoughts but do not say them outright. When one's attitude toward the other is disrespectful, his body language whispers the truth. The other will read it in his facial expression, tone of voice, gestures, and so on. This also blocks the conversation and may cause long-term damage to the relationship.

In conflict we tend to descend to meet. There is an interpersonal gravitation that tends to pull us down to the level of disrespect for the other person. There is an inclination to stereotype the other. When this happens we talk at each other or past each other, not with each other.

For many of us, an act of willpower is needed to fight the gravitational pull into disrespect. The exertion of moral force is required to treat the other as a person of worth with whom we will enter into a dialogue as equals.

Step 2: Listen Until You "Experience the Other Side"

Under the best conditions, effective communication is difficult to achieve. During conflict, when feelings are strong, people are especially prone to misunderstanding one another. You have undoubtedly listened to heated discussions in which the people weren't talking about the same thing but didn't know it—or they may have been in basic agreement but didn't realize it. Whatever goes on between people during conflict, it is rarely accurate communication.

One of the best ways to communicate more accurately during disagreements and to resolve conflict is to institute Carl Roger's rule: "Each person can speak up for himself only *after* he has first restated the ideas and feelings of the previous speaker accurately, and to that speaker's satisfaction."[5]

A "Rap Manual" put out by Eugene Gendlin and some of his associates in a neighborhood center on Chicago's South Side tells how to do this kind of listening:

> You . . . listen and say back the other person's thing, step by step, just as that person seems to have it at that moment. You never mix into it any of your own things or ideas, never lay on the other person any thing that person didn't express. . . . To show that you understand exactly, make a sentence or two which gets exactly at the personal meaning this person wanted to put across. This might be in your own words, usually, but use that person's own words for the touchy main things.[6]

The goal of listening is to understand the *content* of the other person's ideas or proposals, the *meaning* it has for him, and the *feelings* he has about it. That means being able to step into the other person's shoes and *view from his point of view* the things he is talking about.

This kind of listening is different from merely being able to repeat back the other's words or ideas. Dr. Richard Cabot said, "We do not understand an opposing idea *until we have so exposed ourselves to it that we feel the pull of its persuasion,* until we arrive at the point where we really see the power of whatever element of truth it contains."[7] This is what Martin Buber means when he speaks of "experiencing the other side."

It is very difficult to accurately understand and summarize another person's point of view during disagreements. People often hear from their own point of view and reflect back a summary that is correct in many ways but that distorts the other's message. For example, in an argument with her daughter Emily, Marsha Kirshenbaum said:

Marsha: I'm angry that so often when I ask you to complete your household chores you say you can't because you have to do your homework.

Emily: *(trying to summarize her mother's statement):* You want me to forget about my homework and do the chores.

Emily's reflection is seemingly correct but distorts the spirit of what her mother was saying. This is especially evident to a person who overheard the whole conversation to this point. Marsha was unhappy that her daughter put off both the chores and the homework until there was little option but to do one or the other. A more accurate reflection might have been:

Emily: You're upset because you think I use homework as an excuse for not doing my household chores.

Emily does not have to *believe* that she is using the homework as an excuse when she makes this reflection. Her job is to understand, not necessarily to agree. She'll soon have a chance to state her opinion.

Concentrate especially on reflecting *feelings*. It is not enough to hear the other's emotions—they need to be understood and accepted. Sometimes the diatribes of the other will seem like a deliberate attempt to hurt you. You will be tempted to strike back in rage. If you choose to resist that impulse and empathically reflect the other's feeling, you will be amazed at how quickly the other's feelings usually subside.

Don't say, "I know how you feel." The other person will rarely believe it. Don't offer explanations, apologies, or make any other statements at this point. Discipline yourself to understand the opinions and suggestions or feelings of the other person—from her point of view—and then reflect those thoughts and feelings back to the other in a succinct statement. Be silent to let the other think about what you said, indicate that it was essentially correct, and explain his point a bit further or correct any inaccuracies there may have been in his speaking or your listening. If the other person adds to what he said or corrects your reflection, summarize that to his satisfaction. When the other person feels heard, you have *earned the right to speak* your point of view and express your feelings.

Step 3: State Your Views, Needs, and Feelings

After demonstrating respect for the other as a person and conveying your understanding of his feelings and point of view, it is your turn to communicate your meaning to the other. Five guidelines are useful at this step of the conflict resolution process.

First, state your point of view *briefly*. Especially during conflict, you will usually communicate better if you keep your message short and to the point.

Next, avoid loaded words. That can be difficult during tense times. A character in one of Philip Roth's novels said with surprise, "My God! The English language is a form of communication! Conversation isn't just crossfire where you shoot and get shot at! Where you've got to duck for your life and aim to kill! Words aren't only bombs and bullets—no, they're little gifts containing meanings!"[8]

Third, say what you mean and mean what you say. Many times people withhold important information in tense times. Or they talk about one issue when their real concern centers on an entirely different matter. When in conflict people often make much more extreme statements than they really believe. While there may be some occasions when it is best to be guarded, it is often preferable to state the truth as it really is for you.

Fourth, disclose your feelings. The other person may have accused you unjustly and may have stirred up some feelings of anger or resentment. Or you may have a lot of feelings about the subject under discussion. It is difficult to constructively express the alienation you feel toward the person who has offended you, but this normally needs to be done if the conflict is to be resolved. Some of the assertion skills learned earlier may help here. Until the emotional issues are resolved, the sutstantive issues probably can't be settled. Whether you are talking or listening, the conflict resolution method concentrates especially on the feelings.

Finally, there are some occasions when step 3 of the conflict resolution process (stating your own views, needs, and feelings) is unnecessary. Sometimes one person is upset and the other is not. When the angry person vents his feelings and is accepted and treated with respect, the conflict may end.

Though avoiding step 3 may *sometimes* be appropriate, usually it is not. Some people misuse this method by listening to the other while refusing to disclose their feelings or point of view. When this happens repeatedly it undermines the relationship.

THE CONFLICT RESOLUTION METHOD IN ACTION

Because there are three steps involved in it, some people call the conflict resolution process the one-two-three process:

1. Treat the other person with respect.
2. Listen until you "experience the other side" and reflect content, feelings, and meanings.

3. Briefly state your own views, needs, and feelings.

Meg, a student in one of our communication skills courses, used this method for the first time in a discussion she was having with Don, her fiancé. They often got into verbal battles about religion. One day, when she saw a conflict brewing, she decided to try her newly learned skills. Later she wrote out the dialogue. (Note that in the first few interchanges, she was *not* using the conflict resolution method.)

Don: You sure spend a lot of hours helping at your church. Wouldn't you rather do other things?

Meg: Our church is really great. I do a lot for it because I get a lot out of it—and I get a good feeling from it.

Don: I'll take my church anytime. In the Catholic Church, you don't have to do anything and you still reap the benefits.

Meg: Do you like anything else about the Catholic Church besides the lack of work?

Don: Isn't that enough? Look at your church—two hundred families are working their heads off and you're still in the red! I'd never waste my time like that. Besides, the Protestant Church demands all that work and you're forced to do something you *really* don't want to spend time doing. (*Talks at length about this.*)

Meg: Don, it sounds like we have a very different point of view here. I just took a communication-skills course that describes a healthy way to express your own opinions and still listen to understand the other person's opinion. Here's the method. While you make a statement I listen carefully; then restate your views. That way you know I fully understand what you've just said. Then we'll switch—OK?

Don: (*laughing*): You're trying to slow me down! OK, go ahead.

Meg: You think that spare time is important and you'd rather spend it doing something other than volunteer work for a church.

Don: Right. Especially when . . .

Meg: Wait—my turn. I think that if I enjoy doing something, even if it's volunteer work for a church, I should be free to do it, especially when I think it is worthwhile service and not a waste of time.

Don: You do it because you want to, not because the church makes you feel obligated.

Meg: (*Nods, meaning "yes."*)

Don: The Catholic Church is better than the Protestant Church because you don't have to pledge money or be accounted for all the time. Besides, the Catholic Church has made a lot of good changes recently—like you don't have to eat fish on Friday anymore.

Meg: You believe the Catholic Church is more desirable than the Protestant because of healthy changes and no demands.

Don: (*Nods affirmatively.*)

Meg: I prefer the Protestant Church because of close fellowship with friends work-
       ing together and the church service which always includes excellent music
       and helpful sermons.

Don: You like the music and the messages. I'll admit they may be better than in
       the Catholic Church, but I wouldn't listen to that anyway. I'd daydream.
       When I'm in my church I feel I'm worshipping God just by being there.
       That's all I need.

Meg: It sounds like you and I are happy in our own churches because we look for
       different things.

This was Meg's evaluation of the interaction:

I feel so good about this conversation. When we talk about these kinds of things, it
usually gets real bad. I think this is the first time Don listened to my side when we
had a strong disagreement. It helped me, too. Without the skills, I'm sure I would
have gotten preachy and holier-than-thou. By using the skills I avoided using the
roadblocks. And though we've had talks on this topic before, this was the first time I
understood where Don was coming from.

People often think that the skills described in this book are very modern. Not
so. Before the times of Socrates and Jesus individuals with exceptional ability at
interpersonal communication were using similar methods of relating.

For many centuries the essentials of conflict resolution have been known
and practiced. Here is an example of the use of the conflict resolution method
during a tense and dangerous time in a much earlier era.

At the end of the sixteenth century William Shakespeare wrote the play
Julius Caesar which dramatized the conflict and intrigue that surrounded
Caesar's death in 44 B.C. Brutus was among those who assassinated Caesar,
then, with brilliant oratory, convinced the Roman populace that he had done
what was best both for them and for the greater glory of Rome. He stirred up in
the crowd a loathing of Caesar and of those, like Mark Anthony, who had
remained loyal to Caesar.

Moments later, Mark Anthony rose to address that same crowd. Before his
first words were uttered a belligerent voice from the mob yelled, "T'were best he
speaks no harm of Brutus here." Another shrieked, "This Caesar was a tyrant."
Another howled, "We are blessed that Rome is rid of him."

Mark Anthony realized he would be lucky to live through the night. This
speech was a life-or-death matter. Calling upon his knowledge of people, he did
three things in that speech which make it one of the great pieces of oratory in the
world.

First, he treated the crowd with respect. "Friends, Romans, countrymen,"
he said, "lend me your ears. . . ."

Next, having listened carefully, he demonstrated his understanding of the
popular point of view and his acceptance of people's right to their own opinions.

He succinctly reflected back to them the parts of Brutus' speech that had deeply affected them and at the same time demonstrated that he heard the jeers from the crowd. "The noble Brutus," continued Mark Anthony, "hath told you Caesar was ambitious. If it was so, it was a grievous fault, and grievously hath Caesar answered it." He continued in this vein, summarizing their concerns and opinions.

When he thought the people in the crowd knew that he, Mark Anthony, understood the situation from their perspective, the Roman politician proceeded to step 3. He stated his own opinion in noninflammatory words and presented some important evidence. "He was my friend, faithful and just to me; but Brutus says he was ambitious and Brutus is an honorable man. He [Caesar] hath brought many captives to Rome, whose ransoms did the general coffers fill. Did this in Caesar seem ambitious? . . . You all did see that on the Lupercal I thrice presented him a kingly crown, which he did thrice refuse. Was this ambition?" Mark Anthony then produced Caesar's will, which left most of the dead ruler's wealth to the citizens of Rome.

The odds for Mark Anthony's survival that day, March 15, 44 B.C., were slim indeed. He was saved by following the three steps of the conflict resolution method. Shakespeare probably never learned it as a "method," but he knew that Anthony in such a crisis would have to treat the crowd and his opponents with respect and listen attentively and demonstrate his understanding. By doing this he could drain off the anger of the people standing before him. Only after Mark Anthony had dealt with their emotions would people be ready for the facts as he saw them. When the people were ready emotionally, he stated his case. By following these three steps he not only survived the day but lived to take over the reins of Rome.[9]

FOUR WAYS TO USE THE CONFLICT RESOLUTION METHOD

There are four ways of implementing the conflict resolution method. First, one can use this method even when the other person or persons are not using it. By listening to the other with respect and speaking briefly in noninflammatory ways, you can help the other person to simmer down and engage in a more productive discussion.

When you are involved in a dispute or sense that a fight is brewing, a second approach is to explain the method briefly and ask the other person to join you in trying this way of relating.

Bart, a teacher, had repeated conflicts with one of his students, Jim. After learning the conflict resolution method, he decided to try to use it with Jim when the next opportunity arose. He didn't have long to wait. This is Bart's account of what happened:

> Jim started a fight with a child in another class. During the slugfest some school equipment was broken. When Jim and I talked about this type of thing previously we seemed to get nowhere. This time I resolved to use the one-two-three method.
>
> I asked Jim to go to my room and wait for me while I took the rest of the class to the library. When I went to my room, Jim looked like he was ready to "fly off the handle" with me, as he had on so many previous occasions. I sat down next to him in silence for nearly a minute and then said, "Jim, before we begin talking let's make a contract. Each of us will listen to what the other says and say it back before we speak. And when we talk we'll keep it straight and simple."
>
> I paused, leaving a long silence as before. Then, looking at him I said, "What do you say . . . is it a deal?" I extended my hand in the form of a handshake. He took it and said, "It's a deal."
>
> The results? We both understand and like each other a lot better than before. And after we dealt with the feelings we did some problem solving which has licked the problem for over a month.

A third way of introducing the conflict resolution method is to do it when things are calm and peaceful. In a family meeting, class session, or work gathering explain that conflict is inevitable in any group and that there is a way of successfully coping with the emotional elements of conflict so that people can discuss their differences more profitably and resolve them more constructively. Explain the method, perhaps role-play it, and possibly provide a handout that explains the method. Then discuss the desirability of using it in your family or organization when there are strongly felt differences. You may get more resistance to using the method than you expect. If that happens—you've probably guessed it—refrain from answering the objections right away. Instead, treat the other with respect, listen carefully to the objection, and demonstrate that you understand. *Then* you may make a brief statement. After doing a lot of listening, I usually say something like, "I haven't been very happy with the way we've handled disagreements in the past. I don't think it has been satisfying to you, either. I'd like to try this out for a time or two and see if it helps. If not, no point in continuing. Willing to give it a try . . .?"

Lastly, you can use this method to help others resolve their conflicts. If the antagonists agree to your third-party role, your job is to remain neutral and make sure that the conflict resolution process is followed. In very delicate situations the third party may decide to reflect after each person speaks. Less distortion may occur when a neutral party summarizes a statement than when essentially the same words are spoken by an adversary.

It is more common, however, for the third party to explain the three steps of the conflict resolution process and secure the agreement of all parties to use the process. Then he facilitates the process, primarily by reminding people to follow the process when they slip off into other ways of interacting. Occasionally the third party may summarize the major issues raised by each person. The role of the third party is to stay out of the conflict, help others use a method by which they can communicate under stress, and help them learn a method that will enable them to handle future conflicts successfully without third-party assistance.

PREPARATION
FOR THE ENCOUNTER

Psychologist George Bach who has conducted "fair fight training" with couples and businessmen for over a decade, says that the mutual agreement to engage in conflict can be crucial to a productive outcome. According to Bach and Herb Goldberg:

> The fair fight is implemented by the "initiator" who has a beef or complaint. He requests the other person ("fight partner") to engage him in a fair fight. If the "fight partner" agrees to accept, a time and place for the fight is set.
>
> The "engagement" process is critical for offsetting the tendency to jump right in and have it out on the spot. This would only result in one person being caught off guard, and a rapid spiral of destructive encountering would ensue. A fair fight is therefore always conducted upon mutual consent and under agreed-upon conditions.[10]

People commonly plunge impetuously into many of their conflicts without ascertaining whether or not the timing is right for them and whether or not the other person consents to fight, and without securing agreement on the conditions that can make the conflict productive. Once their dander is up, even those people who tend to shy away from conflict are likely to plunge into battle without first seeking agreement on the conditions for a productive dispute.

Here are some things worth checking out. Do each of us have sufficient emotional energy for this conflict? If a friend is going through a painful divorce, I may choose not to confront him on matters that I would bring up under a different set of circumstances.

Who should be there? As a general rule, the people who are involved should be there and people who aren't involved shouldn't be at the scene of conflict. When you are first learning to fight productively it is often easiest to do it unobserved—except perhaps by a mutually agreed-upon third party. Sometimes bystanders take sides or one of the disputants becomes self-conscious. Besides, a strong fight is seldom enjoyable to hear. Why inflict your conflict on other people? One can go too far in this direction, however. Conflict need not always be conducted in secrecy as though it were an evil thing. Then, too, when parents allow children to overhear some of their conflicts it helps the youngsters develop a more realistic understanding of human relationships.

When is the best time? Is there a period when you are both unlikely to be fatigued, when you can take as long for the conflict as is required, and when you can have time afterwards for reconciliation, problem solving, evaluation of how fairly and effectively you fought, and so on?

Where is the best place? Usually you will want to be isolated from the distraction of the telephone, radio, TV, and other people. Another consideration is the neutrality of the turf—should you fight on your ground, in the other person's area, or in space that "belongs" to neither of you (or an area common to both of you)?

While each of these issues can be significant, the most important part of preparation is to refrain from a surprise attack on the other. The fight that begins with mutual consent and agreed-upon conditions (including the use of the conflict resolution method) is off to a good start.

EVALUATING THE CONFLICT

Many of the benefits of conflict listed earlier are not achieved or are only partially achieved because the people did not engage in a productive fight or because they did not take the time afterwards to learn the lessons of their conflict.

After the fight it is well to have a dialogue with your fight partner about how you fought and what you learned. If that is not possible, you may wish to have an inner dialogue about the process and results of the fight. The ideal, of course, is to process the fight with your partner *and* mull it over in your own mind from time to time. Here are some questions that may help you learn from your conflicts:[11]

- What have I learned from this fight?
- Can I learn anything from this fight about one or more of the things that tend to "push my button" or pushes the other person's button? Specifically what "triggering event" started this fight?
- How well did I (or we) use the conflict resolution process: preparation, respect, listening, stating my view, evaluation?
- How badly was I hurt?
- How badly was my partner hurt?
- How valuable was this fight for my partner and me in letting off steam?
- How useful was it in revealing new information about myself, my partner, and the issue in contention?

- Did either of us change our opinions at all? If so, what do I think of the new positions we arrived at?
- What did I find out about my own and my partner's fight style, strategy, and weapons?
- Are we closer together or farther apart as a result of this fight?
- What do I want to do differently the next time I'm in a conflict?
- What do I wish my partner would do differently the next time he and I fight?

EXPECTED OUTCOMES OF THE CONFLICT RESOLUTION METHOD

One of the most dramatic outcomes of the conflict resolution method is its effect on the emotionality of an interaction. This method encourages the genuine and direct expression of feeling by one person at a time. When feelings are expressed, then heard and accepted by another person, they tend to be very transient. This method enables the rapid discharge of heightened emotion so people can then discuss their differences more productively.

A second outcome of this method for me is that I may grow in understanding and change. After all, I do not possess the whole truth. When I really hear another person so deeply that I experience the persuasiveness of some of his convictions, I may adapt some new ideas and methods or integrate part of the other person's approach with mine. Also, when I am really challenged in a fair fight, I discover that which in my own experience is most rooted in reality. So at the same time I am integrating new insights I am strengthening those things that deserve to remain influential in my life and value system.

Another possible result of the conflict resolution method is that the other person may change. As Carl Rogers put it, "If I can listen to what he can tell me, if I can understand how it seems to him, if I can see its personal meaning for him, if I can sense the emotional flavor which it has for him, then I will be releasing potent forces of change in him."[12] Then, too, the skillful way in which I state my own point of view increases the probability of change in the other. However, *the purpose of this method is improved communication in stressful times. It is important to realize that many times the other will not significantly alter his beliefs or behaviors.*

Another frequent result of this approach to conflict resolution is that the two parties may be ready to jointly develop a creative solution to the substantive issues of the conflict. This three-step process, you recall, was designed to deal with the emotional issues of a dispute, not the substantive ones. Once the emotions have subsided, the substantive issues can usually be resolved by means of the collaborative problem-solving process described in the next chapter.

This conflict resolution method can also be used to handle values conflicts constructively. Some of the most damaging fights are over values issues. When people hold different values at the beginning of a conversation it is unusual for them to have a complete meeting of the minds when the interaction ends. When this conflict resolution method is used in values clashes, the goal is to understand one another better, perhaps influence each other to some degree, and to *agree to disagree* on the issues that remain. This process enables the parties in a values conflict to communicate face to face until acceptance of the right to differ occurs. People can remain at odds in terms of some issues without being at odds with each other. The dialogue between Meg and Don demonstrated this type of outcome.

Finally, handling conflict this way tends to deepen and enrich companionships. Relationships tend to falter because the individuals in them don't know how to handle the *differences* between them. To ignore the differences is to resign yourselves to a superficial relationship. To fight over the differences using inadequate methods causes heartache and blows conflicts out of proportion until they may needlessly dominate a relationship. When using the conflict resolution method, the truth and being of each is confronted caringly by the truth and being of the other. As a result, each person meets the other in depth, and after thrashing out the conflict they often experience a deep feeling of harmony and camaraderie.

This kind of harmony at the other side of conflict not only occurs between neighbors, friends, spouses, parents and children, and people in work relationships, it can also be experienced where there is national, religious, or racial hatred. Carl Rogers met with a group of five Protestants and four Catholics during the conflict and terrorism in Northern Ireland. The sister of one participant had been blown up by a bomb. Another had hidden behind mattresses while his home was riddled with bullets. The children of another were brutalized by British soldiers. These people met for a weekend of sharing facilitated by skillful leadership. By the end of the weekend "these centuries-old hatreds were not only softened but in instances deeply changed" and friendships were forged that cut across ideological differences.[13]

A Boston University professor wanted to "demonstrate that it is possible for a group of people with deep differences and antagonisms to learn to communicate with one another as human beings and start working together on solving problems."[14] In collaboration with Boston's WBZ television station, he brought together a group of blacks and whites for a televised encounter lasting for more than a dozen hours. The session was facilitated by professional group leaders. The group began with several hours of attacks and recriminations on each other.

Newsweek reports the change that occurred as participants began using elements of the conflict resolution method:

> A Negro woman teacher set a totally new tone by abruptly giving a long, moving explanation of what it felt like to be black. Mrs. [Louise Day] Hicks [outspoken champion of the "neighborhood" schools], who has been accused by blacks of appealing to racism, responded sympathetically. "I just didn't understand before," she said. "No one ever told me." Then she dropped her own aggressive mien and sorrowfully explained how agonizing it was for her to carry the image of a racist. At the end of her highly candid discourse, another Negro woman exclaimed: "You have been the symbol of everything I've always hated. But now for the first time I've seen you as a human being—and I want to see you again, Louise." . . . [The] Negro militant who had clashed with Mrs. Hicks more than anyone else felt differently enough about things to attempt a little joke. "Tonight . . . I would like to announce my engagement to Louise Day Hicks."[15]

When people use the conflict resolution method skillfully, the effects are usually positive—often dramatically so. Still, conflict is unpredictable, and no method of human interaction can be guaranteed.

SUMMARY

During a conflict, focus on the emotions first. One way of doing this constructively is to use the conflict resolution method:

- treat the other with respect;
- listen and restate to the other's satisfaction; and
- briefly state your point of view.

This method can be used by you alone or by agreement with the other, or it can be facilitated by a neutral third party. Preparation for a conflict is important and includes mutual consent and agreed-upon conditions for the fight. After the conflict a period of evaluation will help you learn from the fight and also learn how to fight more productively the next time. As a result of using this method, emotions are vented and usually subside fairly quickly, one or both parties may change, people can express themselves on values issues and "agree to disagree," and the emotional bonds between people tend to grow stronger. The best human relationships usually exist on the other side of conflict.

CHAPTER FOURTEEN

Collaborative Problem Solving: Seeking an Elegant Solution

The problem-solving approach allows for mental double-declutching. It does not require a direct switch from one point of view to another. It provides a period "in neutral" where there is an openness to facts and, therefore, a willingness to consider an alternative view.[1]

—William Reddin,
management consultant

THREE KINDS OF CONFLICT

There are basically three kinds of conflict. One is a conflict of *emotions*. In any significant relationship, because people are human and differences are inevitable, strong antagonistic feelings will develop. These can usually be resolved using the conflict resolution method outlined in the preceding chapter. Then there are *values conflicts*. There is rarely any "solution" to this type of conflict because nothing concrete or tangible is involved for the person who is upsetting herself. However, the use of the conflict resolution method may help people with opposing beliefs to better understand one another, help them to develop more tolerance for each other's position, and occasionally influence their attitudes and actions.

The third type of conflict, *a conflict of needs*, is the subject of this chapter. After the values issues have been sorted out and the emotional components resolved, there are often substantive issues that remain to be settled.

Here are some examples of recent conflicts of needs in my life:

My Need	Other's Need
To have transportation to do necessary shopping tonight.	To have transportation for an important date.
To have our home telephone "open" for an expected long-distance call.	To talk with friends about a mutual problem.
To have important typing projects completed.	To be with your young children because of problems with a babysitter.
To have the grounds of our Conference Center look well.	To avoid aches caused by the use of heavy equipment.

Each of these problems was settled in such a way that the needs of both parties were met. Before examining the collaborative problem-solving method that I employed to resolve those interpersonal problems, let's review some of the other options which are commonly used.

ALTERNATIVES TO COLLABORATIVE PROBLEM SOLVING

There are four fairly common alternatives to collaborative problem solving: denial, avoidance, capitulation, and domination. Each can be used appropriately on occasion. Repeated use of any of these options, however, leads to predictable negative consequences.

Denial

Conflicts are so threatening to some people that they deny the existence of interpersonal problems. They do nothing about the problem except deny it, that is, exclude it from conscious awareness. The repression of conflict means "pretending" to oneself and others that everything is all right. In every age people have deluded themselves, crying, " 'Peace, peace' when there is no peace."[2]

When a person consistently denies that problems exist, she makes herself unnecessarily vulnerable in a world that can be dangerous. Repeated denial often leads to psychosomatic illness and other forms of psychological distress.

Avoidance

Some people are aware of interpersonal conflicts of needs; they simply do everything within their power to avoid facing them. They withdraw from situations when strife occurs. Or they gloss over the problem, acting as though it doesn't exist. Many couples build a falsely peaceful façade for a marriage that is ridden with conflicts.

Premature forgiveness can be a well-intentioned but destructive way of avoiding conflict. Premature forgiveness is an effort to patch up a relationship without working through the angry and hurt feelings and other conflicted realities of the relationship. Here again, the feelings go underground where they may build to the point of being uncontrollable.

Repeated avoidance of problems results in a greatly diminished existence. The paradox of avoidance is that people often use it to try to keep a healthy relationship. Yet avoidance undermines a relationship and leads to the bleak, chilly distance which I call *ice-o-lation*. Withdrawal often becomes a continuous retreat from the opportunities of the world. Furthermore, continued avoidance leads inevitably to denial and all its negative effects.

Capitulation

When confronted by someone else's need that conflicts with their own need, many people capitulate. They give in, often without a struggle. They go through life without getting their needs met. Some parents use a "permissive" approach to childrearing. In actual practice this may be repeatedly expressed in capitulation to the child's needs, wants, and desires in spite of one's own legitimate needs, which go unmet.

When one habitually capitulates to another person there is a "flow of resentment" toward that person. One psychologist, speaking on the dangers of permissiveness, told a group of parents, "If you want to hate your child, just let him win all the time. That's a sure formula."

Repeated use of any of the three alternatives mentioned—or any combination of them—amounts to submissive behavior. The negative consequences of submissiveness mentioned on pages 130–131 apply to the consistent use of denial, avoidance, or capitulation.

Domination

Another approach to problem solving is domination—imposing one's own solution on the other person. The person who dominates the decision making comes up with a solution designed to meet her needs. We have found that these solutions rarely meet the dominant person's needs as well as other solutions might. She might get her way, or gain a particular result, but the relationship suffers needlessly. The needs of the other person are either not addressed at all or are not as accurately perceived or as fully met as is possible.

As you can imagine, aggressive people tend to rely on domination during a conflict of needs. What has surprised me, however, is the number of primarily submissive people who, when in a position of authority, are likely to impose their solutions on others during a conflict of needs. This often occurs in issues between adults and children. Adults often assume they are right because they have more knowledge and experience than children. Thus they rule out collaborative problem solving. A fairly submissive teacher, for example, said that, in relation to students, "I have really looked for the other to agree to *my* solution. Instead of genuinely wanting to solve a problem, I've wanted the other to capitulate. And I think of myself as nonaggressive?!" In teaching communication skills to thousands of people in positions of power (parents, managers, teachers, etc.) I have discovered that many of the less assertive people capitulate when lacking "position power," but they dominate when in a position that places them over someone else. There are many possible explanations for this phenomenon. I believe that one of the factors is that people have seldom experienced alternatives to domination and capitulation. Thus, when they became authority figures they behave in the way that was modeled for them during their formative years and in their work experience. Thinking up and then imposing "good" solutions seems to be what parents, teachers, and managers are for in the eyes of many.

There are many negative consequences to the overreliance on handing solutions down to others when there is a conflict of needs. For one thing, again there is a flow of resentment. This time it is toward the person imposing the solution. In addition to the normal resentment people tend to feel when dominated, the imposition of a solution may awaken old unresolved resentments of times when other authority figures imposed their will in the past. The authoritarian person, then, may not only have to cope with resentment against his specific act, but with the accumulated resentments of many years. When domination occurs repeatedly the negative results are often dramatic. People resort to sabotage, pilferage, work stoppage, passive resistance, emotional distance, and other destructive ways of striking back.

When solutions are imposed they often have to be followed up rigorously. After all, if the other person's needs are not being met and/or if she has not participated fully in the decision-making process, she is not likely to be highly motivated to make the solution work. So, not only is it difficult to resolve some issues, but even if resolved they may not stay resolved unless the person who imposed the solution devotes considerable energy and attention to overseeing its administration.

The authoritarian approach to resolving conflicts of needs, when used consistently, can be very damaging to the other person(s) in the relationship. Erich Fromm, the noted psychotherapist, writes:

> Inasmuch as social and parental authority tend to break [the child's] will, spontaneity and independence, the child, not being born to be broken, fights against the authority represented by his parents; he fights for freedom not only *from* pressure but also for his freedom to be himself, a full-fledged human being, not an automaton. For some children the battle for freedom will be more successful than for others, although only a few succeed entirely. The scars left from the child's defeat in the fight against irrational authority are to be found at the bottom of every neurosis.[3]

Clark Moustakas, a psychologist at the Merrill-Palmer Institute, studied alienation in children and found that it could be traced in large measure to the way adults dominate children "by loud, demanding orders and by sweet manipulating words." Says Moustakas: "What shocked me . . . is that in spite of all the evidence . . . authoritarian people continue to impose their standards and values on others. . . ."[4]

Capitulation and domination are win/lose strategies—one person wins, the other loses. Denial and avoidance are also win/lose approaches: through lack of awareness or withdrawal one of the parties loses—she does not get her needs met. When one considers the relationship aftermath, it is probably more correct to say that repeated use of any of these four ways of coping with conflict can be called lose/lose. Each of the parties loses something and the relationship itself deteriorates.

Compromise: I'll Meet You Part Way

My dictionary defines *compromise* as "consent reached by mutual concessions." Compromise takes into account the needs and fears of both parties. There are times when it can be extremely important in the settlement of interpersonal differences. Henry Clay, the American statesman who guided the Missouri Compromise through the House of Representatives, said that compromise is the cement that holds the Union together:

> All legislation . . . is founded upon the principle of mutual concession. . . . Let him who elevates himself above humanity, above its weaknesses, its infirmities, its wants, its necessities, say, if he pleases, "I will never compromise"; but let no one who is not above the frailties of our common nature disdain compromise.[5]

In a world of conflicting needs, wants, and values, compromise obviously has its place. It can lead to very undesirable results, however, when used consistently or appropriately, as the ancient story of Solomon's decision makes clear.

In the ninth century B.C., Solomon was king of Israel. In those days, one of the monarch's important duties was to serve as judge in personal disputes. One day two women came before Solomon, each claiming a child as their own:

> The first said, "My lord, this woman and I share the same house, and I gave birth to a child when she was there with me. On the third day after my baby was born, she too gave birth to a child. . . . No one else was with us in the house. . . . During the night her child died because she lay upon it. Then she arose in the middle of the night and took my child from my side while I slept, and laid the child in her bosom and put her dead child in my bosom. Thus when I rose toward morning to nurse my child, behold, it was dead; but when I was able to examine it closely in the morning-light, it was not my son which I had borne."
>
> The other woman said, "No, the living child belongs to me. The dead child is yours." But the first woman was saying at the same time, "No, the dead child belongs to you, the living child is mine!" Thus they wrangled before the king.
>
> The king mused. . . . Then he said, "Fetch me a sword." They brought in a sword and the king gave the order: "Cut the living child in two and give half to one and half to the other."
>
> At this the mother of the living child whose heart yearned for her boy, cried to the king, "O my Lord, give her the living child, never kill it!" The other woman said, "No, divide it; neither of us shall have it." The king said, "Give yonder woman the living child and by no means slay it, for she is its mother."[6]

In that situation, the compromise which was acceptable to one of the women literally meant the death of the child. The repeated use of compromise can be lethal in other, less obvious ways. In many marriages very different personalities are joined together. When they differ, they may consistently resolve problems by compromise. During twenty years of marriage, whenever there is a difference each of them settles for something less than what they really want. Their compromises bring them a temporary domestic peace that is without joy and delight. After years of bland compromises the marriage ends in one of two kinds of divorces—legal or emotional.

In organizations, too, the excessive use of compromise kills creativity, stifles people, and strangles profits. In his book *Up the Organization*, Robert Townsend, a business leader, advised:

> Compromise is usually bad. It should be a last resort. If two departments or divisions have a problem they can't solve and it comes up to you, listen to both sides and then . . . pick one or the other. This places solid accountability on the winner to make it work. Condition your people to avoid compromise.[7]

Since, in compromise, each party settles for something less than its full needs and desires, I call it the mini-lose/mini-lose method. Each side gives something up to end the conflict or solve the problem.

SEEKING AN "ELEGANT SOLUTION" THROUGH COLLABORATIVE PROBLEM SOLVING

In a collaborative problem solving, once the people discover they have conflicting needs, they join together to find a solution acceptable to both. It entails redefining the problem, discovering novel alternatives, and focusing on overlapping interests. In this process, neither person capitulates to or dominates the other. Because no one loses, no one gives up or gives in and because both (all) parties benefit. This is often called a *win/win* way of dealing with conflicting needs. When it is possible to use this method—and it often is—it is usually the most desirable way to resolve the conflicts of needs that occur between people.

Mary Parker Follet illustrated the collaborative approach to problem solving when she wrote of two people in a small stuffy room in a university library. One person wanted the window open; the other wanted it closed. Instead of focusing on solutions (whether the window would be opened or closed) they concentrated on needs and resolved the problem by coming up with another alternative—opening a window in the next room. This provided fresh air for the person who wanted it and, at the same time prevented the north wind from blowing directly on the person who objected to being in a strong draft.[8]

After training thousands of people—managers, teachers, parents, health care professionals, salespersons, therapists, clergy, and so on—our staff believe that it comes as a surprise to most people to discover that a win/win method exists which can actually resolve many of the thorniest interpersonal issues they face. Many have told us how gratifying it is to be released from the win/lose, mini-lose/mini-lose, and lose/lose methods of problem solving that they have been locked into for years.

Of course, many people are skeptical that win/win methods can work in the "real world." When I mention Mary Parker Follett's examples of opening a window in an adjoining room, a workshop participant is apt to say, "Yes, but there may not be a window in the next room."[9] In that case, creative problem solvers might come up with another option that is attractive to both people. A friend of mine in a similar situation where there was no window in an adjoining room found several solutions to the problem that were agreeable to both. These included changing seats, opening the top rather than the bottom half of the window, and searching for a different location in the library in which to study. I have been amazed at the number of really difficult conflicts of needs in my life that have been resolved by collaborative problem solving. This method is not a panacea for all of life's problems. There are some occasions when this method will not work or when another approach is more fitting. However, we've found it to be successful with an extraordinarily high percentage of typical problems which occur between people.

SIX STEPS OF THE COLLABORATIVE PROBLEM-SOLVING METHOD

One of America's greatest philosophers, John Dewey, declared that philosophy must cease to be "a device for dealing with the problems of philosophers" and become, instead, a method, cultivated by philosophers, for dealing with the problems of everyday people.[10] Probably the "most important single emphasis of John Dewey" was his insistence on establishing "universally recognized . . . rules of logic" that could help people problem-solve in such a way that they could achieve better consequences and avert the worse.[11] Dewey's "rules of logic" constitute a process that can be used to solve personal problems and business problems, resolve social conflict, or do critical thinking about scientific and other subjects.[12] Psychologist Thomas Gordon has written helpfully about the application of that process to the resolution of interpersonal problems after people discover through assertion and listening that they have conflicting needs.[13]

Here are the six steps of the process:

1. *Define* the problem in terms of *needs*, not solutions.[14]
2. *Brainstorm* possible solutions.
3. *Select* the solution(s) that will best meet both parties' needs and *check possible consequences*.
4. *Plan* who will do what, where, and by when.
5. *Implement* the plan.
6. *Evaluate* the problem-solving process and, at a later date, how well the solution turned out.

Collaborative problem solving requires the use of listening skills, assertion skills, and the conflict resolution method. In addition you will need to understand this collaborative problem-solving method—which is fairly easy because it is such a logical progression. And you will need to avoid the common pitfalls of using the method. Let's go through the process step by step.

Step 1: Define the Problem
in Terms of Needs, Not Solutions

Most of us agree in the top of our minds that an accurate statement of the problem should precede the other steps of problem solving. In the rough and tumble of life, however, with pressures on our time, emotional stress caused by the problem, and the demanding intellectual effort that it sometimes takes to define a problem clearly, many people settle for a slipshod definition of the problem. A haphazard definition of the problem will probably undermine the entire collaborative problem-solving process. It is important to arrive at a clear, concrete, succinct statement of the problem.

For a win/win outcome, the problem is stated in terms of *needs—not solutions*.[15] This is so crucial to the collaborative problem-solving process that I want to state *what* I mean by this distinction, *why* it is important, and *how* it may be achieved.

First, *what* is meant by defining a problem in terms of needs? Most of the time people think about problems in terms of conflicting solutions. Five members of a religious order lived together in a home. They shared one car. All were active in community affairs and thus were frequently involved in evening meetings. As can be imagined, conflict generated around the use of the automobile. When they tried to define the problem, Sister Veronica said, "I must have the car to go to the School Board meeting tonight at eight o'clock." (The meeting was being held at the eastern edge of the city.) Sister Katherine said, "But I need the car to go to the parish social action task force meeting at eight o'clock." (That n.eeting was held in a suburb ten miles west of the city.) As people usually do, these dedicated women had defined their problem in terms of clashing *solutions*: "I must have the car tonight." "But I need the car tonight to go in the opposite direction at the same time." When a problem is defined in that way—in terms of solutions—a win/win outcome has been eliminated. Either one woman gets the car or the other does. One wins, the other loses.

I asked the sisters to state the problem in terms of need.

Both sisters replied, "I need the car tonight." That was simply restating the problem in terms of their predetermined solutions.

To get at the *need* which lay behind their proposed solutions I asked, "What do you need the car for?"

Sister Veronica said, "I need to get to and from the meeting tonight."

Sister Katherine said, "And I need transportation to the social action committee meeting tonight."

Both women's *need* was *transportation*. Use of the group's car was *one possible solution* to their transportation needs. Once they defined the problem in terms of needs rather than solutions, a whole range of other solutions could be generated. This problem had troubled these two women for over a year. Once they defined it in terms of their need for transportation, they were able to solve the problem in minutes. Six months later I received a letter saying that the transportation solution was still working well and that the "needs approach" had made interpersonal relations in their religious community more constructive.

Remember the two persons in the stuffy library room? They probably began by stating their problems in a solution format. One wanted the window open. The other wanted it closed. If asked, "What do you want to achieve by opening the window?" the answer could have been a statement of need: "To have more fresh air." If the other were asked, "What's in it for you to keep the window closed?" she would undoubtedly reply with a needs statement: "I need to avoid strong drafts as I am fighting off a cold." When the problem is redefined—when it is stated in terms of needs—other options can be discovered which may satisfy both parties, like opening the window in an adjoining room. *To discover needs we try to find out <u>why</u> the person wants the solution she initially proposed. Once we understand the advantages that solution has for them, we have discovered their "need."*

Why bother to define interpersonal problems in terms of needs rather than solutions? The reason, already suggested, is that solution-type definitions of interpersonal problems lead, inevitably, to win/lose results.

Ross Stagner says conflict is "a situation in which two or more humans desire goals which they perceive as being attainable by one or the other *but not by both.*"[16] The word *perceive* is the key to that sentence. If the perception of the problem is changed at the outset from a win/lose orientation to a win/win perspective, the chances for a mutually beneficial outcome are greatly increased. A false and limited perception of the nature of the problem undermines most problem-solving efforts.

Redefinition of the problem in terms of needs leads to conflict re-solution in which both (or all) parties can get their needs met.

How does one go about defining a problem in terms of needs?

Sometimes it is obvious that there is a conflict of interests. For the two women in the religious order, the broad outlines of the problem were clear. Their task was to redefine the problem in terms of needs. Had a third party not been present, they would have had to listen empathically and speak assertively to understand each other's needs. One way of doing this is to distinguish between *means* and *ends*. What is the ultimate goal that Sister Veronica has for the means she has selected (using the community's car)? A friend of mine uses the following formula in defining needs: "*I need to. . . .* [statement of the goal, not a solution]." He finds this helpful in asserting. In listening he searches for the same kind of information: "You need to. . . . [after careful listening—a statement of the other's goal—not the solution she may have proposed].

The stress of conflict or even of anticipated conflict makes it likely that people will often unwittingly disguise their needs in language that is more heavily coded than usual. Then, too, under stress, people's ability to listen usually decreases significantly. Therefore, it can take a surprisingly long time to define a problem in terms of needs—even when important aspects of the conflict are obvious at the outset.

Often, however, the conflict of needs is camouflaged. One or both parties may be unaware of the other person's need at the outset of a conversation. The person who is aware of her needs may assert and find herself up "against a brick wall" because the other has equally strong counterneeds. When this happens the asserter moves to conflict resolution skills (when the other is in the grip of great emotion) and then to collaborative problem solving. Because it is important to know the precise nature of the other's need, and because the other may not state it clearly, quite a bit of time may be required to understand and to be able to accurately state the problem in terms of needs.

Sometimes a person may be listening to another unfold her dreams when all of a sudden the listener is given data that, unknown to the other, conflicts with the listener's needs. The listener then has to reflect the other's needs clearly, state her own needs assertively, and then, once the problem is stated to the satisfaction of both parties, the remainder of the problem-solving process can be followed. It is a difficult thing, however, to listen accurately and empathically, assert respectfully and forthrightly, and state both sets of needs objectively—especially when one is experiencing the stress of conflict.

For example, a mother was listening to her 17-year-old daughter, Joan, tell about how excited she was about graduating from high school in January (a half year earlier than the rest of her class). Joan felt relieved that all her high school requirements were behind her and proud that she had obtained a job for the period before she began college.

Joan's mother, who teaches communication skills, was able to listen empathically to Joan's description of her achievements and her hopes for the future.

Joan then stated her plans to visit Arizona (from her home in New York State) to visit two young men and then travel to San Diego to visit a third. This plan conflicted with her mother's value system and the mother was triggered out of her empathic listening and began sending roadblocks.

Later, when the mother realized what had happened, she reopened the conversation and disciplined herself to listen empathically. Then she asserted her concerns and the mother and daughter proceeded to find a mutually agreeable solution.

Participants in our courses tell us that one of the most difficult things about collaborative problem solving is the fact that they are often unaware they need this skill at the start of an interaction because they are unaware of the other person's strong need. Discerning that need and then switching methods (i.e., from assertion) is difficult and time-consuming when first learning communication skills. With practice, however, it becomes much easier and somewhat quicker.

Defining the problem in terms of needs, which is the first step of the problem-solving method, often takes about half of the time required for the whole process. To repeat, it requires *asserting one's own needs, listening reflectively until you understand the other person's needs,* and then stating both sets of needs in a one-sentence-long summary of the problem. Except for very simple or very difficult problems I figure on five to twenty minutes for this step. It's well worth the time involved. As the old saying has it, "A problem well defined is half-solved."

Step 2: Brainstorm Possible Solutions

Once the problem is adequately defined, the search for possible solutions begins. I usually use the brainstorming method. *Brainstorming* is defined as the rapid generation and listing of solution ideas without clarification and without evaluation of their merits. Many a seemingly insoluble problem has been constructively resolved through the use of this method.

In brainstorming you try for quantity, not quality. Seasoned brainstormers realize that most of the ideas generated will be excluded in later stages of the process. But they could care less. They are after high volume now.

There are basic guidelines for brainstorming which, when followed, lead to more productive sessions. These guidelines are designed to secure a climate in which a powerful flow of creative thinking energy is directed at conceiving possible solutions in a short time period (usually less than five minutes). Deviation from any of the guidelines will probably slow the flow of ideas and decrease the group's creativity. These, then, are the all-important guidelines:

1. *Don't evaluate.* Evaluation thwarts creativity. It tends to make people defensive and they are likely to keep their ideas to themselves. This is a time to suspend critical judgment:

Brainstorm ....Nobody says, "No."
Brainstorm ....Nobody says, "That will never work."
Brainstorm ....Nobody says, "That is a *dumb* idea."
Brainstorm ....Nobody says, "That will cost too much."
Brainstorm ....Nobody says, "That has already been tried."
Brainstorm ....Nobody says, "That's a terrific idea."

Later on there will be a time to state what solutions look best to you. But for now hold rigorously to the "Don't evaluate" rule—even when "positive" evaluations seem called for.

2. *Don't clarify or seek clarification.* Explanatory remarks interfere with the rapid and creative generation of possible solutions. When people begin to explain what they mean in the middle of the brainstorming process ("The reason I want to post notices on doors is . . .") or are asked what they mean by others, the ideas often slow down to a trickle.

3. *Go for zany ideas.* A far-out idea may seem nonsensical but it may provide, in seed form, the solution that is finally adopted. I am told that the managers of a major airport were brainstorming ways of removing snow from the runways. One of the participants suggested putting a giant frog on the control tower which could push the snow aside with its enormous tongue. In time that idea was reshaped to the solution they ultimately selected—a revolving cannon that shoots a jet airstream.

Beyond their occasional usefulness, zany ideas often serve as relaxants to a pair or group, and may thereby foster greater creativity.

4. *Expand on each other's ideas.* Brainstorming generates a lot of incomplete ideas. Some of the best solutions come from adding to or combining or going beyond ideas that have already been contributed. One young couple was brainstorming ways of sheltering themselves from the elements on their vacation. He said, "Buy a van." Piggybacking on that idea, she said, "Rent a recreation vehicle for two weeks each year."

5. *List every idea* (or ask the other person if she would like to list them). Be sure *each* idea is recorded in a few of the *speaker's* key words when possible. The

person holding the pen should not become a self-appointed editor, censor, or judge—just a recorder. When brainstorming in a group it is often helpful to have two or more recorders working at newsprint pads on easels.

6. *Avoid attaching people's names to the ideas they suggest or listing each person's contribution separately.* School teachers will often list their ideas in one column and students' ideas in another column. Many parents make the same mistake unthinkingly. The goal is for the two people or group to come up with the best ideas they can. All parties contribute to the climate which nurtures creativity, each puts forth ideas which triggers the thinking of others—so in fact, even if one person makes a contribution which is adopted, it is a group effort. Focusing on *who* gave words to the idea is dysfunctional.

Research findings demonstrate that it is important not to come into a problem-solving session with the attitude that there is only one adequate solution to this conflict.[17] *Solution rigidity* is responsible for the failure of many problem-solving efforts. Once you begin utilizing this process regularly, you will probably be amazed at the number of "elegant" solutions there are for very difficult problems.

Step 3: Select the Solution (or Combination of Solutions) That Will Best Meet Both Parties' Needs

If clarification is necessary on some of the solutions that emerged in the brainstorming, this is the time to do it. The clarification should be as succinct as possible. The "no evaluation" guideline applies to the clarification period as well as to the generation of the ideas. If no clarification is needed, begin the selection process.

The following guidelines have proven helpful in evaluating what proposed solution or combination of solutions will be selected:

1. *Ask the other what proposed alternatives she would favor in the solution of the problem.* Do *not* eliminate solutions one by one. This consumes needless time and can decrease people's problem-solving attentiveness and effectiveness.
2. *State which alternatives look best to you.* Make sure your needs get met.
3. *See which choices coincide.*
4. *Jointly decide on one or more of the alternatives.* Usually, if the needs were well defined at the start, several of the same alternatives will be selected by *both* people.

Be sure the other person is satisfied with the solution arrived at. It is to your advantage as well as hers that both of you accept the choice. If it meets her needs, she will be far more motivated to see that the solution is implemented. As someone wisely said, "People do things for their reasons, not for ours."

Consensus is the decision-making method most appropriate in the collaborative problem-solving process. Consensus means finding "a sense of the meeting," a willingness to accept the group's decision. Rensis and Jane Likert write:

> The process of arriving at a consensus is a free and open exchange of ideas which continues until agreement has been reached. The process assures that each individual's concerns are heard and understood and that a sincere attempt has been made to take them into consideration in the search for and the formulation of a conclusion. This conclusion may not reflect the exact wishes of each member, but since it does not violate the deep concerns of anyone, it can be agreed upon by all.* [18]

When two people are working the collaborative problem-solving method, it may seem too formal to say that decisions are arrived at by consensus. However, the spirit of consensus pervades the collaborative process whenever it is used. Majority votes, parliamentary procedures, adherence to *Robert's Rules of Order*—these are not used in collaborative problem solving. (Straw votes may help to determine the sense of a sizable group—but these are not binding and often are not necessary.)

Once both parties have selected a solution which seems mutually desirable, it is important to try to foresee the possible consequences of that solution or combination of solutions. Seemingly desirable solutions are often ambushed by unforeseen consequences. While it is impossible to accurately predict all outcomes, people who are skilled in problem solving do not overlook this important activity.

Step 4: Plan Who Will Do What, Where, and by When

Sometimes people are so elated at arriving at a decision that meets everyone's diverse needs that they celebrate prematurely rather than work out the nitty-gritty of how the solution will be implemented. However, a solution is no better than its implementation. The parties involved need to decide who will do

---

*In one-to-one problem-solving, it has been my experience that both individuals are usually pleased with their mutually arrived-at solution. Sometimes in groups (and occasionally when only two people are involved) the mutually arrived-at solution "may not reflect the exact wishes of each member." You may be asking, "How is this different from compromise?" Compromise is achieved by "mutual concessions." Consensus is a process that arrives at "group solidarity"—a "general agreement." There is a fine but important line between compromise and consensus that deserves longer treatment than is possible in this chapter. One of the major differences between the two is emotional: People usually like a consensus better than a compromise. Also, there is frequently a relational difference. The process of consensus tends to create closer relationships than does compromise

what, where, and by when. Sometimes determining the how—the methods to be utilized—is also important. It is helpful, too, to specify times when the people involved will get together to check how the implementation of the solution is going.

Many people are forgetful. Others have memories which are inexact. It is usually desirable to *write out* the agreement that was reached, including the details of who will do what by when. The written agreement is not meant to be anything more than a reminder. Some people like to keep a statement of the problem, the ideas brainstormed, the solution, and the implementation decisions on one page. In one family I know, people date and sign the papers and keep all the agreements in a folder in a particular drawer. They enjoy reading agreements from years ago in much the same way that other families enjoy looking at photographs of various events in the family's history.

Step 5: Implement the Plan

Until this point in the process we have been thinking and talking. Now we are at the point of *action*. There has been mutual agreement about who will do what by when. Now is the time to do it.

The first four steps usually are part of a discussion that takes place at one period of time. When the discussion is completed the parties usually separate and do their part of the agreed-upon action steps. As a gesture of good faith, it is important to complete your action steps on schedule. If the other was a full participant in the problem-solving process, and if her needs were met by the solution, there is a high likelihood that she, too, will carry out her part of the agreement.

Still, people are human and sometimes they do not live up to agreements which were made with great sincerity. In these situations an assertion message, followed by reflective listening, may be appropriate.

As you do collaborative problem solving with another person, skip Step 5 (implementing) and move directly to Step 6. Implementation of the plan is of crucial importance, but it doesn't begin until you and the other person have completed this discussion.

Step 6: Evaluate the Problem-Solving Process and, at a Later Date, How Well the Solution Turned Out

After a problem-solving session I like to take a few minutes to discuss how the process went. The kinds of things we discuss include some of the following topics:

- How each of us feels in general about the process we just went through.
- What each liked most about the process.
- What each liked least about the process.
- Something that bothered me.
- Something that bothered the other.
- Something I wish I hadn't done or said.
- Something the other wishes she hadn't said or done.
- What each of us can do better next time.

Toward the end of the problem-solving session I always make sure we set a time to see how well the solution is working for us. Some action plans do not stand the test of time—either in total or in part. If an action plan is not working, it should be corrected, or a new one should be instituted. If it is working well, why not celebrate having worked through a difficult issue with success?

WHAT THIS PROBLEM-SOLVING METHOD COMMUNICATES

A consultant-friend, Peter Lawson, points out that each step of the collaborative problem-solving method has an important mutually affirming message that may be communicated at a conscious or subconscious level. Through the years I have added some of my ideas to his. This is the message I find in each step of the problem-solving process:

Step	Message
I. Define the problem in terms of needs.	Your needs are important to me; you are important to me. I am important enough to have my needs expressed and heard. We really can understand one another.
II. Brainstorm possible solutions.	I value your creative thinking and mine, and believe that together we can be even more creative in dealing with our common problem.
III. Select the solutions(s) that will meet both (all) parties' needs—and check possible consequences.	I want you to have your needs satisfied, I want my needs satisfied, and I won't accept either one of us denying our uniqueness.
IV. Plan who will do what, where, and by when.	You and I are willing to make joint decisions and coordinated plans to assist each other in getting our needs met.
V. Implement the plan.	You and I have the power to change our behaviors in ways that can enhance our lives and improve our relationship. Our

	commitment to each other is expressed in action as well as in words.
VI. Evaluate the process . . .	You and I want to continually improve the way we solve problems that arise between us. In honesty and caring we will discuss our feelings about this interaction.
and the solution.	We are not locked into any solution, policy, or program. If our decision is not as good for us as we had hoped, we have the power to remake it—better.[19]

COLLABORATIVE PROBLEM SOLVING IN ACTION

Before and After

Sonje and her husband, Woody, have had frequent conflicts about one issue in their life. Sonje is a violinist in a symphony orchestra and has to practice at least an hour each day. During this time, Woody often turns the stereo on at high volume. The stereo spoils Sonje's concentration and grates on her nerves. Sonje gave this description of her behavior before—and then after—learning collaborative problem-solving skills.

My usual response to his action was to say, "Will you turn that damned thing down!" or "You're being very inconsiderate!"

One day I decided to answer his blaring of the stereo with an assertion message. I said, "Woody, when you turn the volume up on the stereo when I am practicing, I get very frustrated because my concentration suffers."

After reflective listening (in which I found out a lot of other things) I learned that my husband also had a problem. He didn't like listening to me while I worked out bowings and fingerings for difficult sections in a piece of music. So he tried to drown out those sounds when I practice.

Our brainstorming produced several alternative solutions, including:

I practice directly after school before he comes home.

We install soundproofing in my practice room at home.

I practice on my free period in school (Sonje is a public school teacher).

We buy headphones for his stereo.

Et cetera.

Of the twelve solutions, eleven were not feasible for one reason or another. We purchased a set of headphones and Woody can crank up the volume on his stereo as loudly as he wants with no inconvenience to me or our neighbors.

Of course, this wasn't textbook-smooth in the real-life situation. A few roadblocks slipped in and my reflective listening left something to be desired. But by the frequent use of the skills of the communication skills course we are becoming more aware of each other at the feeling level and are better at meeting each other's needs. Our relationship has improved and we both feel more fulfilled.

Third-Party Problem Solving

One person who has collaborative problem-solving abilities can act as a facilitator to other people who are struggling with an interpersonal conflict of needs.

A high school teacher described his third-party role in problem solving:

Student A and student B were fighting in the corridor. I separated them and took them to my room. After I listened to them for a while, they calmed down. This was the situation they described. As the end of the marking period approached, the students' industrial arts projects were due. Both students were involved with complicated projects, each requiring the use of a special clamp. The shop was equipped with only one of these clamps, and, since both students were aware of this, each had decided he would use it first. Their anxiety over not being able to complete the project resulted in the fight in the hall.

At my suggestion, the two boys decided to try using the collaborative problem-solving method. The problem was that each boy needed to complete his project before the end of the term which was close at hand.

Five possible solutions were generated by the brainstorming:

1. Student A would complete his project first, then student B.
2. Student B would complete his project first, then student A.
3. One or both students would change to a different project.
4. Another clamp would be obtained.
5. A method would be worked out to allow both students to complete their projects as planned by sharing the clamp.

When we evaluated these options, solutions 1 and 2 were impractical because there wasn't enough time remaining in the term to complete one project and then the other. Number 3 was also ruled out for lack of time (and because neither student liked that alternative). Solution 4 was the most popular. Unfortunately, the industrial arts instructor told us that the particular clamp had to be ordered from an out-of-town supplier and couldn't be received in time to help the boys. Solution 5 was all that was left. By analyzing the steps involved in the individual projects, we realized that student A needed the clamp in the early stages of his project and student B would not need it until one of his final steps. With cooperation and coordination the two would be able to successfully complete their projects without undue delay to either.

The students planned a specific schedule. Student A completed his use of the clamp while student B worked on the parts of his project which did not require the clamp. A then turned the the clamp over to B, and both completed their projects on time.

Some days later we evaluated the solution. Each had been able to complete his project on time and of such quality as to receive high grades and present the projects as gifts to their families. They were thoroughly satisfied with the results of their problem solving.

HANDLING THE CRUCIAL PRELIMINARIES

Deal with strong feelings *before* problem solving. Emotions are often strong when there is a problem between people. If the other has strong feelings, or if both of you do, use the conflict resolution method to reduce the emotional stress. If you are the only one with strong feelings, before you begin problem solving find a way to "dump your bucket without filling the other person's bucket." Failure to first deal with the emotion is one of the most common barriers to successful use of this method.

Be sure the right people are involved in the problem-solving session. The people who should be present are (1) those who are affected by the outcome, and (sometimes) (2) those who have the needed data.

Negotiate a time and place in which to do the problem solving. Make sure the location is suitable. I like privacy so I can let my hair down, the TV and radio off, a way to intercept incoming telephone calls, and so on. Furthermore, I usually ask for one-half to three-quarters of an hour. I rarely need that much time, but it is important to complete the process in one sitting for all but the most complicated problems. Then, too, you never know when you will run into a snag that will take longer than anticipated to work out.

If someone says, "What do you want to see me about?" I may simply say, "Let's wait until we can have more time to discuss it." This may raise the other's tension level, but that could be better than getting into difficult issues in an inopportune time and place. You may have to use the conflict resolution method if you continue to avoid mentioning the topic. On the other hand, there will be times when it is appropriate to disclose what you want to discuss.

The next preliminary is to write out the assertion message with which you will start out the problem-solving session. Yes, *write* it out. It is very important for you to be very clear about your own needs and able to state them accurately and nonjudgmentally. By now, you may think you are a seasoned pro at writing assertion messages. Nontheless, there is a high probability that the problem-solving session will be more productive if you are prepared with a well-worded message that you have committed to writing (usually for your eyes only).

When you begin the problem-solving session, explain the method you would like to use and why you would like to use it. I find two compelling reasons for using the method. First, all the other options are so bad. It may be that the last time you and the other person interacted about conflicting needs, the result was disappointing to one or both of you and that one or both experienced anger, resentment, frustration, or "all of the above." The second major reason for my wanting to use the method is that both of us will get our needs met.

When you spell out the problem-solving process and your reasons for wanting to use it, you may well encounter strong resistance. (The resistance is usually far stronger if you try to lead the other through the process without advance notice.) The other person may suspect that you are trying to gain an upper hand by changing the rules. She may feel uneasy that you know how to use this process and she doesn't. And she may be very skeptical that both of you can get your needs met. She may think that this is a contradiction in terms.

If the other person is resistant, become a listener to her resistance energy. You will probably be tempted to explain or even to persuade. These tend to be roadblocks and using them will probably only stiffen the resistance. Reflective listening, however, usually enables the other to express herself, reduce her stress, develop more trust, and ultimately begin the problem-solving process. This is not a manipulative technique. ("OK, she's being resistant so I'll use listening on her.") It is an honest attempt to understand the other person's emotions while allowing her to vent her "negative" feelings. As we saw earlier, when a person feels understood, she feels better. If my goal is to work cooperatively with someone toward a common goal, we need to have all our energies directed as positively as possible toward that goal. Reflective listening to resistance about this way of resolving the needs, then, is the final step of preparation, though this may have to be followed by your reasons for wanting to use this method. Sometimes there is no resistance and this phase of preparation is not required.

WHAT DO I DO WHEN COLLABORATIVE PROBLEM SOLVING DOESN'T WORK?

People taught by my associates and myself tell us that they have a high success rate with these skills. When the process doesn't work well for them, they have usually fallen into one of the common traps in this process, or one of the parties has a hidden agenda, or the process needs to be recycled—or they are using the skill in too difficult a situation for their level of competence.

Avoid the Common Traps in the Process

People commonly fall into one or more of the following five traps when doing collaborative problem solving.

Not handling the emotions first. If emotions are high, they need to be brought into normal range through the use of the conflict resolution method before the problem-solving process begins. Many businessmen have told us that they have used this six-step process before taking the course. Most of them said it worked fairly well for them sometimes, but was ineffective on other occasions. Most of the times when it didn't work were when strong emotions were involved but were ignored. A central teaching of this program is the *"Primacy of the emotions."* When feelings are strong they must be addressed *first*—before anything else is done.

Not defining the problem properly. Many people do not listen long enough, acceptingly enough, or effectively enough to understand the other person's need. And they may not have specified their own need accurately enough through a well-stated three-part assertion message.

Sometimes people try to use this method when no tangible needs are involved—only values issues. This process is not intended for use in values conflicts.

Evaluating or clarifying during brainstorming. The majority of people we have taught are strongly tempted to interrupt the brainstorming step with evaluations, clarifications, comments, giving examples, and so on. This hinders and may ultimately kill effective brainstorming. Since the quality of your solution hinges so largely on the effectiveness of your brainstorming, it is important to avoid falling into this trap. If the other begins to evaluate or digress in this step, be quick, yet gentle and firm, in bringing her back to the process. If your intervention is experienced as a put-down, that in itself may disrupt the brainstorming.

Not working out the nitty-gritty details. Once harmony has been established in the relationship and a mutually agreeable solution is discovered, many people end the problem-solving process. It seems to some people that it signals a lack of trust to work out the details of implementation at this time.

Other people become impatient. They are not used to spending so much time working out problems with other people. So they do not spell out the specific next steps to be taken; the solution does not get implemented and they are apt to say, "That process just doesn't work."

Not following up to see that the action steps are carried out. Just because you arrived at a harmonious agreement doesn't mean it will be put into practice. Many people have crowded schedules, numerous priorities, and other complications that may interfere with their efforts on behalf of your common plan. Lack of follow-through on the other person's part doesn't necessarily mean that they don't care about you or about the agreed-upon solution. It can be important, therefore, to set and use realistic checkpoints to evaluate the progress you are making in the resolution of your joint problem.

Smoke Out Hidden Agendas

Sometimes when people are not making adequate progress in the problem-solving process it is due to an underlying problem that has not been brought into the open. This problem constitutes a large emotional barrier between the two people. When this seems to be the case, you may wish to offer a door opener like, "Seems like something is hanging us up. Is there something else in our relationship that we should talk about first?" Sometimes the other person will say, "No, there's nothing wrong"—and then will gradually spell out the hidden barrier.

Recycle the Process

Sometimes when you cannot reach consensus on a solution it is because one or two steps of the process need to be done more effectively. The problem usually becomes evident at Step 3 (selecting the solution). It is often helpful to try again. Assert your needs clearly and succinctly. Listen long and hard until you have discovered the other's need. Then, with the joint problem clearly in mind brainstorm freely without evaluation, clarification, explanation, or digression. Many times a mutually beneficial solution is reached on the second time through the process.

APPLICATIONS OF COLLABORATIVE PROBLEM-SOLVING

Goal Setting

When goals are being established, the collaborative problem-solving process can often be used effectively. For example, Red decided that he and his wife Eilene should place $1,000 per year in a long-term savings account. Their income was limited, however, and that goal seemed to conflict with Eilene's objective of quitting her job and returning to graduate school. Previously, Red and Eilene would have fought about the issue. He would ultimately have won and she would have sulked. That's the pattern they had developed over the years. This time, however, they both stated their needs, brainstormed solutions, and went through the remainder of the collaborative problem-solving process. They decided not to save at all for three years while she went to school and to save $1,700 per year for the first six years after she began working again. Each was pleased because the needs of both would be met.

A high school teacher wanted to involve her students in planning their next unit of study. Her primary need was to adequately cover the material in the unit so students would be able to pass the statewide test (Regents' Examination) at the end of the year. The students shared that need but they had other concerns. They placed more emphasis on one part of the unit which was applicable to them, wanted fewer lectures, and desired a way of sorting out and discussing the critical issues—and no tests on Fridays (when many of the other teachers gave tests). The class listed the top-priority items for them and selected a committee of five to work with the teacher in planning the who-will-do-what-by-when steps and to assist in implementation. At the end of the unit, the teacher and most of the students were generally pleased with the results, but they learned some things that could be improved the next time around. Moreover, the class did exceptionally well on the statewide tests.

Harlow was a manager in a plant that pays lip service to a system of managing called Management by Objectives (MBO). One of the basic ideas of MBO is that the boss and his subordinate are to collaborate in determining the objectives which the employee will be accountable for achieving in the coming year and by which he will be evaluated at the end of the year. Harlow said, "Up until now, the whole thing has been a farce because none of us had been taught the interpersonal skills to make the system work."

After he and his boss had taken a course in management communication skills, they discussed the accomplishments and problems of the past year and then began to set goals for the coming year. Harlow's boss briefly outlined the company's objectives for the year, the division's objectives, and his own objectives to help the division and company meet their objectives. The boss's *needs* were to meet his objectives, and in order to do that, Harlow would have to find a way of contributing to those goals.

Then Harlow was asked what he most wanted to achieve in the coming year. Once his needs were clear, Harlow and his boss combined their needs into one statement, brainstormed ways of meeting both sets of needs, and developed a set of mutually acceptable goals for the coming year. The action plans were developed at a later meeting. According to Harlow, "MBO never made any sense before. Now I know what my boss and division wants and needs and why. And we've found a way to use my skills and harness my interests better than ever. If the periodic review sessions we've scheduled go this well, I think I should get the results the company needs and yet meet many of my own needs, too."

In a One-to-One
"Helping Relationship"

When another person has a strong need, listening skills are appropriate. Sometimes, however, after listening reflectively through the presenting problem to the real problem, the process may become stalemated because the person with the need lacks skill in problem solving and decision making. If you think you have listened long enough to the other to understand her core issue, it may be desirable to explain the problem-solving model to her and ask if she would like to try it in her situation. If she accepts, your role is to help her proceed step by step through the process. Since this is not collaborative problem solving, only her need is stated in Step 1. In Step 2, your job is to keep her brainstorming and not evaluating or explaining her solutions. (Sometimes it is appropriate for you to contribute some—not most!—of the possible solutions in Step 3.) The selection of the best possible alternative is hers alone to decide, though you may ask her to anticipate the possible consequences of choosing each of the most desirable possibilities. The remaining steps of the process are handled in a similar manner. In this way you enable the other person to solve her own problems and at the same time to learn a problem-solving process that can help her handle future problems.

Other Applications

This process has many other applications. I will mention two more. It has been successfully used in setting rules and policies. Whether they are spoken or unspoken, rules are a part of every relationship, family, and organization. It is desirable for the people affected by rules or policies to participate in determining them. In large groups this may have to be done by representatives. At the beginning of the year some classroom teachers work with the class in mutually setting the rules for their behavior during the year using the collaborative problem-solving method. As the need for new rules arises during the year, the group adds them. When some rules prove unnecessary, they are dropped by group action. When the "principle of participation" is employed in the setting of rules, they tend to make more sense to people and to be observed with greater regularity.

Someone once said that life is a procession of problems. This six-step problem-solving process can also be used by a single individual for the various personal problems in her life that could benefit from a systematic approach.

SUMMARY

There are several alternatives to collaborative problem solving—including denial of the problem, avoidance, capitulation, domination, and compromise. Any one of these may be appropriate in certain occasions, but consistent use of these methods leads to negative consequences.

The collaborative problem-solving method usually has favorable consequences. Its six steps include:

1. *Define* the problem in terms of *needs*, not solutions.
2. *Brainstorm* possible solutions.
3. *Select* the solution that will best meet both parties' needs (after having checked out possible consequences).
4. *Plan* who will do what, where, and by when.
5. *Implement* the solution.
6. *Evaluate* how you worked the problem-solving process and, at a later date, how well the solution turned out.

The "preliminaries" that take place before people begin the first step of the process are usually of critical importance. If the problem-solving process doesn't work, recheck to make sure you avoided the common traps that are barriers to the effectiveness of this method, look for hidden agendas, and/or recycle the process.

This method has many applications at home, at work, and in school. It can be used in goal setting, as a supplement to listening at a certain stage in helping relationships, in rule setting, and in individual problem solving.

This is a most important skill. As George Prince says, "When you fail to use your creative problem-solving talent, you strike at the quality of your own life."[20]

CHAPTER FIFTEEN

Three Essentials for Effective Communication

Guard your inner spirit more than any treasure,
for it is the source of life.[1]
                                    —An ancient sage

IN COMMUNICATION, SKILLS ALONE ARE INSUFFICIENT

Researchers and theorists in the behavioral sciences claim there are three key qualities that foster improved communication: genuineness, nonpossessive love, and empathy.

Genuineness means being honest and open about one's feelings, needs, and ideas. It is a stubborn refusal to let one's real self "travel incognito."

Nonpossessive love involves accepting, respecting, and supporting another person in a nonpaternalistic and freeing way.

Empathy refers to the ability to really see and hear another person and understand him from his perspective.

In the late 1950s, psychologist Carl Rogers hypothesized that these three qualities are essential to constructive communication.[2] Since then, over one hundred research studies have been conducted which support Rogers's theory. Empirical data show that high levels of these key attitudes in therapists lead to constructive relationships with clients. Low levels are associated with harmful therapist-client interactions. Other data show that teachers who embody these qualities foster greater student achievement than teachers who are deficient in them. A student with these qualities is likely to improve his roommate's grade-point average substantially.

Physicians and nurses can facilitate a patient's return to health through the expression of these characteristics as well as by their surgical and pharmaceutical techniques. Managers with these attitudes elicit greater motivation and less resistance from their employees. Salespersons with these qualities tend to have customers who are more satisfied, and this is reflected positively in sales volume. Genuineness, nonpossessive love, and empathy create fulfilling marriages and constructive parent-child relationships.

Communication flows out of basic attitudes as well as through specific methods and techniques. Communication techniques are useful only insofar as they facilitate the expression of essential human qualities. The person who has mastered the skills of communication but lacks genuineness, love, and empathy will find his expertise irrelevant or even harmful. Important as they are, the techniques of communication by themselves are unable to forge satisfactory relationships.

GENUINENESS

Genuineness means being what one really is without front or façade. The authentic person experiences his feelings and is able to express those feelings when appropriate. A genuine person can spontaneously be himself with another so they know him as he truly is. "What you see is what you get."

By contrast, that inauthentic person conceals his real thoughts, feelings, values, and motives. His defensiveness and concealment before others unfortunately block his own self-awareness. Soon, that which is most authentic and spontaneous in him is buried so deep that not even he can recognize it.

Genuineness is essential to all vital relationships. To the degree that I lack authenticity, I am unable to relate significantly to any other person. I must dare to be me to be able to relate to you.

Nathaniel Hawthorne wrote a short story about a man who would not be himself with others. The man vanished into thin air whenever the people around him left the room. His whole identity was dissipated by his efforts to be the kind of person he thought others wanted him to be. No core self was left when the "audience" was gone.

No one can be fully self-revealing. Everyone pretends to be something other than he really is—at least part of the time. Indeed, the word *personality* comes from the Latin *persona*—an actor's mask. The genuine person knows it is impossible to be completely self-revealing, but is committed to a responsible honesty and openness with others.

Genuineness has three ingredients: self-awareness, self-acceptance, and self-expression.

Self-Awareness

The noted nineteenth-century political cartoonist Thomas Nast once attended a party with a group of friends. Someone asked him to draw a caricature of everyone present. This he did with a few skilled strokes of his pencil. The sketches were passed around for the guests to identify. Everyone recognized the other persons, but hardly anyone recognized the caricature of himself.

Though Freud and others have demonstrated that it is not easy to know oneself, it is clearly possible to grow in that ability. Many techniques have been devised to foster self-understanding.[3]

To increase one's self-awareness, however, it is not necessary to read books, attend workshops, or employ an Eastern spiritual discipline. *Each person has more understanding of himself than he is now using.* It is common to tune out the messages from our inner self or to ignore them if and when they have made themselves heard. For example, a person may feel lonely and then try to distract himself from this unpleasant awareness by turning on the TV set. Another person may feel insignificant and become a "work-aholic" to drive that awareness from consciousness. One of the quickest ways of following the Socratic injunction "Know thyself" is to refuse to tune out or ignore the awareness about self that is at least dimly perceived by the conscious mind.

Self-Acceptance

People ignore their inner promptings primarily because they do not accept the full range of their feelings and thoughts. Many people are ashamed of their anger or their sexual impulses and fantasies. Though these are part of every normal life, many people have been at least partially programmed to think these dimensions of themselves are "bad" or "sinful." Sometimes we compare ourselves with the façade others present us, intimidate ourselves, and become less self-accepting.

Many types of experience can lead to increased self-acceptance. Encounter groups under effective leadership, psychotherapy with a genuine, insightful, and understanding therapist, friendships with accepting people, religious conversion, and many other life experiences help build self-acceptance.

Often, improved acceptance of oneself is derived from training in communication skills. Many participants in our workshops say that the most important result of the training for them is that they are more comfortable with all of their feelings and that they like themselves better after having taken the course than they did before. The ability to communicate effectively seems to effect an increase of self-esteem in many persons.

Self-Expression

Self-expression is the third ingredient of genuineness. The self-expressive person is aware of his innermost thoughts and feelings, accepts them, and, when appropriate, shares them responsibly. Even in circumstances of great anxiety, he can reveal what he feels at the moment in a frank and disarming way. David Duncombe, whose writing has significantly influenced the discussion in this section, says the authentic person's openness touches every area of his life.[4]

When bereaved or worried or embarrassed, the real person is able to disclose much of what he feels. When his actions violate his own expectations or those of others, he can admit his shortcomings. He can also give unselfconscious expression to his joy and speak freely about his successes.

When the genuine person is angry, he expresses it (as discretion permits) in a way that has maximum likelihood of removing the frustration, clearing the air, and restoring and improving his relationships. He may also responsibly express his affection without apology or excuse.

Every human being has conflicting feelings. The authentic person can openly express the degree to which his friendships, marriage, and work provide both satisfaction and frustration. When he behaves in a way that falls below his own expectations, the genuine person can express his real sorrow but can also speak of the joy he may also have experienced.

In the preceding paragraphs, several qualifying words and phrases were used. The authentic person *can* disclose his feelings, and be truly himself when it is *appropriate*. Being authentic does *not* mean unreservedly associating aloud to every person one meets about every reaction one experiences. It is simply not appropriate to be totally open about all of one's feelings with every person at all times and places.

While the authentic person does not express every feeling he has, neither does he present himself in a phony manner. He does not erect a façade that will misrepresent him. Those feelings which he *persistently* experiences will be expressed responsibly.

Genuineness does not stand alone. Love and understanding create the climate that nourishes genuineness, and these qualities enable authentic communication to be a beautiful rather than a brutal thing. One of the most delightful descriptions of the way genuineness develops is found in a children's story, *The Velveteen Rabbit*:

> "What is REAL?" asked the Rabbit one day. "Does it mean having things that buzz inside you and a stick-out handle?"
>
> "Real isn't how you are made," said the Skin Horse. . . . "When a child loves you for a long, long time, not just to play with, but REALLY loves you, then you become real. It doesn't happen all at once," said the Skin Horse. "You become. It takes a long time. . . . Generally, by the time you are Real, most of your hair has been loved off and your eyes drop out and you get loose in the joints and very shabby. But these things don't matter at all, because once you are Real, you can't be ugly, except to people who don't understand."[5]

NONPOSSESSIVE LOVE

Nonpossessive love is the second key quality that can foster meaningful communication. Many terms have been used to describe the quality that I am calling "nonpossessive love." Some of the most commonly used labels—"respect," "acceptance," "positive regard"—convey only a portion of the meaning I want to communicate. Even though *love* has such a wide range of usage that the word has been rendered almost meaningless in modern English, there are enough desirable, personal, and historical overtones to the word *love* to justify using it.

Carl Rogers says of this general characteristic that it "means a kind of love for the person as he is, providing we understand the word love as the equivalent of the theologian's term 'agape' and not in its usual romantic and possessive meanings."[6] Another noted psychotherapist, Karl Menninger, speaks of this quality as a person's "patience, his fairness, his consistency, his rationality, his kindliness, in short—his real love" for the other person.[7]

The ancient Greeks distinguished between three kinds of love. One, *Philia*, stands for friendship. It is the love of a David and a Jonathan in the Bible. It is the kind of relationship celebrated in Tennyson's *In Memoriam*. Many ancients thought of *philia* as the happiest and most fully human of all loves.[8]

Eros is affectionate love. It includes the drive of love to create and procreate but is far more inclusive than sexual love alone. It is the love of Romeo and Juliet, or of Tony and Marie in *West Side Story* (a modern version of Shakespeare's love story).

Agape (pronounced ah-GAH-pay) is concern for the well-being of other people. As Waldo Beach and H. Richard Niebuhr note, this love is "not an emotional sentiment of liking, nor romantic attraction, seeking love in return, nor yet an intellectual attitude," but "the will of the self in devotion to the neighbor."[9]

The most rewarding relationships have more than one of these components in them. The love of a man for a woman, which may begin as *eros*, is enriched by *philia* and deepened and stabilized by the commitment of *agape*. The dedication of this book refers to a relationship in which all three of these ingredients are present.

Loving Is Not Necessarily Liking

One of the basic issues that at one time or another confronts virtually everybody is this: How do I love somebody that I think I should love but whom I don't even like? Teachers often believe they should care for every child in their classes, but of course there are always some they dislike. Some managers think they should like every person reporting to them, but, alas, they invariably find that they dislike some of their employees. Parents often believe they should love their children equally, but when they are aware of their feelings, they may note a greater fondness for one child than another. There may even be stages in a child's development when the parent simply does not like his own child. *Frequently people do not like the people they believe they are supposed to love.* This is a major problem for both the theory and practice of effective interpersonal communication.

The group of scholars who have wrestled most seriously with the theoretical aspects of this problem are theologians of the Judeo-Christian tradition. Because their ethic calls for love of neighbor and because they typically have found it difficult to even like some of the people they were commanded to love, many theologians addressed this issue rigorously. Their insights on this topic are relevant to the relational problems all of us face, whatever our religious convictions (or lack of them).

The theologians overwhelmingly believe that commanded (or ought-to) love has a largely nonemotional meaning. Millar Burrows in his *Outline of Biblical Theology* asserts that what is demanded "is not an emotion but an attitude of the will. . . . to love one's neighbor is not to feel affection for him but to wish and seek his good."[10] The Jewish philosopher and theologian Martin Buber put it this way: "The act of relation is not an emotion or a feeling. . . . Feelings accompany love, but they do not constitute it. . . . Hence love is not the enjoyment of a wonderful emotion . . . but the responsibility of an *I* for a *Thou*."[11]

In his *Basic Christian Ethics*, Paul Ramsey gives the best explanation I have ever read of what nonemotional, willed love is like. Dr. Ramsey compares "willed love" for others with the tendency in humans to seek their own good:

> How exactly do you love yourself? Answer this question and you will know how a [person] should love his neighbor. You naturally love yourself for your own sake. You wish your own good, and you do so even when you may have a certain distaste for the kind of person you are. Liking yourself or thinking yourself very nice, or not, has fundamentally nothing to do with the matter. After a failure of some sort, the will-to-live soon returns and you . . . lay hold expectantly on another possibility of attaining some good for yourself. . . .
>
> [Agape] means such love for self *inverted*. Therefore, it has nothing to do with feelings, emotions, taste, preference, temperament, or any of the qualities in other people which arouse feelings of revulsion or attraction, negative or positive preferences in us. . . . [Love] depends on the direction of the will, the orientation of intention in an act, not on stirring emotion. The commandment requires [a person] to aim at his neighbor's good just as unswervingly as man by nature wishes his own.[12]

Willed love, then, should not be confused with liking another person. To suppose I can *like* everyone I meet leads to phoniness and guilt. Affection can often be nurtured, but it cannot be turned on or off like a faucet. I'm so glad to be rid of the idea that I am supposed to like everybody! There are people I don't like. Their behaviors are disagreeable to me. Our personal chemistries do not seem compatible. There is no reason to force myself to be fond of people I do not like. But I can will to do good and not evil to them. I can will to seek the highest good for them. Within the meaning of this definition, I can love even those people whom I do not like.

It is often not the most lovable individual who stands most in need of love, but the least lovable. Within any given individual's life, the moments when he seems most impossible are the times he stands most in need of love. Lorraine Hansberry's *Raisin in the Sun* makes this point. A grown son, Walter, has squandered the family's money, with the result that they must live in a less desirable environment than they had planned to. He has trampled on the family pride. His sister is furious with him. It seems like there is nothing in him left to love, and she feels only contempt for him. His mother is also hurt and disappointed, but she knows that love can persist when liking has all but disappeared. At this moment of crisis, she reminds the family of the essence of agape when she says:

> There is always something left to love. And if you ain't learned that, you ain't learned nothing. Have you cried for that boy today? I don't mean for yourself and for the family 'cause we lost the money. I mean for him; what he been through and what it done to him. Child, when do you think is the time to love somebody the most; when they done good and made things easy for everybody? Well then, you ain't through learning—because that ain't the time at all. It's when he's at his lowest and can't believe in hisself 'cause the world done whipped him so. When you starts measuring somebody, measure him right, child, measure him right. Make sure you done taken into account what hills and valleys he come through before he got to wherever he is.[13]

Fortunately, loving and liking often do go hand in hand. But when they do not, we can love the people we do not like—we can will them good. Genuineness reminds us not to feign affection when it is not felt. No one is helped by an insincere expression of liking. Because we are human, there will be times when we cannot will love for specific other persons. In those times, I generally choose to avoid that person during the period when I am not able to love him.

Acceptance Is an Important Expression of Love

Acceptance is best defined as an attitude of *neutrality* toward another person or persons. When a person is accepting, he offers an atmosphere largely uncontaminated by evaluations of the other's thoughts, feelings, or behaviors. The other person can cry or laugh or be angry—and even if his *behavior* is disliked, *he* is accepted. For that reason, I sometimes call acceptance *"in-spite-of-love."* I can often provide an atmosphere of neutrality for the other *in spite of* the fact that his behaviors and outlooks may not correspond with my values, and may even conflict with them.

Every person stands in need of acceptance. No one is perfect. Everyone has fallen short of what he could be. Each has failed to fulfill his responsibilities at times. Each of us has done things that are hurtful to ourselves and others. When I am different from others, or less than my best self, acceptance by another helps me realize that despite my inadequacies and eccentricities, I can be loved as I am. Acceptance nourishes constructive self-love and helps mobilize my resources to maximize my potential.

As I endeavor to be more accepting, I find it helpful to be aware of several facts about human nature:

1. *No one is perfectly accepting.* Human beings are finite creatures. Some measure of nonacceptance is part of what it means to be a member of the species *Homo sapiens.* We are people, not gods.

2. *Some people tend to be more accepting than others.* A number of factors, including early experiences in one's family and possibly even one's genetic inheritance, influence a person's general level of acceptance.

3. *The level of acceptance in a person is constantly shifting.* Thomas Gordon points out that changes in one's self, in the other person, and in the environment cause fluctuations in one's level of acceptance.[14] When a person is rested, unhurried, and happy, for example, he is more likely to be accepting than when he is unhappy, tired, tense, and rushed. Instead of striving for the impossible goal of total consistency in human relationships, it is more feasible to strive for congruence with one's inner feelings and responsiveness to the situation in which one finds himself.

4. *It is natural to have favorites.* When a person tries to express love equally to all his children, friends, or students, he often ends up relating on the basis of the lowest common emotional denominator. Or he offers a phony niceness and friendliness to those he likes least—thereby increasing the distance in those relationships.

5. *Each of us can become more accepting.* Some of the skills described in this book help people increase their level of acceptance. It is important to remember, however, that no one can become perfectly accepting and that some people, as a result of family environment and many other factors, have a head start in the ability to be accepting.

6. *Pseudoacceptance is harmful to other people and to relationships.* Some people pretend to be accepting of another's behavior but are merely playing a role. They may be playing the role of a "good parent" or a "good teacher" or a "nice guy." They try to show acceptance, but inwardly they feel nonaccepting. When a person feels nonaccepting inwardly, he or she may say they are not irritated by the other and that they are happy about the relationship. But their nonverbals communicate the truth. The look in the eyes and the tone of voice shout one's nonacceptance so loudly that the verbal expression of acceptance is

drowned out. The person feigning acceptance ultimately communicates nonacceptance. If one cannot become genuinely accepting of another person, it is better to admit it openly. Though conflict may occur through such honesty, reconciliation can also be achieved and a meaningful relationship ultimately established.

7. *Lastly, acceptance is not synonymous with approval.* I can accept another person's feelings and still not approve of his behaviors. It is possible to be accepting and confrontative at the same time.

Respect: Another Core Element of Love

Genuine love respects what Buber refers to as the "elemental otherness of the other." It recognizes the sanctity of the other's privacy, it supports his self-direction, and it fosters greater potency rather than greater dependency on the other's part. Love maintains a reverence—a distance—in the relationship.

Real love is not intrusive. It does not violate the privacy of others. It does not try to force its way into the inner sanctum of another's personality.

Parents are often tempted to pry into their children's lives. They would like to prolong the period of self-disclosure that is typical of many young children. But children have a psychological need to develop a private life. They need to keep some things secret from their parents and others. When their child becomes more closed to them, parents often become frustrated or irritated. They typically ply the child or teenager with many questions. Some even turn into detectives and watch stealthily from a hiding place to see what their child is doing and with whom he is doing it.

This tendency to push into the secret places of another's life is not limited to the relationship between parents and children. Spouses often intrude on each other's privacy, teachers on their pupils' private lives, and managers and supervisors on the personal domain of their employees; counselors sometimes force their way into areas that their clients are not yet ready to disclose; and so on.

The development of each person's individuality hinges on his ability to keep self-selected parts of his life secret. The Swiss psychotherapist Paul Tournier has written a marvelous small book entitled *Secrets*, in which he says:

> To have secrets, to know how to keep them to one's self, to give them up only willingly, constitutes the first action in the formation of the individual. . . . To respect the secrecy of whoever it may be, even your own child, is to respect his individuality. To intrude upon his private life, to violate his secrecy, is to violate his individuality. . . . Every man, to feel respected as an individual, needs to feel absolutely free to say what he wishes and to keep as a secret what he wishes.[15]

Genuine love does not trespass on the secret places of another's life. *Real love supports the other's self-direction.* Genuine love persistently refrains from possessiveness, domination, or the imposition of values. It allows and encourages the other to be "himself in freedom." The questions Carl Rogers raises for psychotherapists are relevant to us all:

> Do we respect [the other person's] capacity and his right to self-direction, or do we basically believe that his life would be best guided by us? To what extent do we have a need and a desire to dominate others? Are we willing for the individual to select and choose his own values, or are our actions guided by the conviction (usually unspoken) that he would be happiest if he permitted us to select for him his values and standards and goals?[16]

Genuine love fosters great potency in the other. It diminishes his dependency. It does not conspire with his weakness, but calls forth the other's strength. Love holds back from "helping" another when that "help" is likely to diminish the other's responsibility for his own life. Some of the most successful work with drug-dependent persons carefully avoids many of the things that therapists, teachers, parents, managers, and others typically do that diminish the strength, resourcefulness, and self-esteem of others. David Deitch describes the attitude engendered in the early Daytop program:

> I will relate to you in a manner that benefits the dignity of man. It means that I refuse to act as though you are fragile, or crippled, or damned. I will, instead, regard you as capable of fulfilling your aspirations, and I will expect you to try to be productive.[17]

Love is being present with another person in his time of need. But love does not do for the other person those things that are his to do for himself. True love is a highly disciplined caring that resists the many enticing ways of helping that tend to enfeeble the other.

Love maintains a reverence—a distance—in the relationship. People commonly think of love as closeness—and that is certainly an important aspect of love. But distance is needed, too. As H. Richard Niebuhr says:

> Love is reverence: it keeps its distance even as it draws near; it does not seek to absorb the other in the self or want to be absorbed by it; it rejoices in the otherness of the other; it desires the beloved to be what he is and does not seek to refashion him into a replica of the self or to make him a means to the self's advancement. As reverence love . . . seeks knowledge of the other, not by way of curiosity nor for the sake of gaining power but in rejoicing and wonder. In all such love there is an element of "holy fear" which is not a form of flight but rather deep respect for the otherness of the beloved and the profound unwillingness to violate his integrity.[18]

Warmth: "Love" Tends to Generate "Like"

A person may accept me and treat me with respect but still not like anything about me. Acceptance and respect may or may not be accompanied by warmth. I may be able to *survive* on an interpersonal diet of acceptance and respect, but it will take more than that for me to *flourish*. If I am to blossom, I need some warm, positive, emotional contact with people. I crave having my uniqueness noticed *and* valued. Appreciation—and to a much greater degree, affection—provide that warmth.

When there is little or no liking between people, respect and acceptance can often be willed. Once we accept and respect a person, he tends to be more himself with us. As we get to really know him, feelings of liking often follow. Willed love leads to liking much of the time.

One of the ironies of human relationships, though, is that people often tend to be less accepting and respectful of those they like most (and/or with whom they have intimate ties, such as husband/wife, child/parent, etc.) There is a tendency to try to impose our values on, and to be more judgmental and less respectful or accepting with, precisely those persons whom we like most. Our intimate relationships need the disciplined will of love as well as the warmth of liking.

EMPATHY

Empathy is the third key quality that can enrich interpersonal communication.

Two centuries ago, John Woolman walked barefoot from Baltimore to Philadelphia. He did it to receive in his own body some measure of the pain that black slaves suffered when they were forced to walk barefoot over long distances. By putting himself in the slave's place, he better understood what slavery meant to the slave. He had empathy.

An executive of a steel company in Cleveland resigned his position and applied for work as a day laborer in another city. Some of his friends thought his behavior was "bizarre." Subsequently working side by side with laborers, experiencing their life as fully as he could, he gained a very different perspective on worker's problems. He then entered the field of labor relations and became a recognized authority partly because of his ability to understand the laborer's plight. He had empathy.

Richard Watson Guilder served on a New York City commission dealing with tenement housing. He wanted to understand the plight of families burned out of their homes and to discover the cause of the many fires that destroyed that type of housing. He had a fire department gong placed in his bedroom. Every

269

tenement fire in the Lower East Side was reported on his gong so that he might personally inspect the blaze, meet the people, and investigate the causes. He had empathy.

At the close of the Civil War when many in the North felt a passionate hatred for southerners and wanted to impose a punitive peace, Abraham Lincoln tried to serve the whole country "with malice toward none, with charity for all." How did he avoid the vindictive spirit that was so common in the North? One clue comes from his statement to a friend: "I have not suffered *by* the South," he said. "I have suffered *with* the South. Their pain has been my pain. Their loss has been my loss." He had empathy.

The word *empathy* comes to us as a translation of the word used by German psychologists, *einfühlung*, which literally means "feeling into." It is the ability to understand another person pretty much as he understands himself. The empathic person is able to "crawl into another's skin" and see the world through his eyes. He listens to others in a nonprejudicial, nonjudgmental way. He hears the other person's story as the other chooses to present it and notes the special significance the story has for the other.

The Apathy-Empathy-Sympathy Continuum

I find it easier to understand empathy when I see it on a continuum that ranges from apathy to sympathy (see the following table).

Apathy	Empathy	Sympathy
"I don't care."	"Looks like you're really feeling down today."	"You *poor* thing . . ."
"That's your problem!"	"Sounds as if you were really hurt by that."	"I feel just *dreadful* for you!"

Apathy is defined in the dictionary as "a lack of feeling or a lack of interest or concern." When I am apathetic, I am uninvolved. Usually I send a nonverbal message which means something like this:

"You go your way, and I'll go mine. I wish you no harm, but I'll give you no help. I don't care to be burdened with your problems or lifted by your joys. Do me the favor of leaving me alone."

In modern urban society, it is impossible to really relate to all the people we meet. Some selective apathy is required for psychic survival. Otherwise, our interpersonal circuits would become overloaded, we would "blow a fuse" and be shut down interpersonally for a while, or we would drain our interpersonal energy and all our relationships would glow less brightly.

While selective apathy is necessary, many people are inappropriately apathetic. Some are reclusive and hide from contact with virtually all people. Some are exclusively task-oriented and only interact with others when it furthers one of their goals. Others are with people a great deal but avoid feeling-level interactions. Excessive detachment from other people and from their feelings results in a dwarfed and stunted existence.

Sympathy lies at the other end of the continuum. Sympathy is an overinvolvement in the emotion of another person or persons. Sympathy can so undermine the strength and separateness of the "helper" that he is incapable of helping when he is most needed. I have seen sympathetic people so overcome by the grief of another at a funeral home that the bereaved had to console his supposed comforter.

Sympathy is defined as "feeling *for*" another person in contrast to *empathy*, which is "feeling *with*" the other. Sympathy, though it does not come from a position of strength, is often condescending. It frequently conveys an "Oh-you-poor-thing" attitude. It weakens its receiver just when the person most needs to maintain his own strength.

There is a strong tendency for sympathy to sink into sentimentality. Sentimentality is the inappropriate experience and enjoyment of one's emotions. In this regard, Tolstoy wrote of the wealthy Russian ladies who cried at tragedies enacted at the theater but were oblivious to the discomfort of their own coachmen sitting outside in the freezing cold.

Apathy, when it is prevalent in significant relationships, can be very destructive. Consistent undiluted sympathy, I believe, is even more harmful than apathy. The condescension of pity and the inappropriate experience of emotion that is sentimentality are harmful to both the sympathizer and the object of his or her emotional binge. Sympathy, however, is seldom expressed without some empathy present. To the degree that empathy is involved, the experience of sympathy/empathy can be partially constructive.

Empathy is walking with another person into the deeper chambers of his self—while still maintaining some separateness. It involves experiencing the feelings of another without losing one's own identity. It involves accurate response to another's needs without being infected by them. The empathic person feels the hurt of the other but is not disabled by it. He senses the other person's bewilderment, anger, fear, or love *as if* it were his own feeling, but he does not lose the "as if" nature of his involvement. When a person loses the ability to separate his own feelings from the feelings of another person, he is no longer empathic.

Empathy is hard to describe because it is made up of components that seem to be opposite and contradictory. Empathy is a close identification with another person—but if the identification becomes excessive, it is no longer empathy.

Empathy is a kind of detached involvement with the feeling world of another person or persons.

The Three Components of Empathy

Recent definitions of *empathy* have suggested that this quality is comprised of three components.

First, the empathic person has a sensitive and accurate understanding of the other person's feelings while maintaining a certain separateness from the person.

Second, empathy means understanding the situation that contributed to or "triggered" those feelings. Milton Mayeroff has provided an almost poetic description of these first two elements of empathy:

> To care for another person, I must be able to understand him and his world as if I were inside it. I must be able to see, as it were, with his eyes what his world is like to him and how he sees himself. Instead of merely looking at him in a detached way from outside, as if he were a specimen, I must be able to be *with* him in his world, "going" into his world in order to sense from "inside" what life is like for him, what he is striving to be, and what he requires to grow.[19]

Finally, the empathic person communicates with the other in such a way that the other feels accepted and understood. *The communication of one's empathic understanding is crucial.* Lewis and Wigel write:

> The evidence . . . suggests that those who are perceived as being understanding have no better intellectual understanding of a subject than those who are perceived as not being understanding. . . . [If] we intend to stimulate in others a feeling of being understood, it is not important that we gain considerable information about them but rather that we help them see that we are able to perceive others and situations as they do.[20]

Specific methods that foster empathic understanding of others and help communicate that understanding to them were discussed in Part II of this book (Chapters 3–7), "Listening Skills."

Research data indicate that empathy is a potent force for good. Teachers with high levels of empathy foster greater academic growth in students than teachers with low levels of this quality. Carl Rogers says, "It is the most effective agent we know" for fostering personal growth and "improving a person's relationships and communications with others."[21]

Not only does the empathic person foster constructive change in others, but his empathy helps him develop in positive directions himself. His horizons are widened and his sensitivities are deepened by empathic contact with others.

Some psychologists believe empathy is one of the best single indices of psychological maturity.

IMPLEMENTATION OF THE CORE ATTITUDES

Genuineness, nonpossessive love, and empathy are attitudes that foster improved relationships with people. The dictionary defines an *attitude* as "a mental or emotional orientation to some object." When these three attitudes are missing, a person's relationships are diminished. When these attitudes are present, the relationships can flourish. I believe that genuineness, nonpossessive love, and empathy are *necessary conditions* for optimal communication.

Merely to hold these attitudes, however, will do limited good. Genuineness, nonpossessive love, and empathy have little or no effect on a relationship until they are communicated to the other party. These attitudes need to be expressed behaviorally. They require skills that are possible to develop and which are strong in their impact. Many of these basic interpersonal skills are taught in this book.

Some people disparage skill development in the interpersonal realm. They condescendingly call communication skills "mere techniques." They believe skill training in human relationships depersonalizes relationships. They believe that techniques may be appropriate when dealing with the world of things but that they have no place in interpersonal relationships.

In my life, however, many relationships were strained and some were destroyed because I lacked the skills to express the constructive attitudes I felt toward other people. When I did not know how to communicate the attitudes I had, the relationships gained little, if anything, from them.

One of the greatest deficiencies in our culture, it seems to me, is that a few people are highly skilled at expressing these key attitudes. It is unusual for a person to have been taught the methods by which to express his unique self and his genuine love for and understanding of others. Yet these skills are very important factors in achieving personal fulfillment and vocational effectiveness.

While some people overlook the usefulness of communication skills, other people become legalistic about them. They believe the only way you can listen to another is to follow a certain formula to the letter and that the only way to assert yourself is to follow another formula to a "t." Certain guidelines are very helpful in making the core qualities operational much of the time. The attitudes, however, can be expressed in other ways. Attitudes are broader and more basic than the guidelines that suggest specific responses. Guidelines for communication skill development are invaluable to most people—but it is helpful to remember that there is more than one way to express genuineness, or nonpossessive love, or empathy. The more a person develops his communication ability, the greater the number of constructive alternatives that become open to him. The goal, after all, is more creative and responsible freedom in relationships.

People sometimes say, "What if I lack these core attitudes? Am I fated to experience relationships that are bland at best and destructive at worst?"

It is well to remember that each of us has some degree of these attitudes within us. The pioneering psychiatrist Alfred Adler spoke of an *inborn* social feeling, an *inescapable characteristic* of empathy, that exists in all of us. Some of the core attitudes may have atrophied from disuse, some may be blocked by our reactions to life experiences, but none of us is totally deficient in these qualities.

Then, too, when we express our attitudes by means of effective communication skills, the attitudes are strengthened and nourished. The more we practice the art and skills of loving, the more loving we become. My own experience and observation of trainees makes me utterly convinced that learning and using the *skills* taught in this book will foster an increase in the *attitudes* of genuineness, nonpossessive love, and empathy.

T. S. Eliot told of people who dreamed of creating systems so perfect that no one will need to be good. In our saner moments we all know that this concept is a fallacy. Communication skills, no matter how finely structured, cannot be a substitute for authenticity, caring, and understanding. But they can help us express these qualities more effectively than many of us have been able to do in the past. And the expression of these core qualities nourishes and reinforces these characteristics. As we manage to communicate more genuinely, lovingly, and empathically, we grow into the more that we can become.

Four Steps to Improved Communication

It is one thing to read about communication skills in a book; it is quite a different matter to apply them effectively in daily life. In teaching communication skills to thousands of people, I have found that five factors strongly affect whether the skills will be used in their lives—a quantified commitment to use the skills, the application of the skills in appropriate situations, a willingness to be undaunted by occasional failure, preparing others for the fact that you will be trying to communicate differently sometimes, and engaging in skill training.

A QUANTIFIED COMMITMENT TO USE THE SKILLS

In the realm of interpersonal communication, as in so many other matters, people's intentions tend to outrun their actions. Thus, when the typical reader finishes this book, she is liable to think, "I will work on each of these skills so that I can improve relationships with important others in my life." In actual fact, however, after a few attempts at using the skills, the reader may tend to lapse back into the comfort of her old, but often less effective, ways of communicating. It's not that she *decided* not to use the skills. Quite to the contrary, she may have thought she made a decision to use the skills frequently.

The word *decision* has been watered down by imprecise usage. So when I teach communication skills to someone (as I have been teaching them to you in this book), I urge the person to *commit* herself to a *specific number* of uses of each of the skills per week for a period of three months.

The specific number of uses of the skill is as important as the commitment to use the skill. Unless you pin yourself down to a specific number of uses, it is easy to think you are utilizing the skills more than you really are. Following is the commitment one of our workshop's participants made:

From October 16 - January 16

Name: Harry Ogden

Skills	Commitment	Frequency of usage: Week of												
		Oct		November				December					Jan	
		20	27	3	10	17	24	1	8	15	22	29	5	12
Attending	5/wk	6	4	5	0	3	12	8	3	4	6	14	6	4
Reflective Listening	2/wk	3	2	1	0	4	6	3	3	1	2	0	4	3
Logical Consequences	2/mo	1	0	1	0	1	1	0	1	1	0	1	0	0
3–Part Assertion	1/wk	3	2	3	1	2	1	1	1	0	1	0	2	1
Descriptive Recognition	4/wk	4	3	0	0	0	14	5	6	4	7	18	8	9
Conflict Reduction	2/mo	0	1	1	0	1	0	0	1	2	0	1	0	0
Collaborative Problem Solving	2/mo	1	0	2	0	0	1	2	0	1	1	0	1	1

Every Friday afternoon, Harry reviewed his commitment and recorded on the chart the number of times he used each skill. He said, "It's amazing how using the chart helped me to persist in using the skills. There were times, like the week of November 10, when I virtually ignored the skills all week and didn't even realize I wasn't using them. If you hadn't urged us to develop a schedule that I could measure myself against, I'm afraid the skills would have fallen into disuse—like so many other good things that I've learned."

I asked Harry how he remembered to review the schedule.

"That part was easy," he said. "The day I made the commitment, I wrote 'Comm. Chart' in my datebook on every Friday afternoon for three months. Also, I scotch-taped the chart in a visible place in my office so that I could review my progress once in a while. Incidentally, the chart helped me to be aware of the seasons in my life. On Thanksgiving and Christmas weeks, I tried to greatly increase the use of my attending and descriptive-recognition skills. The same was true of birthdays and other special events. I began to give more of myself to others—as well as giving the more materialistic kind of presents."

SELECT APPROPRIATE SITUATIONS

When people are exposed to the skills taught in this course, they often want to try them out in some of the most difficult interpersonal problems in their lives. They may use reflective listening in situations that are most likely to trigger them into pronouncing judgments or giving advice. They tend to want to be assertive with the persons least likely to respond to an assertion message.

Just as it would be foolhardy to start jogging one day and enter a marathon the next, so it is unwise to use the skills in difficult situations before you have tried and mastered them in less-dramatic settings.

UNDAUNTED
BY OCCASIONAL FAILURE

These skills aren't panaceas. When used well, they have a high probability of being successful and enriching relationships. Even the most skilled and genuine users, however, have occasional failures.

Presumably you are not yet one of the world's most skillful practitioners of communication skills. If the pros occasionally have their failures, you will undoubtedly have your share too. When the skills don't work well for you, you have the option of giving up or figuring out what went wrong and learning how to correct that the next time. Persistence in the face of occasional failure is a necessity for persons who are committed to develop any skill.

PREPARE OTHERS
FOR THE CHANGE

After learning communication skills, some people have a strong desire to keep the skills a secret. Others want to prepare the important others in their work and personal lives for the fact that they will be trying to use some different approaches to communication some of the time. Our research suggests that it is usually beneficial to tell the people with whom you are likely to be using the skills that you will be trying to utilize some new approaches to communication, why you are doing it, and what these will be.

After participating in a workshop, Harry Ogden wrote his wife:

Dear Midge,

It has been a long time since I've sent a letter to you. You may be wondering why I'm sending this letter. As you know, I've been taking a course on Management Communication Skills that means a lot to me. Well, many people in the course expressed frustration over the fact that those who meant so much to them were not there to share in the experience. They also said how hard it is to convey the feelings and skills to other people. I felt that same frustration and have decided to attempt to express what the experience has meant to me and to share some of that with you.

You may have some feelings about this—some positive, some of anxiety, or some even of threat. So I want to tell you how I think the course may affect me.

One of the main things we learned is how to listen when a person has a need to be listened to. Essentially the listener should have genuine concern for the speaker, should reflect facts and feelings (I'll explain more of what I mean by that when we talk), and, most importantly, be nonevaluative and refrain from giving advice. I really want to learn how to listen this way. I hope that this will enable you to be more "you" and me to be more "me."

One of the major benefits of listening is the establishing of trust in a relationship.

When a relationship has trust, you don't have to be defensive about yourself; being yourself becomes easier.

So I really want to learn to be a nonjudgmental, reflective listener. It's not going to be easy, and I may seem a little phony at times, so I ask you to be patient with me as I try to overcome some bad communication habits and learn some new skills.

We learned a lot of other skills, some of which you and I have discussed already. In this letter I'm not going to go into the other skills, though soon I'd like to explain how and why I hope to use them.

Well, in closing, I would like to say that the course was a most unusual experience for me that opened up some important avenues of communication and self-discovery. I decided to try to share some of that meaning with you in this letter. Thank you for listening—and for being you.

> With all my love,
> Harry

P.S. It was fun talking about the three-part assertion message on Wednesday night. And I promise to put my dirty clothes in the hamper!

In addition to the letter to his wife, Harry told his children about the course and that he was going to try to communicate differently. At work he called a meeting with all his subordinates and told them about the course content and how he hoped to implement it on the job. In each setting, Harry admitted that he didn't know the skills well yet and that he might forget to use them at crucial times. He also said that sometimes the skills might seem strange and perhaps even unproductive to people. He asked for a three-month period in which to give the skills a fair trial. After being kidded a bit about "things certainly couldn't get much worse," everyone agreed to give Harry three months to try to develop and use the skills.

"I'm glad I negotiated that trial period," Harry told me. "Several times people said, 'You're doing that communication thing on me.' And, after reflecting their discomfort, I would say, 'Yeah, it doesn't seem to be working too well right now—but we said we'd give it a three-month try. Let's see if I got the gist of what you were saying.' And we'd be into the conversation again.

"At the end of the three months everyone agreed that the experiment was a success. Sure, it bugged people some of the time. But all agreed that the reflections were better than the roadblocks and the assertion was better than nagging or aggression. And now it's easier to agree to disagree on values issues and to solve real problems on a win/win basis."

SKILL TRAINING

Skill-building workshops can be a tremendous asset in developing one's ability to communicate better. This book describes the concepts and tells what the central communication methods are. But reading a book is not the equivalent of learning in a workshop situation in which the skills are modelled by the trainer and on audio and video tape and where practice sessions with feedback are held. Most people find that a skill-training workshop is very helpful in fostering increased interpersonal effectiveness.

It is important to note, however, that the research indicates that training in interpersonal communication can be "for better or for worse."[1] Two frequent problems with ineffective training are the educational design and the inability of the trainer to utilize the skills or express the key qualities (see Chapter 15) while teaching the course. When these problems are not present, research suggests that participants can increase their ability with the skills in a remarkably brief period.[2]

It is my strong conviction that, with rare exceptions, a high level of communication effectiveness is seldom achieved without an intensive and well-designed training program. For these reasons I would encourage you to be highly selective and critical in choosing a communications training program if that is a possible direction for you. Organizations that desire more information about the training programs that my colleagues and I designed to teach the skills described in this book may direct inquiries to:

> Communication Skills
> Ridge Consultants
> 5 Ledyard Avenue
> Cazenovia, New York 13035

Notes

Preface

1. William Turner, A *New Herball Wherein Are Contayned the Names of Herbes* (London, 1551).

PART ONE: INTRODUCTION

1. George Gazda, *Human Relations Development: A Manual for Educators* (Boston. Allyn & Bacon, 1973), p. 34.

Chapter One:
Skills for Bridging
the Interpersonal Gap

1. Richard Wright, *The Outsider* (New York: Harper & Row, 1969).
2. Karl Jaspers, *The Way to Wisdom* (New Haven: Yale University Press, 1951), p. 147.
3. Harry Stack Sullivan, *Interpersonal Theory of Psychiatry* (New York: W. W. Norton, 1953).
4. David Riesman, Nathan Glazier, and Reuel Denney, *The Lonely Crowd: A Study of the Changing American Character* (New York: Doubleday, 1950).
5. T. S. Eliot, *The Cocktail Party* (New York: Harcourt Brace Jovanovich, Inc.; London: Faber & Faber Ltd), p. 140. Copyright 1950.
6. Virginia Satir, *Peoplemaking* (Palo Alto, Calif.: Science and Behavior Books, 1972), p. 197.
7. Quoted in Ann Landers, "Survey Results Shock Reader," *Syracuse Herald-Journal*, 29 March 1976.
8. Gabriel Marcel, *The Mystery of Being* (Chicago: Regnery, 1960).
9. Carl Rogers, *On Becoming a Person: A Therapist's View of Psychotherapy* (Boston:

Houghton Mifflin, 1961), p. 330. Copyright © 1961 by Carl R. Rogers. Reprinted by permission of Houghton Mifflin Co., and that of Constable Publishers, London.

10. *Second Chance* (motion picture) (Nutley, N.J.: Hoffman-LaRoche Laboratory).

11. Erich Fromm, *The Art of Loving* (New York: Harper and Brothers, 1956), p. 83.

12. Gerard Egan, *The Skilled Helper: An Introduction to Systematic Counselor and Human Relations Training* (Monterey, Calif.: Brooks/Cole, 1975), p. 22. Copyright © 1975 by Wadsworth Publishing Company, Inc. Reprinted by permission of the publisher, Brooks/Cole Publishing Company, Monterey, California 93940.

13. Charles B. Truax and Robert Carkhuff, *Toward Effective Counseling and Psychotherapy* (New York: Aldine/Atherton, 1967), p. 108.

14. Robert Havighurst, *Developmental Tasks and Education* (New York: Longmans, Green, 1952); Erik Erikson, *Childhood and Society* (New York: W. W. Norton, 1964).

15. Alvin Toffler, *Future Shock* (New York: Random House, 1970). Toffler says that one of the three abilities we need in our "survival kit" for the future is learning how to relate.

16. H. Richard Niebuhr, *The Purpose of the Church and Its Ministry* (New York: Harper and Brothers, 1956), p. viii.

17. One of the most important issues in communication skills training is the selection of skills to be taught. From my perspective, Dr. Thomas Gordon's choice of basic communication skills in his *Parent Effectiveness Training: The "No-Lose" Program for Raising Responsible Children* (New York: Peter H. Wyden, 1970) represented a major step forward in communication skills training. Though there are differences in what is considered most fundamental in Gordon's books and those highlighted in this volume, my indebtedness to him on this (and many other topics covered in this book) is considerable.

Chapter Two:
Barriers to Communication

1. Reuel L. Howe, *The Miracle of Dialogue* (New York: The Seabury Press, Inc., 1963), pp. 23–24. Copyright © 1963 by the Seabury Press, Inc.

2. Thomas Gordon, *Parent Effectiveness Training: The "No-Lose" Program for Raising Responsible Children* (New York: Peter H. Wyden, 1970), pp. 44, 108.

3. Carl Rogers, *Client-Centered Therapy: Its Current Practice, Implications, and Theory* (Boston: Houghton Mifflin, 1951); note especially 31. See also Carl Rogers, *On Becoming a Person: A Therapist's View of Psychotherapy* (Boston: Houghton Mifflin, 1961). Copyright © 1961 by Carl R. Rogers. Reprinted by permission of Houghton Mifflin Co. Howe, *The Miracle of Dialogue*, pp. 18–35. Haim Ginott, *Between Parent and Child: New Solutions to Old Problems* (New York: Macmillan, 1965). See also Ginott's *Between Parent and Teenager* (New York: Avon, 1969) and *Teacher and Child: A Book for Parents and Teachers* (New York: Macmillan, 1972). Jack Gibb "Defensive Communication," in *Leadership and Interpersonal Behavior*, edited by Luigi Petrullo and Bernard M. Bass (New York: Holt, Rinehart and Winston, 1961), pp. 66–81.

4. Gordon, *Parent Effectiveness Training*, pp. 41–47, 108–117 and 321–27.

5. Rogers, *On Becoming a Person*, p. 330. *Copyright* © 1961 by Carl R. Rogers. Reprinted by permission of Houghton Mifflin Co.

6. Ibid., pp. 330–31. Copyright © 1961 by Carl R. Rogers. Reprinted by permission of Houghton Mifflin Co.

7. Quoted in Robert Sherwood, *Roosevelt and Hopkins* (New York: Harper, 1948), p. 282.

8. Clark Moustakas, *Individuality and Encounter: A Brief Journey into Loneliness and Sensitivity Groups* (Cambridge, Mass.: Howard A. Doyle, 1971), pp. 7–8.

9. Ginott, *Between Parent and Teen-Ager*, p. 113.

10. David Augsburger, *The Love Fight* (Scottsdale, Pa.: Herald Press, 1973), p. 110.

11. Jacques Lalanne, "Attack by Question," *Psychology Today*, November 1975), p. 134.

12. Norman Kagan, *Interpersonal Process Recall: A Method of Influencing Human Interaction* (Ann Arbor: Michigan State University Press, 1975), p. 29.

13. Dag Hammarskjold, *Markings* (New York: Alfred A. Knopf, 1964), p. 190.

14. Ginott, *Between Parent and Child*, pp. 29–30.

15. Luke 11:24–26.

PART TWO:
LISTENING SKILLS

1. Quoted in Ralph Nichols and Leonard Stevens, *Are You Listening?* (New York: McGraw-Hill, 1957), p. 49.

Chapter Three:
Listening Is More Than
Merely Hearing

1. A letter from a patient quoted in Paul Tournier, *The Meaning of Persons* (New York: Harper & Row, 1957), p. 165.

2. Ralph G. Nichols and Leonard A. Stevens, *Are You Listening?* (New York: McGraw-Hill, 1957), pp. 6–7.

3. Ibid., pp. 6–10.

4. Quoted in B. Harvey Branscomb, *The Teachings of Jesus: A Textbook for College and Individual Use* (New York: Abingdon, 1931), p. 23. This saying comes from an apocryphal "New Testament" book.

5. Ralph G. Nichols and Leonard A. Stevens, "Listening to People," *Harvard Business Review*, September–October 1957.

6. Franklin Ernst, Jr., *Who's Listening? A Handbook of the Transactional Analysis of the Listening Function* (Vallejo, Calif.: Addresso 'set, 1973).

7. John Drakeford, *The Awesome Power of the Listening Ear* (Waco, Tex.: Word, 1967), p. 17.

8. Allen Ivey and John Hinkle, "The Transactional Classroom," unpublished manuscript, University of Massachusetts, 1970.
9. Norman Rockwell, "My Adventures as an Illustrator," edited by T. Rockwell, *Saturday Evening Post*, April 2, 1960, p. 67. President John Kennedy had this ability, too. See Drakesford, *The Awesome Power of the Listening Ear*, p. 65.
10. Albert Scheflen with Norman Ashcraft, *Human Territories: How We Behave in Space-Time* (Englewood Cliffs, N.J.: Prentice-Hall, 1976), pp. 6, 42.
11. C. L. Lassen, "Effect of Proximity on Anxiety and Communication in the Initial Psychiatric Interview," *Journal of Abnormal Psychology* 18 (1973): 220–232.
12. Ernst, *Who's Listening?* p. 113.
13. Charles Truax and Robert Carkhuff, *Toward Effective Counseling and Psychotherapy: Training and Practice* (New York: Aldine/Atherton, 1967), pp. 361–62.
14. Quoted in Gerald Nierenberg and Henry Calero, *How to Read a Person Like a Book* (New York: Pocket Books, 1975), p. 28.
15. Paul Ekman and Wallace Friesen, *Unmasking the Face: A Guide to Recognizing Emotions from Facial Expressions* (Englewood Cliffs, N.J.: Prentice-Hall, 1975), pp. 14–16.
16. Silvan Tomkins, in *Challenges of Humanistic Psychology*, edited by James Bugental (New York: McGraw-Hill, 1967), p. 57.
17. Anthony G. White, *Reforming Metropolitan Governments: A Bibliography* (New York: Garland, 1975).
18. Allen Ivey, *Microcounseling: Innovations in Interviewing Training* (Springfield, Ill.: Thomas, 1975).
19. John Moreland, Jeanne Phillips, and Jeff Lockhart, "Open Invitation to Talk," manuscript, University of Massachusetts, 1969, p. 1
20. Eugene Herrigel, *The Method of Zen*, edited by Herman Tausend and R. F. C. Hull (New York: Pantheon, 1976), pp. 124–25.
21. Halford Luccock, *Halford Luccock Treasury* edited by Robert Luccock, Jr. (New York: Abingdon, 1963), p. 242.
22. Quoted in Nathan Scott, *Man in the Modern Theater*, (Richmond, Va.: John Knox, 1965), p. 86.
23. Ecclesiastes 3:7.

Chapter Four:
Four Skills of Reflective Listening

1. John Powell, *The Secret of Staying in Love* (Niles, Ill.: Argus, 1974), p. 140. Reprinted from *The Secret of Staying in Love* by John Powell © 1974 Argus Communications. Used with permission from Argus Communications, Niles, Illinois.
2. Quoted in Haim Ginott, *Group Psychotherapy with Children* (New York: McGraw-Hill, 1961), pp. 180–82.

3. Steven Danish and Allen Hauer, *Helping Skills: A Basic Training Program* (New York: Behavioral Publications, 1973), p. 27.

4. William James, *Varieties of Religious Experience* (New York: Longmans, Green, 1902), p. 397.

5. Norman Kagan, *Interpersonal Process Recall: A Method of Influencing Human Interaction* (Ann Arbor: Michigan State University Press, 1975), pp. 60–62. Kagan goes on to state that because people have some ability at reading feelings, they don't need to be taught how to do it. I believe most of us can improve this ability through an educational process—which in fact is what Kagan's program is designed to do, too.

6. Robert Carkhuff, *The Art of Helping: A Guide for Developing Helping Skills for Parents, Teachers, and Counselors* (Amherst, Mass.: Human Resource Development Press, 1973), p. 78.

7. Ernest Jones, *The Life and Work of Sigmund Freud*, edited and abridged by Lionell Trilling and Steven Marcus (New York: Basic Books, 1961), p. 253.

8. Quoted in Gerard Egan, *The Skilled Helper: A Model for Systematic Helping and Interpersonal Relating*, (Monterey, Calif.: Brooks/Cole, 1975), p. 139. Copyright © 1975 by Wadsworth Publishing Company, Inc. Reprinted by permission of the publisher, Brooks/Cole Publishing Company, Monterey, California 93940.

9. Ibid., p. 138. Copyright © 1975 by Wadsworth Publishing Company, Inc. Reprinted by permission of the publisher, Brooks/Cole Publishing Company, Monterey, California 93940.

Chapter Five:
Why Reflective Responses Work

1. J. M. Shlien. I am unable to locate the source of this quotation.

2. Richard Bandler and John Grinder, *The Structure of Magic: A Book about Language and Therapy* (Palo Alto, Calif.: Science and Behavior Books, 1975), 1: 22–23.

3. Alfred North Whitehead, *Adventures of Ideas* (New York: Mentor, 1933), p. 286.

4. Quoted in *Life*, 14 October 1966.

5. T. S. Eliot, "Burnt Norton." *Four Quartets* (New York: Harcourt Brace Jovanovich, Inc., 1952; London: Faber & Faber Ltd). Copyright 1952.

6. Haim Ginott, *Between Parent and Child: New Solutions to Old Problems* (New York: Macmillan, 1965), pp. 35–36.

7. John Drakeford, *The Awesome Power of the Listening Ear* (Waco, Tex.: Word, 1967), pp. 19–20.

8. Perry London, *Behavior Control* (New York: Harper & Row, 1969), p. 88.

9. Anti-Defamation League of B'nai B'rith, *Rumor Clinic*.

10. Jiddu Krishnamurti, *The First and Last Freedom* (New York: Harper and Brothers, 1954), p. 19.

11. Thomas Carlyle, *Sartor Resartus* (New York; Stokes, 1883), p. 172. Italics added.

Chapter Six:
Reading Body Language

1. Julius Fast, *Body Language* (New York: Pocket Books, 1971), pp. 7–8. From *Body Language* by Julius Fast. Copyright © 1970 by Julius Fast. Reprinted by permission of the publishers, M. Evans and Company, Inc., New York, New York 10017.

2. Randall Harrison, "Nonverbal Communication: Exploration into Time, Space, Action, and Object," in *Dimensions in Communication: Readings* edited by James Campbell and Hall Hepner (Belmont, Calif.: Wadsworth, 1970), p. 258.

3. Albert Mehrabian, "Communication Without Words," *Psychology Today*, September 1968, p. 53.

4. Quoted in Gerald Nierenberg and Henry Calero, *How to Read a Person Like a Book* (New York: Pocket Books, 1973), p. 23.

5. Isaiah 3:9, as translated by George Adam Smith, *The Book of Isaiah* (New York: Harper and Brothers, 1927), 1:31.

6. Paul Ekman and Wallace Friesen, *Unmasking the Face: A Guide to Recognizing Emotions from Facial Clues* (Englewood Cliffs, N.J.: Prentice-Hall, 1975), p. 18.

7. Gerard Egan, *The Skilled Helper: A Model for Systematic Helping and Interpersonal Relating* (Monterey, Calif.: Brooks/Cole, 1975), p. 63.

8. D. Huenegardt and S. Finando, "Micromomentary Facial Expressions as Perceivable Signs of Deception," paper presented to Speech Association of America, New York, Quoted in C. David Mortensen, *Communication: The Study of Human Interaction* (New York: McGraw-Hill, 1972), pp. 222–24.

9. Ralph Nichols and Leonard Stevens, *Are You Listening?* (New York: McGraw-Hill, 1957), p. 59.

10. Quoted in John Woolman, *The Journal of John Woolman*, edited by Janet Whitney (Chicago: Henry Regnery, 1950), p. 132.

11. Rollo May, *Love and Will* (New York: W. W. Norton, 1969), p. 241.

12. Len Sperry, *Developing Skills in Contact Counseling* (Reading, Mass.: Addison Wesley, 1975), p. 40.

13. Erle Stanley Gardner, "How to Know You're Transparent When You'd Like to Be Opaque," *Vogue*, July 1956, pp. 45–47.

14. B. G. Rosenberg and J. Langer "A Study of Postural-Gestural Communication," *Journal of Personality and Social Psychology* 2: 593–97.

15. Abne Eisenberg and Ralph Smith, Jr., *Nonverbal Communication* (Indianapolis: Bobbs-Merrill, 1971), pp. 34–35.

16. Quoted in Nierenberg and Calero, *How to Read a Person Like a Book*, p. 18.

17. Edward Sapir, "The Unconscious Patterning of Behaviors in Society," *Selected Writings of Edward Sapir in Language, Culture, and Personality*, edited by David Mandelbaum (Berkeley: University of California Press, 1949), p. 556.

Chapter Seven:
Improving Your Reflecting Skills

1. David Augsburger, *The Love Fight: Caring Enough to Confront* (Scottdale, Pa.: Herald Press, 1973), p. 23.

2. Carl Rogers, *On Becoming a Person* (Boston: Houghton Mifflin, 1961), pp. 21–22. Copyright © 1961 by Carl R. Rogers. Reprinted by permission of Houghton Mifflin Co.

3. *McCall's*, September 1968.

4. I John 3:18 (Moffatt translation).

5. Gerard Egan, *The Skilled Helper: A Model for Systematic Helping and Interpersonal Relating* (Monterey, Calif.: Brooks/Cole, 1975), pp. 153–54. Copyright © 1975 by Wadsworth Publishing Company, Inc. Reprinted by permission of the publisher, Brooks/Cole Publishing Company, Monterey, California 93940.

6. Clark Moustakas, *Creativity and Conformity* (Princeton, N.J.: D. Van Nostrand, 1967), p. 23.

7. Quoted in Douglas Steere, *On Beginning from Within/On Listening to Another* (New York: Harper & Row, 1943), p. 197.

8. George Gazda et al., *Human Relations Development: A Manual for Educators* (Boston: Allyn & Bacon, 1973), pp. 81–82.

PART THREE:
ASSERTION SKILLS

1. *Pirke Avot* ("Ethics of the Fathers"), Talmud.

Chapter Eight:
Three Approaches to
Relationships

1. Sherwin Cotler and Julio Guerra, *Assertion Training: A Humanistic-Behavioral Guide to Self-Dignity* (Champaign, Ill.: Research Press, 1976), p. 201. Used with permission.

2. Virginia Satir, *Peoplemaking* (Palo Alto, Calif.: Science and Behavior Books, 1972), pp. 78–79. This is her rough estimate. Satir uses the word *leveling* rather than *asserting*.

3. Anne Morrow Lindbergh, *Dearly Beloved* (New York: Harcourt, Brace and World, 1962), p. 10.

4. L. Z. Bloom, Karen Coburn, and Joan Pearlman, *The New Assertive Woman* (New York: Dell Books, 1975), p. 219. I believe the statistics are significant despite the limitations inherent in self-assessment procedures.

5. W. H. Auden, *About the House* (New York: Random House, 1965). Reprinted by permission of Curtis Brown, Ltd. Copyright © 1963 by Edward Mendelson, William Meredith, and Monroe K. Spears, executors of the Estate of W. H. Auden (first appeared in *The New Yorker*).

6. Georg Simmel, "Secrecy and Group Communication," in Talcott Parsons et al., *Theories of Society* (New York: Free Press, 1961), p. 320.

7. Theodore White, *The Making of the President 1960* (New York: Atheneum, 1961), p. 171.

8. Ashley Montague, *The Nature of Human Aggression* (New York: Oxford University Press, 1976), p. 249.

9. Albert Scheflen with Norman Ashcroft, *Human Territories: How We Behave in Space-Time* (Englewood Cliffs, N.J.: Prentice-Hall, 1976), p. 167.

10. Eliot Howard, *Territory in Bird Life* (London: William Collins, 1920). See also Konrad Lorenz, *On Aggression*, trans. Marjorie Wilson (New York: Bantam, 1967). Robert Ardrey, though not a scientist, did much to popularize the research and theories of numerous scholars in this book *The Territorial Imperative: A Personal Inquiry into Animal Origins of Property and Nations* (New York: Atheneum, 1968).

11. Lois Timmins, *Understanding through Communication* (Springfield, Ill.: Charles C. Thomas, 1972), pp. 116–117.

12. Quoted in Gerald Kennedy, *Fresh Every Morning* (New York: Harper & Row, 1966), p. 75.

13. Abraham Maslow, in *Challenge of Humanistic Psychology*, edited by James Bugental (New York: McGraw Hill, 1967), pp. 280–81.

14. Thomas Moriarity, "A Nation of Willing Victims," *Psychology Today*, April 1955, pp. 43–50.

15. Carolina Maria de Jesus, *Child of the Dark: The Diary of Carolina Maria de Jesus*, trans. David Saint Clair (New York: Signet, 1962), p. 47.

16. Many years ago Dr. Martin Seldman introduced me to assertion training. Our numerous conversations and his assertion training classes have had much influence on some of the assertion sections of this book. Some of Dr. Seldman's ideas on the subject are found in Martin Seldman, Ph.D., and David Hermes, *Personal Growth Thru Groups: A Collection of Methods* (San Diego, Calif.: The We Care Foundation, Inc., 1975).

17. Frederick Perls, *Gestalt Therapy Verbatim* (Lafayette Calif.: Real People Press, 1969), p. 19.

18. The phrase is from George Bach and Herb Goldberg, *Creative Aggression* (Garden City, N.Y.: Doubleday, 1974), p. 43.

19. As has been noted, the submissive person often controls the aggressive person, but this is a lose/lose kind of control. In the lose/lose situation, the submissive person does not do what she wants, and the aggressive person's actions are frustrated.

20. Robert Emmons and Michael Alberti, *Stand Up, Speak Out, Talk Back* (New York: Pocket Books, 1975), p. 39. See also Arthur Lange and Patricia Jakubowski, *Responsible Assertive Behavior*, p. 53.

21. Quoted in Marshall Rosenberg, *A Manual for Responsible Thinking and Communicating* (Saint Louis: Community Psychological Consultants, 1972), p. v.

22. Byron Butler, quoted in Lawrence LeShan, "Psychological States as Factors in the Development of Malignant Disease: A Critical Review," *Journal of the National Cancer Institute*, 22, no. 1 (1959).

23. Bach and Goldberg, *Creative Aggression*, pp. 194ff.

24. Thomas Huxley, *The Struggle for Existence: A Programme* (London, 1888). Many scientists believe Huxley's emphasis on destruction and competition was a serious distortion of Darwin's theory and that it is contradicted by evidence from the world of

nature. See, for example, Peter Kropotkin, *Mutual Aid: A Factor of Evolution* (London, Heinemann, 1902).

25. Quoted in *Fortune*, May 1973.

26. Esther 7:10 (Moffatt translation).

27. *The Essaies of Sir Francis Bacon* (London: John Beale, 1612).

28. Georg Bach and Ronald Deutsch, *Pairing* (New York: Peter H. Wyden, 1970), p. 53.

29. Quoted in Albert Camus, *The Rebel: An Essay on Man in Revolt*, revised and translated by Anthony Bower (New York: Vintage Books, 1958), p. 251.

30. Albert Speer, *Inside the Third Reich: Memoirs of Albert Speer* (New York: Macmillan, 1970).

31. Herbert Fensterheim and Jean Baer, *Don't Say Yes When You Want to Say No* (New York: David McKay, 1975), p. 14.

32. Howard Clinebell, Jr. and Charlotte Clinebell, *The Intimate Marriage* (New York: Harper & Row, 1943), p. 179.

33. Harry Emerson Fosdick, *On Being a Real Person* (New York: Harper and Brothers, 1943), p. 179.

Chapter Nine:
Developing Three-Part
Assertion Messages

1. David Seabury, *The Art of Selfishness* (New York: Simon and Schuster, 1964), p. 59.

2. Manuel Smith, *When I Say No, I Feel Guilty: How to Cope—Using the Skills of Systematic Assertive Therapy* (New York: Dial Press, 1975), pp. 7–14.

3. Many assertiveness trainers disagree. Robert Alberti and Michael Emmons claim, "It almost doesn't matter *what* you say!" *Stand Up, Speak Out, Talk Back* (New York: Pocket Books, 1975), p. 85. In their earlier pioneering work they said, "Although *what* you say is clearly important, it is often *less* important than most of us generally believe." *Your Perfect Right*, 2nd ed. (San Luis Obispo, Calif.: Impact, 1974), p. 32. By contrast, my colleagues and I believe that what you say, your precision of speech in assertion situations, is usually *more* important than most of us believe.

4. Thomas Gordon, *Parent Effectiveness Training: The "No-Lose" Program for Raising Responsible Children* (New York: Peter Wyden, 1970), p. 108.

5. John Wallen's unpublished paper "Behavior Description: A Basic Communication Skill for Improving Interpersonal Relations" (1970) has been a helpful resource here.

6. Hazen Werner, "In Marriage—Tremendous Trifles Count," *Together*, February 1962, pp. 19–21.

7. Andrew Salter, *Conditioned Reflex Therapy: The Direct Approach to the Reconstruction of Personality* (New York: Capricorn Books, 1949).

8. John Powell, *The Secret of Staying in Love* (Niles, Ohio: Argus Communications, 1974), p. 108. Reprinted from *The Secret of Staying in Love* by John Powell © 1974 Argus Communications. Used with permission from Argus Communications, Niles, Illinois.

9. Salter, *Conditioned Reflex Therapy*, p. 47.
10. Thomas Gordon with Noel Burch, *T.E.T.: Teacher Effectiveness Training* (New York: Peter Wyden, 1974), p. 143. As far as I can ascertain, the three-part assertion message began with the two-part feedback message developed by the National Training Laboratory Institute. The feedback message included a nonjudgmental description of behavior and a disclosure of one's feelings about that behavior. Dr. Gordon began to use that method and then he or one of his instructors added the "concrete or tangible effect," a most significant improvement for many situations. Thomas Gordon calls these three-part messages "I Messages."
11. In teaching the three-part assertion message I have discovered that persons who do not want to confront in situations where there are tangible results ("because those things really don't matter to me") tend to have a strong desire to confront on values issues. When people become more assertive about matters where there is a tangible effect, it appears that there is a diminished desire to control other people's values.

Chapter Ten:
Handling the
Push–Push Back Phenomenon

1. Reuel Howe, *The Miracle of Dialogue* (New York: The Seabury Press, Inc., 1963), p. 84. Copyright © 1963 by The Seabury Press, Inc.
2. Abraham Maslow, *Toward a Psychology of Being*, 2nd ed. (Princeton, N.J.: D. Van Nostrand, 1968), pp. 46–47.
3. Gregory Baum, *Man Becoming: God in Secular Experience* (New York: Herder and Herder, 1971), pp. 49, 54.
4. Jack Gibb, "Defense Level and Influence Potential in Small Groups," in *Leadership and Interpersonal Behavior*, edited by Luigi Petrullo and Bernard M. Bass (New York: Holt, Rinehart and Winston, 1961), pp. 66–81.
5. Carl Rogers, *Carl Rogers on Encounter Groups* (New York: Harper & Row, 1970), pp. 52–53.
6. Robert Alberti and Michael Emmons, *Stand Up, Speak-Out, Talk Back: The Key to Self-Assertive Behavior* (New York: Pocket Books, 1975), p. 90.
7. Frederick Stoller, "A Stage for Trust," in *Encounter: The Theory and Practice of Encounter Groups*, edited by Arthur Burton (San Francisco: Jossey-Bass, 1970), p. 90.
8. Richard Walton, *Interpersonal Peacemaking: Confrontations and Third Party Consultation* (Reading, Mass.: Addison Wesley, 1969), p. 86.
9. Sharon and Gordon Bower have an interesting chapter on defensive responses in their book *Asserting Yourself: A Practical Guide for Positive Change* (Reading, Mass.: Addison-Wesley, 1976). The authors analyze the various ways people try to "detour" the asserter from her destination. There are significant differences between their approach to handling defensive responses and the methods advocated in this chapter.
10. Allen Frank, "Conflict in the Classroom," in Fred Jandt, *Conflict Resolution through Communication* (New York: Harper & Row, 1973), p. 249.

Chapter Eleven:
Increasing Your Assertive Options

1. Herbert Fensterheim and Jean Baer, *Don't Say Yes When You Want to Say No!* (New York: David McKay, 1975), p. 41.

2. Sidney Jourard, *The Transparent Self*, rev. ed. (New York: Van Nostrand Reinhold, 1971), pp. vii, viii.

3. T. S. Eliot, *The Elder Statesman* (New York: Farrar, Straus, 1959), p. 102. A selection from *The Elder Statesman* by T. S. Eliot. Copyright © 1959 by Thomas Stearns Eliot. Reprinted with the permission of Farrar, Straus & Giroux, Inc., and Faber & Faber Ltd, London.

4. Rollo May, *Power and Innocence: A Search for the Sources of Violence* (New York: Dell, 1972), p. 245.

5. Basil of Caesarea, *Longer Rule*. Quoted in John McNeill, *A History of the Cure of Souls* (New York: Harper and Brothers, 1951), p. 95. A somewhat similar point of view is propounded by modern psychologists.

6. John Powell, *The Secret of Staying in Love* (Niles, Ill.: Argus Communications, 1974), p. 68. Reprinted from *The Secret of Staying in Love* by John Powell © 1974 Argus Communications. Used with permission from Argus Communications, Niles, Illinois.

7. Psalms, 12:2.

8. Haim Ginott, *Between Parent and Child: New Solutions to Old Problems* (New York: Macmillan, 1965).

9. Gregor Piatigorsky, *Cellist* (New York: Doubleday, 1965).

10. William Wordsworth, *Lines Composed a Few Miles above Tintern Abbey*, 1.33.

11. Franklin Ernst Jr. *Who's Listening? A Handbook of the Transactional Analysis of the Listening Function* (Vallejo, Calif.: Addresso 'set, 1973), p. 113.

12. Paul Weiss and Jonathan Weiss present different points of view on this topic; see their book *Right and Wrong: A Philosophical Dialogue between Father and Son* (New York: Basic Books, 1967), pp. 46ff.

13. George Prince, *The Practice of Creativity: A Manual for Dynamic Group Problem Solving* (New York: Harper & Row, 1970), p. 39.

14. Ibid., p. 40.

15. Ibid., p. 39.

16. Erich Fromm, *The Anatomy of Human Destructiveness* (Greenwich, Conn.: Fawcett Publications, 1973), p. 224.

17. Quoted in Rudolf Dreikurs and Pearl Cassel, *Discipline without Tears*, 2nd ed. (New York: Hawthorn Books, 1972), p. 65.

18. Rudolf Dreikurs with Vicki Soltz, *Children: The Challenge* (New York: Hawthorn Books, 1964), pp. 72–75. For a contrasting viewpoint, see B. F. Skinner, *About Behaviorism* (New York: Alfred A. Knopf, 1974).

19. Rudolf Dreikurs, Bernice Grunwald, and Floy Pepper, *Maintaining Sanity in the Classroom: Illustrated Teaching Techniques* (New York: Harper & Row, 1971) p. 81.

20. Haim Ginott, *Between Parent and Child: New Solutions to Old Problems* (New York: Macmillan, 1965) has a helpful chapter on the topic of this section: pp. 91ff.

21. Compare Mark 3:5 and Matthew 23:1–36; see Hosea 11:9.
22. Manuel Smith, *When I Say No, I Feel Guilty: How To Cope—Using the Skills of Systematic Assertive Therapy* (New York: Dial Press, 1975), and Fensterheim and Baer, *Don't Say Yes When You Want to Say No!*
23. Weiss and Weiss, *Right and Wrong*, p. 79.
24. Albert Camus, *The Rebel: An Essay on Man in Revolt* (New York: Vintage Books, 1958) emphasizes the danger of an exclusively negative focus and the importance of being aware of the affirmations that lie behind one's *no*, pp. 13ff.
25. Matthew 5:37. Some translators render the second sentence, "Anything more than this comes from evil."
26. For greater detail on this method, see Thomas Gordon with Noel Burch, *T.E.T.: Teacher Effectiveness Training* (New York: Peter Wyden, 1974), pp. 156ff.

PART FOUR:
CONFLICT MANAGEMENT SKILLS

1. Harvey Seifert and Howard Clinebell, Jr., *Personal Growth and Social Change: A Guide for Ministers and Laymen as Change Agents* (Philadelphia: Westminster Press, 1969), p. 174.

Chapter Twelve:
Conflict Prevention and Control

1. Richard Walton, *Interpersonal Peacemaking: Confrontations and Third Party Consultation* (Reading, Mass.: Addison-Wesley, 1969), p. 5. Italics are his. Reprinted with permission.
2. Alexander Hamilton, James Madison, and John Jay, *Federalist Papers*, No. 10. (New York: New American Library, 1961.)
3. Florence Allshorn, *The Notebooks of Florence Allshorn* (London: SCM Press, 1957), p. 66.
4. J. H. Oldham, *Florence Allshorn and the Story of St. Julians* (London: SCM Press, 1951), p. 88.
5. Gibson Winter, *Love and Conflict: New Patterns in Family Life* (Garden City, N.Y.: Doubleday, 1958), pp. 102–4. Italics added.
6. Harry Harlow, "Affectional Responses in Infant Monkeys," *Science* 130 (1959).
7. Konrad Lorenz, *On Aggression* (New York: Harcourt, Brace and World, 1966).
8. Stanley Coopersmith, *The Antecedents of Self-Esteem* (San Francisco: W. H. Freeman, 1967).
9. John Dewey, *Human Nature and Conduct* (New York: Modern Library, 1930), p. 300.
10. Lewis Coser, *The Functions of Social Conflict* (Glencoe, Ill.: Routledge & Kegan Paul, 1956).
11. McAlister Coleman, *Men and Coal* (New York: Farrar and Rinehart, 1943).
12. Walton, *Interpersonal Peacemaking*, p. 5.
13. Muzafer Sherif, O. Harvey, B. White, W. Hood, and Carolyn Sherif, *Intergroup Conflict and Cooperation: The Robber's Cave Experiment* (Norman, Okla.: University Book Exchange, 1961).

14. Robert Blake and Jane Mouton, *Group Dynamics: Key to Decision Making* (Houston: Gulf, 1961).

15. Ruth Benedict's ideas on this subject were preserved and expanded upon by psychologist Abraham Maslow. See also Maslow's "Synergy in the Society and in the Individual," *Journal of Individual Psychology*, 20 (1964) and his *Eupsychian Management* (Homewood, Ill.: Irwin, 1965), pp. 88–107.

16. Albert Ellis has written many books on this subject. One of the most popular is Albert Ellis and Robert Harper, *A New Guide to Rational Living* (North Hollywood, Calif.: Wilshire, 1975).

17. Roger Fisher, "Fractionating Conflict," in *International Conflict and Behavioral Sciences: The Craigville Papers*, edited by Roger Fisher (New York: Basic Books, 1964), pp. 91–110.

18. Ibid., pp. 91–110.

19. Eugene Litwak, "Models of Bureaucracy Which Permit Conflict," *American Journal of Sociology* 67 (1961); 177–184.

20. Rensis Likert and Jane Likert, *New Ways of Managing Conflict* (New York: McGraw-Hill, 1976).

21. Robert Nye, *Conflict among Humans* (New York: Springer, 1973), p. 93.

22. Robert Blake, Herbert Shepherd, and Jane Mouton, *Managing Intergroup Conflict in Industry* (Houston: Gulf, 1964), pp. 18–33.

23. Robert Blood, "Resolving Family Conflicts," in *Conflict Resolution Through Communication*, edited by Fred Jandt (New York: Harper & Row, 1973), p. 230.

24. Daniel Katz, "Current and Needed Psychological Research in International Relations," in *Conflict Resolution: Contributions of the Behavioral Sciences*, edited by Clagett Smith (Notre Dame, Inc.: University of Notre Dame Press, 1971), p. 86.

25. Orson Bean, *Me and the Orgone* (New York: St. Martin's Press, 1971), pp. 26–27, 112–113. Bean's book is the story of his attempt to incorporate Wilhelm Reich's insights into his own daily life.

Chapter Thirteen:
Handling the Emotional Components of Conflict

1. John Powell, *The Secret of Staying in Love* (Niles, Ill.: Argus Communications, 1974), p. 74. Reprinted from *The Secret of Staying in Love* by John Powell © 1974 Argus Communications. Used with permission from Argus Communications, Niles, Illinois.

2. George Odiorne, *Objectives—focused Management* (New York: Amacom, 1974), p. 35.

3. Clark Moustakas, *Who Will Listen? Children and Parents in Therapy* (New York: Ballantine Books, 1975), pp. 12–13.

4. Martin Buber, *The Knowledge of Man*, edited by Maurice Friedman (New York: Harper & Row, 1967), p. 69.

5. Carl Rogers, *On Becoming a Person: A Therapist's View of Psychotherapy* (Boston: Houghton Mifflin, 1961), p. 332. Copyright © 1961 by Carl R. Rogers. Reprinted by permission of Houghton Mifflin Co. Italics are in the original. Rogers' thinking

on this subject was originally presented in a speech at the Centennial Conference on Communications at Northwestern University in 1951. A quarter of a century earlier Elliott Dunlop Smith proposed that managers take a fresh look at a topic under discussion by viewing it from the perspective of the other person. In his book *Psychology for Executives* (New York: Harper, 1928), he called this "the bilateral check."

6. Quoted in Carl Rogers, *Carl Rogers on Personal Power* (New York: Delacorte Press, 1977), p. 123.

7. Richard Cabot, M.D., quoted in a manuscript by George Peabody. Italics are mine.

8. Philip Roth, *Portnoy's Complaint* (New York: Random House, 1969).

9. William Shakespeare, *Julius Caesar*. Some people complain that these communication skills can be used for evil purposes as well as for good purposes. That's true; they can be used manipulatively. Anthony's speech in *Julius Caesar* is an example of this. It is clear from the whole play that Mark Anthony was an unscrupulous man manipulating the crowd. Like all good things—intelligence, charisma, wealth, fire, and so on—these skills can be used for direct mutual communication by people of integrity, or they can be used manipulatively. My goal in writing this book is to foster genuine interaction.

10. George Bach and Herb Goldberg, *Creative Aggression* (Garden City, N.Y.: Doubleday, 1974), p. 379.

11. Several of these questions come from George Bach and Peter Wyden, *The Intimate Enemy: How to Fight Fair in Love and Marriage* (New York: William Morrow, 1964), p. 94.

12. Rogers, *On Becoming a Person*, p. 332. Copyright © 1961 by Carl R. Rogers. Reprinted by permission of Houghton Mifflin Co., and that of Constable Publishers, London.

13. Rogers, *Carl Rogers on Personal Power*, pp. 129–33. This group interaction was filmed; the result, the movie *The Steel Shutter*, is available for rental through the Center for Studies of the Person, 1125 Torrey Pines Road, LaJolla, California 92037.

14. *Newsweek*, January 27, 1965, p. 5.

15. *Newsweek*, January 13, 1969, p. 60.

Chapter Fourteen:
Collaborative Problem Solving

1. William Reddin, *Managerial Effectiveness* (New York: McGraw-Hill, 1970), p. 170.

2. Jeremiah 6:14, 8:11.

3. Erich Fromm, *Man for Himself: An Inquiry into the Psychology of Ethics* (Greenwich, Conn.: Fawcett Publications, 1947), p. 161.

4. Clark Moustakas, *Loneliness and Love* (Englewood Cliffs, N.J.: Prentice-Hall, 1972), p. 27.

5. Quoted in John Kennedy, *Profiles in Courage* (New York: Pocket Books, 1957), p. 4.

6. I Kings 3:16–27.

7. Robert Townsend, *Up the Organization* (New York: Alfred A. Knopf, 1975), p. 35.

8. Mary Parker Follett, *Freedom and Co-ordination* (London: Management Publications Trust, 1949), pp. 65–66.

9. Sidney Verba, in his *Small Groups and Political Behavior* (Princeton, N.J.: Princeton University Press, 1961), p. 223, raised the same concern in almost the same words.

10. John Dewey, *Creative Intelligence: Essays in the Pragmatic Attitude* (New York: Henry Holt, 1917), p. 65.

11. Lewis Hahn, in *Guide to the Works of John Dewey*, edited by Jo Ann Boydston (Carbondale: Southern Illinois University Press, 1970), p. 31.

12. The guidelines John Dewey advocated for problem solving were set forth in many books and articles. His *How We Think*, rev. ed. (Boston: D. C. Heath, 1933; originally published 1910) provides a simpler statement of his method. A more sophisticated treatment may be found in Dewey's *Studies in Logical Theory* (Chicago: University of Chicago Press, 1903), which he revised, expanded, and brought out under a new title: *Essays in Experimental Logic* (Chicago: University of Chicago Press, 1916). Applications of this method are found in many of Dewey's books, including *Democracy and Education: An Introduction to the Philosophy of Education* (New York: Macmillan, 1916), pp. 163f.

13. Thomas Gordon with Noel Burch, *T.E.T.: Teacher Effectiveness Training* (New York: Peter H. Wyden, 1974), pp. 217f.

14. Gordon, *T.E.T.*, pp. 229–30, makes the very useful distinction between stating a problem in terms of needs and stating it in terms of solutions.

15. Thomas Gordon, *Leader Effectiveness Training (L.E.T.): The No-Lose Way to Release the Productive Potential of People* (New York: Wyden Books, 1977), p. 195. This step of stating the problem in terms of competing needs rather than colliding solutions, which I learned from Dr. Gordon and his associate Ralph Jones, is one of the most important keys to the successful use of the collaborative problem-solving method.

16. Ross Stagner (ed.), *The Dimensions of Human Conflict* (Detroit: Wayne State University Press, 1967), p. 136.

17. Daniel Druckman, "Dogmatism, Prenegotiation Experience, and Stimulated Group Representation as Determinents of Dyadic Behavior in a Bargaining Situation," in *Conflict Resolution through Communication*, edited by Fred Jandt (New York: Harper & Row, 1973), p. 123.

18. Rensis Likert and Jane Likert, *New Ways of Managing Conflict* (New York: McGraw-Hill, 1976), p. 146.

19. Peter Lawson developed this idea in an unpublished manuscript. Much of the wording is his, but some is mine, as I have adapted Peter's ideas to my usage.

20. George Prince, *The Practice of Creativity: A Manual for Dynamic Group Problem Solving* (New York: Harper & Row, 1970), p. 171.

Chapter Fifteen:
Three Essentials
for Effective Communication

1. Proverbs 4:23.

2. Carl Rogers, "The Necessary and Sufficient Conditions of Personality Change," *Journal of Consulting Psychology* 22 (1957); 95–110.

3. John O. Stevens, *Awareness: Exploring, Experimenting, Experiencing* (New York: Bantam Books, 1973).

4. David Duncombe, *The Shape of the Christian Life* (New York: Abingdon Press, 1969).

5. Margery Williams, *The Velveteen Rabbit, or How Toys Become Real* (New York: Avon, 1975), pp. 16–17.

6. Carl Rogers, *On Becoming a Person: A Therapist's View of Psychotherapy* (Boston: Houghton Mifflin, 1961). Copyright © 1961 by Carl R. Rogers. Reprinted by permission of Houghton Mifflin Co., and that of Constable Publishers, London.

7. Karl Menninger, *Theories of Psychoanalytic Technique* (New York: Basic Books, 1958).

8. An interesting discussion of *philia* is found in C. S. Lewis's *The Four Loves* (London: Geoffrey Bles, 1960), pp. 69–70.

9. Waldo Beach and Richard H. Niebuhr (eds.), *Christian Ethics: Sources of the Living Tradition* (New York: Ronald Press, 1955).

10. Millar Burrows, *Outline of Biblical Theology* (Philadelphia: Westminster Press, 1946), p. 163.

11. Martin Buber, *I and Thou* (New York: Charles Scribner's Sons, 1958), p. 14. See also Buber's *Two Types of Faith* (New York: Macmillan, 1952), pp. 66ff.

12. Paul Ramsey, *Basic Christian Ethics* (New York: Charles Scribner's Sons, 1950), pp. 99–100.

13. Lorraine Hansberry, *A Raisin in the Sun* (New York: Signet Books, 1959), p. 121.

14. Thomas Gordon, *Parent Effectiveness Training: The "No-Lose" Program for Raising Responsible Children* (New York: Peter H. Wyden, 1970), pp. 15ff.

15. Paul Tournier, *Secrets* (Richmond, Va.: John Knox Press, 1965), pp. 9, 23, 28.

16. Carl Rogers, *Client-centered Therapy* (Boston: Houghton Mifflin, 1951), p. 20.

17. David Deitch, "The Role of the Ex-addict in Treatment of Addiction," *Federal Probation*, December 1967.

18. H. Richard Niebuhr, *The Purpose of the Church and Its Ministry: Reflections on the Aims of Theological Education* (New York: Harper and Brothers, 1956), p. 35.

19. Milton Mayeroff, *On Caring* (New York: Harper & Row, 1971), pp. 41–42.

20. William Lewis and Wayne Wigel, "Interpersonal Understanding and Assumed Similarity," *Personnel and Guidance Journal* 43, no. 2 (1964): 155–58.

21. Rogers, *On Becoming a Person*, p. 332. Copyright © 1961 by Carl R. Rogers. Reprinted by permission of Houghton Mifflin Co., and that of Constable Publishers, London.

Afterword:
Four Steps to Improved Communication

1. Robert Carkhuff, *Helping & Human Relations: A Primer for Lay and Professional Helpers* Volume II, Practice and Research (New York: Holt, Rinehart & Winston, Inc., 1969), p. 6.

2. Allen Ivey, *Microcounseling: Innovations in Interviewing Training* (Springfield, Ill.: Charles C. Thomas, Publishers, 1971), p. 117.

Index